Green Growth and Low Carbon Development in East Asia

T0271872

The concept of green growth, coupled with one of green economy and low carbon development, is a global concern especially in the face of the multiple crises that the world has faced in recent years – climate, oil, food, and financial crises. In East Asia, this concept is regarded as the key in transforming cheap-labour dependent, export-oriented industries towards a more sustainable development.

Green Growth and Low Carbon Development in East Asia examines the beginnings of low carbon, green growth in practice in East Asia and how effectively it has directed East Asian nations, especially South Korea, China, Taiwan, and Japan, to put environment and climate challenges as the core target zone for investment and growth. Special focus is paid to energy and international trade – areas in which these nations compete with pioneered nations of Europe and the United States to develop renewable energy industries and enhance their international competitiveness.

On the basis of the lessons learned in East Asia, together with a comparison of Russia, this book discusses the applicability and limitations of this developmental approach taken by the developing nations and resource-rich emerging economies, including conditions and contexts in which nations are able to transition into sustainable development through the use of low carbon, green growth strategies.

Fumikazu Yoshida is Professor of Economics at Hokkaido University, Japan.

Akihisa Mori is Associate Professor of Global Environmental Economics at Kyoto University, Japan, and the Director and Secretary General of the East Asian Association of Environmental and Resource Economics.

Routledge studies in ecological economics

Green Growth and Low Carbon Development in East Asia

Edited by Fumikazu Yoshida and Akihisa Mori

Routledge
Taylor & Francis Group

LONDON AND NEW YORK

First published 2015
by Routledge
2 Park Square, Milton Park, Abingdon, Oxfordshire OX14 4RN

and by Routledge
711 Third Avenue, New York, NY 10017

First issued in paperback 2017

*Routledge is an imprint of the Taylor & Francis Group,
an informa business*

British Library Cataloguing-in-Publication Data
A catalogue record for this book is available from the British
Library

Library of Congress Cataloging-in-Publication Data
Green growth and low carbon development in East Asia /
   edited by Fumikazu Yoshida and Akihisa Mori.
      pages cm. — (Routledge studies in ecological economics)
   1. Economic development—Environmental aspects—East Asia.
   2. Environmental policy—Economic aspects—East Asia.
   I. Yoshida, Fumikazu, 1950– II. Mori, Akihisa, 1970–
      HC460.5.Z9E546 2015
      338.95'07—dc23
      2014046567

ISBN 13: 978-1-138-06728-8 (pbk)
ISBN 13: 978-1-138-83264-0 (hbk)

Typeset in Galliard
by Apex CoVantage, LLC

Contents

PART II
Trade and industrial structural change

PART III
Perspectives

Figures

Tables

Contributors

Pongsun Bunditsakulchai is IGES Fellow at the Institute for Global Environmental Strategies (IGES), Japan.

Soyoung Kim is a PhD candidate in Global Environmental Studies, Kyoto University, Japan.

Satoshi Kojima is Principal Researcher at the Institute for Global Environmental Strategies (IGES), Japan.

Chun-Hsu Lin is a researcher at the Center for Green Economy, Chung-Hua Institution for Economic Research, Taiwan.

Etsuyo Michida is a researcher at the Institute of Developing Economies, Japan External Trade Organization (JETRO), Japan.

Akihisa Mori is Associate Professor of Global Environmental Economics at Kyoto University, Japan, and the Director and Secretary General of the East Asian Association of Environmental and Resource Economics.

Mustafa Moinuddin is a policy researcher at the Institute for Global Environmental Strategies (IGES), Japan.

Yasuhiro Ogura is a PhD Candidate at Kyoto University, Japan.

Jinsoo Song is Distinguished Professor at Silla University, South Korea.

Nikita Suslov is Professor at the Institute of Economics and Industrial Engineering SB RAS, Russia.

Kazuhiro Ueta is Professor at Kyoto University, Japan.

Lei Wang is Assistant Professor at Hokkaido University, Japan.

Lih-Chyi Wen is Head of the Center for Green Economy, Chung-Hua Institution for Economic Research, Taiwan.

Fumikazu Yoshida is Professor of Economics at Hokkaido University, Japan.

Haruyo Yoshida is a part time teacher at Sapporo University, Japan.

Acknowledgements

This book is part of a research result titled "A Fundamental Study of the Economic Growth of East Asia and Its Sustainable Development." This research project aims to find out ways to redirect the existing economic growth modality toward sustainable development. Since 2008, the world has suffered from the dual global crisis of economic and climate change. But crisis is said to bring opportunities to break through barriers that were locked-in in the existing socio-economic system. We take discourses of green growth and low carbon development that are initiated from East Asia to see if they can provide strategies and policies for greening economic growth in East Asia and the world.

This book would not have been possible without the efforts of many. First of all, we want to thank the Japan Society for Science Promotion (JSPS) for their support. This research project is carried out by the JSPS grant (grant number 23310029) in 2011–2013. Of course we are very grateful to all of the authors who have contributed to this book. We also want to thank participants of the Sapporo workshop and two anonymous reviewers for their comments, critical remarks and suggestions to improve the content and structure of this book. Participants include Zhong Xiang Zhang, Kwon Rae Chung, Helmut Weidner, and Young Ho Lee. We also want to thank all of the people involved in the process of making this book, including YongLing Lam from Routledge and Yoshie Kondo of Hokkaido University. Last but not least, we thank Kumiko Kawarabayashi and Eriko Iida for their assistance in the production of the book.

Fumikazu Yoshida
Akihisa Mori

Green growth and low carbon development in East Asia
An introduction

Akihisa Mori

Background

During periods of rapid economic growth, many Asian countries have suffered from various types of environmental degradation, ranging from pollution of the local air, water, and soil to air pollution that crosses national boundaries. These countries have also seen increases in their greenhouse gas (GHG) emissions. China now emits more GHGs annually than any other country, and India is fourth largest emitter worldwide.

High-growth Asian countries have gradually come to recognize that excessive use of natural resources will be followed by a depletion of those resources; this pattern is known to be a bottleneck in economic growth (The Organisation for Economic Co-operation and Development [OECD], 2011: 9). These countries also recognize the adverse impacts of climate change on themselves and others, and are beginning to take adaptive measures. These measures include efforts toward sustainable development; adoption of environmental laws, regulations, and administrative orders; and the establishment and development of government organizations to implement these measures.

However, many governments in Asian countries fear that focusing on only environmental protection will result in end-of-pipe solutions, which may impair economic growth and weaken their legitimacy. Governments tend to place priority on economic growth and accordingly provide insufficient resources, authority, status, and incentives for environmental administration organizations to effectively enforce policies and measures at the street level. Sustainable development has come to be regarded as political rhetoric and a means of obtaining funding from international donors. However, the policy and institutional changes sought by international donors tend to require political, economic, and social costs that are too high for host countries to implement the changes (Mori, 2011).

Green growth and low carbon development as a global agenda

Against this background, a feasible and achievable paradigm (Chung, 2010: 6) was urged as a way to achieve sustainable development in Asia. In response, the United Nations Economic and Social Commission for Asia and the Pacific

(UNESCAP) declared green growth a basic principle of its work and defined such growth as improving the ecological quality of economic growth (UNES-CAP, 2008). UNESCAP defines the eco-efficiency of economic growth as maximal social benefit with minimal ecological impact, and this is regarded as a key principle of sustainability. To improve eco-efficiency, a country should adopt a long-term perspective and seek fundamental changes in socio-economic activity and the improvement of decision-making processes that impact the use of natural resources. Several areas are of particular interest: (a) eco-tax reform; (b) sustainable infrastructure; (c) greening of business; and (d) sustainable consumption.

Discourse on green growth has spread globally since 2008, when multiple global crises occurred. The most significant of these was a global financial crisis, which was followed by global recession. As part of the recession, consumption in developed countries shrank dramatically, as did global trade. These changes increased unemployment in both developed and developing countries, widened the income gap both within and between countries, and might have worsened poverty globally. To recover from the recession, many countries increased public spending with the aim of providing economic stimulus.

In the same year, the world suffered from energy and food crises. The price of crude oil reached a peak of US$ 145 per barrel in the middle of 2008. During the global recession, the crude oil price reached a low of US$ 36, but had increased to US$ 127 in 2011, as demand increased in emerging countries. Food prices also rose during this time, in part due to increasing conversion of agricultural production to energy crops.

A global environmental crisis has been recognized by researchers around the world. The Intergovernmental Panel on Climate Change has warned that the world should take actions to prevent a 2°C rise in average global temperature by 2100 in order to avoid catastrophic damage from climate change. The Stern Review has argued that although human activities may induce major disruptions to economic and social activities on the scale of the great wars and economic depression of the first half of the 20th century, the benefits of strong earlier and effective actions to protect the environment nevertheless considerably outweigh the costs (Stern, 2007). On the same topic, Millennium Ecosystem Assessment (2005) warned of the rapid loss of global biodiversity and the degradation of ecosystem services. It is predicted that the poor would be the most strongly affected by both rising prices and global environmental crises.

The results of studies on the topic suggest that conventional economic stimulus cannot overcome all of these crises. Governments may increase consumption by enacting stimulus packages and may protect the poor from rising prices by increasing fuel subsidies, but these actions will increase energy consumption, carbon emissions, and fiscal deficits, which will intensify carbon lock-in.

The infeasibility of conventional solutions has led to the idea of a Green New Deal-style program. At the 2009 G20 Summit, the leaders stressed their commitment to "ensuring a fair and sustainable recovery for all" by making "the transition towards clean, innovative, resource efficient, low carbon technologies and infrastructure" (Barbier, 2010: 18). The United States made a commitment to increase investment in clean energy and transmission lines. The United Kingdom, Germany, Japan, South Korea, and China followed suit, committing to either increase government investment in green projects or provide fiscal incentives for green products and services (Table 1.1). At the 2010 G20 Summit, South Korea, backed by the United Kingdom and Canada, shifted the agenda from immediate and short-term measures of financial reform and stabilization to long-term policy coordination in order to implement the framework needed to ensure global prosperity. South Korea took a leading role at the summit, choosing green economy as a theme at the Rio+20 (Dodds et al., 2014).

It was in this context that the concept of green growth was recognized globally. UNESCAP has initiated research and programs for the extension of green growth throughout Asia as a way to improve the ecological quality of economic growth. The OECD, partly funded by South Korea, has published reports on strategies and progress indicators of green growth, and conducts research on green growth underway in many countries.

However, green growth is not the only discourse that emerged in this period. The United Nations Environment Programme (UNEP) has presented the concept of a *green economy* as a way to reconcile economic recovery with natural resource depletion (UNEP, 2011). The concept of low carbon development emerged as a major challenge in both developed and developing countries as the multilateral climate negotiation became heated over setting the target for 2020. Although developed countries are reported to be responsible for 75 percent of historic GHG emissions (WRI, 2005), emissions have rapidly increased in emerging economies, and they are receiving increasing criticism for their inaction on GHG emissions, citing the principle of "Common But Differentiated Responsibility." China, India, and Brazil have recognized the benefits of low carbon development through a clean-development mechanism (CDM), which offers them the opportunity to gain from carbon emissions reduction (CER), as well as access to the most advanced low carbon technologies and a reduction in local environmental pollution.

Low carbon development is defined as development based on climate-friendly low carbon energy. Such development follows principles of sustainable development, makes a contribution toward avoiding dangerous climate change, and adopts patterns of low carbon consumption and production (Urban and Nordensvärd, 2013). Such development entails components of low carbon *growth*, such as access to climate-friendly modern energy as an alternative to traditional fuels and fossil fuels; the promotion of low carbon technology innovation and business models; the avoidance of carbon lock-in; and sustainable use of forest and land resources. In addition, low carbon development addresses social justice, aiming for poverty reduction and seeking to gain the benefit of development, while mitigating its harm (Urban and Nordensvärd, 2013). Thus, priority is given to emitters with development needs, and both institutional and technological approaches toward mitigation are used. In contrast to this type

Table 1.1 Green New Deal package in major countries

Country	Policy summary	Amount of planned investment	Expected new green jobs
United States	Investment on clean energy and transmission lines	US$ 150 billion for a decade	5,000,000 for two decades
United Kingdom	Prime minister announced the transition to low carbon society in 2008. Investment more than GBP 100 billion on ocean wind power by 2020	GBP 50 billion for coming three years	16,000 by 2020
Germany	A fiscal stimulus package amounting to 100 billion euro Renewable energy industry has a market of 240 billion euro and generates 250 thousand jobs. Germany provides environmental bonus and tax exemption to those who purchase new automobiles.	5 billion euro	900,000 by 2020
France	A fiscal stimulus package in 2008 amounting to 26 billion euro for two years France legislated an act that stipulates green job creation.	-	500,000
China	Published a fiscal stimulus package in 2008 to spend 4 trillion yuan by 2010 Invest 100 million yuan in 2008, of which 10% is directed to pollution control and energy saving	210 billion yuan	-
South Korea	The Framework Act on Low Carbon Green Growth in 2009	KWN 50 trillion during 2009–2012	960,000
Japan	The Green New Deal Plan and fiscal stimulus amounting to JPY 57 trillionPlan to expand market to JPY 70–120 trillion	JPY 2.2 trillion	1,400,000
Taiwan	The Dawning Green Energy Industrial Program Economic Revitalization Policy Project to Expand Investment in Public	NTD 500 billion during 2009–2012	-

Source: Ikuma and Wang (2010: 54) and Lin et al. (2014).

of approach, Mitchell and Maxwell (2010) emphasize adaptation, defining it as development that minimizes the harm caused by low emissions, while working toward a more resilient future.

In response, multilateral and bilateral donors, such as the Asian Development Bank, the African Development Bank, the United Kingdom, and Germany have created programs and projects in the name of green growth/economy and low carbon development to assist developing countries. The World Bank has created special carbon funds that invest in climate mitigation activities. In response, several developing countries have implemented green growth/economy strategies. As examples, Vietnam implemented a green growth strategy in 2012 that focuses on carbon emissions reduction, and Ethiopia has implemented the Climate Resilient Green Economy Strategy to address both climate change through both adaptation and mitigation.

As a result of the global spread of the concept of green growth, green economy, and low carbon development, the market for low carbon environmental goods and services has grown up to reach £3.4 trillion (US$ 5.4 trillion) in 2011/2012 (Department of Business Innovation and Skills, UK, 2013).

Targets, policies, and measures in Northeast Asia

Northeast Asian countries have published a number of targets, policies, and measures in the name of green growth and low carbon development (Table 1.2).

South Korea was the pioneer in establishing a framework for this. It formulated a low carbon green growth strategy in 2008 and enacted the Framework Act on Low Carbon Green Growth in 2009 as part of the Five-Year Green Growth Plan for 2009–2013. As financial support for this plan, the government agreed to spend 50 trillion won during 2009–2012, 30 percent of which would be spent for rehabilitation of the four major rivers. After years of debate, the South Korean government committed to a 30 percent reduction in carbon emissions by 2020, measured against the projected emissions under a business-as-usual scenario. To work toward reduced GHG emissions, the South Korean government published the 2008 National Basic Energy Plan, which set targets for 2030 of a 46 percent reduction in energy intensity as well as the targets of having 11 percent of power generated from renewable sources and 59 percent generated by nuclear power plants. Recognizing that a feed-in-tariff (FIT) provides little or no incentive for technological development, the government replaced the FIT with a renewable portfolio standard (RPS) in 2012. Under the RPS, the 13 largest power producers are mandated to generate or purchase a rising share of power from renewable sources to ensure the steady growth of renewable energy. The mandated share is scheduled to rise up to 10 percent by 2022, from 2 percent in 2012. RPS is complemented by several programs and measures, such as the requirement that an increasing share of electricity be obtained from renewable sources, and the adoption of a renewable-fuel standard intended to increase the relative use of biodiesel for transportation (Duffield, 2014). In 2013, the Seoul Metropolitan government implemented

Table 1.2 Plans, strategies, targets policy, and measures for green growth and low carbon development in four countries

	China	South Korea	Japan	Taiwan
Laws and Plans	12th five-year plan in 2011 Long-term Renewable Energy Development Plan in 2007 Renewable Energy Law in 2006	Framework Act on Law-Carbon, Green Growth in 2009 National Basic Energy Plan (in 2008 and 2014)	Growth strategy in 2006, 2010 Strategic Energy Plan (in 2010 and 2014)	Renewable Energy Development Statute in 2009
Targets				
GHG emissions reduction in 2020	40%–45% per unit GDP compared with 2005 level (8.5% reduction compared to BAU)	30% compared with BAU scenario (4% compared with 2005 level)	25% compared with 1990 level (suspended in 2013)	0% compared with 2000 level (in 2025)
Renewable energy	11.4% for non-fossil fuel energy, with 35GW of solar PV capacity by 2015	11% by 2030 (in 2007)11% by 2035 (in 2014)		6500MW by 2030 (in 2009)12502MW by 2030 (16.1%)
Energy intensity reduction	16% by 2015	46% by 2030 and 11% by 2012		More than 20% by 2015 and 50% by 2025
Policies				
Renewable Energy	RPS in 2006 FIT for wind power in 2010, solar power in 2012, and offshore wind power in 2014	Fixed FIT in 2002 RPS in 2012	RPS in 2002 Fixed FIT with mandatory purchase in 2012	Fixed FIT in 2009

Emissions Trading Scheme	Pilot scheme at five cities and two provinces by 2013Nationwide scheme in 2015	Nationwide scheme in 2015	Tokyo Metropolitan area in 2010
Carbon–energy tax	Replacing toll fee and fuel tax with transport fuel tax in 2008 Greening automobile purchasing tax in 2009		Carbon tax as a surcharge to the Coal and Oil Tax in 2012
Measures			
Government procurement	Local content requirements in bidding wind power development projects		
Subsidy/Subsidized loan	Fiscal stimulus to purchase energy efficient electric appliances Compensation for the loss by FIT from the Energy Development Fund in 2009 Subsidized loan from China Development Bank	Subsidy from Renewable Energy Development Fund	Subsidy and tax exemption for certified energy efficient appliances and low emission automobiles

Source: Author compilation.

a premium FIT for rooftop solar photovoltaics (PV) that exceeded the target set by the RPS. To increase grid connectivity, the government enacted a smart grid law, describing its roadmap and attracting large firms to a pilot project in Jeju Island.

In response to the 2008 global financial crisis, China implemented the world's largest fiscal stimulus. This stimulus included low carbon components, such as the development of a high-speed train network and a subsidy for rural consumers who purchase energy-efficient electric appliances. Although China initially expressed skepticism about climate change, CDM projects have caused the government to recognize that CDMs offer an opportunity to sustain economic growth without suffering from the trilemma among increases in reliance on coal, inefficient energy use, and air pollution with which China has struggled for the past two decades (Mori and Hayashi, 2012). China enacted the Renewable Energy Law in 2006, which set an RPS for wind power. It also published the Long-Term Renewable Energy Development Plan in 2007 to reframe renewable energy, which had previously been regarded as a measure for rural electrification, as a measure for industrial development. China also launched pilot low carbon city projects with two aims: to demonstrate good practices and to include performance on carbon emissions reduction as part of the evaluation system for local leaders.

Committing to a 40–45 percent reduction in carbon intensity by 2020 in the National Appropriate Mitigation Action, China also set mandatory targets of a 16 percent reduction in energy intensity, an increase in non-fossil energy to 11.4 percent of total energy, and a 17 percent reduction in carbon intensity. These targets are part of the 12th Five-Year Plan (covering 2011–2015). The Renewable Energy 12th Five-Year Plan was published in 2012. This plan sets targets for the share of renewable energy at 9.5 percent for primary energy consumption and at 20 percent for electricity generation. To attain these targets, China replaced its RPS with an FIT and mandated that state transmission companies must purchase all available onshore wind power in 2010, expanding the scope to include solar power in 2012, and offshore wind power in 2014. The National Development and Reform Committee implements pilot low carbon economic reforms in five provinces and eight cities. Accordingly, many provinces and cities are taking measures to promote a low carbon economy; some of these locations obtain international funding, but others do not (Oberheitmann and Ruan, 2013). The committee aimed to launch a pilot emissions trading scheme in four cities and one province by 2013,[1] and the most successful one is scheduled to be applied as a nation-wide scheme in 2016. Although carbon tax is under scrutiny, the government replaced the toll fee and fuel tax with a transport fuel tax in 2008 and a greening automobile purchasing tax in 2009.

Bolstered by the expansion of the Asian market and pressured by a global rise in energy prices, the Japanese government made resource productivity and recycling part of the 2008 Growth Strategy. This led to the inclusion of environmental and climate components in the fiscal stimulus as a policy response to the 2008 global financial crisis. These components provided subsidies and tax exemptions to consumers who purchased certified energy-efficient electric appliances or certified low-emissions/high-fuel-efficiency automobiles. Japan instituted a fixed FIT for solar power, although this was limited to surplus power and power generated by rooftop PV. In addition, green innovation was promoted as a key strategy, inspiring the Future City Initiative. This initiative aimed to develop a package of infrastructure for mass production and use of renewable energy in the designated cities and towns as part of the 2010 National Growth Strategy. It was not until the Fukushima nuclear disaster, however, that the Japanese government decided to implement a fixed FIT mandating that incumbent electric power companies must purchase *all* renewable energy, and a carbon tax added as a surcharge to the current Coal and Oil Tax. However, the government abandoned its mid-term GHG emissions reduction target in 2013 and has hesitated to set targets for renewable energy and nationwide energy efficiency, let alone a new GHG emissions reduction target. This is a direct consequence of the shutdown of nuclear power plants after the Fukushima nuclear disaster.

Taiwan has not officially submitted a Nationally Appropriate Mitigation Action plan to the United Nations Framework Convention on Climate Change, but it has set the amount of year-2000 level of GHG emissions as the target for 2025. To attain this target, it enacted the Renewable Energy Development Statute in 2009, which implemented a fixed FIT and set targets for the share of renewable energy and energy intensity.

Features

The targets, plans, and policies described above demonstrate the features characteristic of green growth, low carbon development in Northeast Asia. These features are as follows. First, although green growth and green economies, in particular, are intended to address a wider range of global environmental challenges, Northeast Asian countries have paid most of their attention to renewable energy development and, to a lesser extent, nuclear power. UNEP (2011) and Barbier (2010) identify reducing coal dependence, protecting biodiversity, and conservation of water as key areas for a green economy. UNESCAP (2008) defines green growth as eco-efficient economic growth and include broad ecological challenges. In practice, however, countries in Northeast Asia have paid the most attention to renewable energy.

This focus is related to the second feature: climate management is being reframed from least-cost climate mitigation and adaptation to a means of economic opportunity (Zadek, 2013: 199). Environment and the associated climate challenges have been made the primary target for investment and growth, which has encouraged the development of domestic low carbon industries as a means to enhance national innovation capacity; such innovation will not only use imported low carbon technologies for and in production but also develop the knowledge and expertise to create such technologies (Bell, 2012). Capturing a share of the global market in low carbon goods and services will be sought through export. This is in line with the existing export-oriented industrialization strategy in East Asia, which aims to increase the export share in gross domestic product and to shift production upstream in the supply chain. This shift occurs through diversifying products and services, which also enhances resilience to external shocks such as the 1997 Asian economic crisis.

Third, the governments of countries in Northeast Asia have centralized their administrative structure so that the president and/or prime minister can directly command and control the related issues. In the past, the authority and responsibility for climate issues was split among a variety of ministries, which deterred coordination among ministries, integration among related policies, and implementation of integrative policies. Toward that end, South Korea established the Presidential Committee on Green Growth as the headquarters for green growth and appointed ministers and industrial associations as members. China appointed the task to the National Development and Reform Commission, the most powerful commission in the government, to integrate climate concerns into energy policy. In Japan, the Prime Minister's Office took over the headquarters function to advance GHG emissions reduction through management by objective and results.

Evaluation criteria

How do we evaluate green growth, low carbon development in Northeast Asia?

The first group of criteria is development and job creation in the green sector. Green growth, green economy, and low carbon development have been initiated as part of fiscal stimulus packages to overcome the global financial crisis, but with a greener approach. In addition, Northeast Asian countries are framing the issues as an economic opportunity, and so green industrial policies receive especial focus, particularly in renewable energy industries. Governmental policies have induced domestic companies to make investments in a few specific sectors as a way of localizing production and increasing exports. In the process, participating companies can acquire the production capacity to adapt to customers' needs and can take advantage of economies of scale to compete in the global market.

The second group of criteria includes changes in socio-economic activity and improvements to the decision-making processes that affect the use of natural resources. Green industries may remain niche industries and become ultimately unprofitable unless they are associated with changes in the socio-technical regime. The growth of renewable energy will be limited because economic, political, social, environmental, technical, and geographic barriers impede the transformation of energy systems (Urban, 2014: 13–14). Transformation of energy systems has three possible transitional pathways: the "transitional pathway," which is characterized by further hybridization of the current infrastructure; the "reconfiguration pathway," which features internationalization and a scale increase of renewable generation leading to the emergence of a super grid; and the "de-alignment and re-alignment pathway," which is dominated by decentralized distribution of electricity with local or regional generation and balancing (Verbong and Geels, 2010). The transformation may go hands in hand with the removal of fossil fuel subsidies and carbon–energy taxation. However, there is a risk that the transformation might be implemented at the expense of the poorest people in societies, especially in places where the government does not always spend its budget for public goods and services that benefit the poor. Higher upfront capital requirements will deter companies and households from installing energy management systems, despite a substantial net benefit in the long term. Top-down technological approaches will face political, economic, social, and technological barriers. Full inclusion of the views of the end users will be important in any scale-up of renewable energy. This makes it imperative to change the decision-making process in such a way that it integrates bottom-up policies as part of governance.

The third group of criteria is environmental side effects. Although green growth and low carbon development are intended to enhance resource productivity, they may cause cross-media transfer of the problems or displace problems to other countries, as typically seen in exploitation of natural resources and recycling in foreign countries. This will increase the global environmental load unless importing countries properly manage the effects. Ongoing liberalization of international trade and foreign direct investment can accelerate this geographical transfer, resulting in the concentration of dirty activities to certain areas, which will become severely polluted. Although multilateral agreements, such as the Basel Convention on the Control of Transboundary Movements of Hazardous Wastes and their Disposal may prevent exports of listed hazardous wastes, they do not prevent the export of re-usable and/or recyclable goods that are likely to be improperly managed at the destination, which would cause severe environmental pollution.

In addition, green/low carbon consumption in one country may not be always adopted in other countries. Codes and standards ensure certain levels of environmental performance of building and products. Certificates help enhance the credibility of products with consumers, leading consumers to make greener choices. Green purchasing and procurement help companies to enjoy economies of scale, allowing them to supply greener products at a competitive price. All of these things encourage companies to implement green supply chain management globally so as to minimize and control pollutants in the lifecycle of products. In the process, companies select suppliers that can comply with the required product standard and avoid those that do not. However, non-exporting companies and companies that do not transact with exporting companies may continue the production and sale of dirtier and more dangerous products in less regulated markets because these can be offered at a lower price. This may result in some places attracting companies that produce dirty and dangerous products, and these companies are then likely to pressure governments to block enforcement of stringent product regulations. Several exporting countries may collectively establish an alternative certificate with less stringent codes and standards as a countermeasure. Such a certificate may cause a race to the bottom as it attracts an increasing number of producers that keep employing less environmentally friendly process.

Research questions

This book aims to address the following four questions in relation to the discussion above:

(a) How much have the green growth and low carbon development strategies and policies increased production and export of green technology, goods, and services?
(b) To what extent have the green growth and low carbon development strategies and policies encouraged socio-technical system transformation for sustainability?
(c) How serious have the abovementioned side effects of green growth and low carbon development been?
(d) What are the implications of the Northeast Asian experience of green growth and low carbon development for developing and emerging economies outside of that region?

About the chapters

Part I of this book focuses on the transformation of energy systems, the core aspect of green growth and low carbon development. Northeast Asian countries have implemented renewable energy promotion policies as a way to boost renewable energy, both in industry and among energy consumers. However, the expected transition pathways, progress, and barriers vary among these nations.

In Chapter 1, Jinsoo Song describes the development of renewable energy in South Korea, showing its progress and future transformation pathway. Assuming that South Korea is going to take the "reconfiguration pathway," he examines the idea of a super grid in Northeast Asia, coupled with massive renewable power generation in the Gobi Desert, as a tool to promote renewable energy in the region. In Chapter 2, by contrast, Fumikazu Yoshida and Haruyo Yoshida focus on the impact of renewable energy on local economy, with an expectation that Japan will take "de-alignment and re-alignment pathway" in increasing renewable energy. They take renewable resource-rich Hokkaido as an example to analyze renewable energy's potential and actual economic benefits with respect to revitalization of local economies.

In reality, Japanese government seems to take a small step toward the "transition pathway." The Fukushima nuclear disaster opened a window for the Japanese government to change the extant policy hierarchy and decision-making process regarding energy policy. However, it hesitates to take the "de-alignment and re-alignment pathway." Using his involvement as a government committee chair as background, Kazuhiro Ueta in Chapter 3 discusses the decision-making processes on renewable energy development under the Cost Verification Committee, and the Energy and Environment Council and analyzes how changes in the decision-making process impacted energy and climate policy in Japan.

The Chinese government seems to be taking the "transition pathway," because it has promoted increases in both nuclear and renewable power generation and keeps a centralized system of electricity supply intact. In the process, it changed the focus of wind-power development policy from adoption to industrial development in 2003, enhancing policies intended to foster local manufacturers while making use of foreign technology and financing at the outset. In Chapter 4, Rei Wang and Fumikazu Yoshida analyze how CDM projects pushed the development of wind power in China.

Part II extends the scope, examining the impacts of green growth and low carbon development strategy on the pattern of international trade and evaluating the environmental and economic consequences. In addition to multilateral negotiation under the auspices of the World Trade Organization, a number of negotiations on regional trade and investment liberalization are ongoing, including those for the Association of Southeast Asian Nations (ASEAN) Economic Integration, the Trans-Pacific Partnership, and USA–EU Free Trade Area. Countries pay little if any attention to the environmental consequences and impact on green growth and low carbon development of such agreements during the negotiation process. As the spread of freer trade accelerates, green growth and low carbon development strategy are likely to have a marginal impact on the industrial and trade structure so long as they cover only a limited range of industries.

In Chapter 5, Yasuhiro Ogura and Akihisa Mori quantitatively analyze the extent to which green growth strategy has changed the industrial and trade structures in South Korea, China, and Japan, with special focus on pollution-intensive and environmental industries. In Chapter 6, Lih-Chyi Wen and Chun-Hsu Lin examine the policy and state of green technology and environmental industries in Taiwan, using a questionnaire survey to explore the challenges and barriers that Taiwanese environmental industries face. In Chapter 7, Satoshi Kojima, Pongsun Bunditsakulchai, and Mustafa Moinuddin present a global computable general equilibrium model with endogenous investment allocation across countries and regions with sector-specific capital stock to analyze the economic and carbon impacts of trade and investment liberalization in the ASEAN Plus Six (ASEAN nations, plus Japan, South Korea, China, Australia, New Zealand, and India) under several scenarios. This analysis discusses the implications of reconciling trade and investment liberation with low carbon development.

Chapters 8 and 9 focus on the side effects of the green growth and low carbon development strategy. In Chapter 8, Soyoung Kim and Akihisa Mori examine South Korea's export of used electric appliances and analyze the incidence of costs and benefits to various stakeholders, such as producers, recyclers, and the government of South Korea, as well as Vietnam, an importing country, under the South Korean's Extended Producer's Responsibility (EPR) program. In Chapter 9, Etsuyo Michida examines product-related environmental regulations to quantitatively demonstrate how these stringent environmental regulations in developed countries affect trade and industrial structures in developing countries through the transnational supply chain. She uses data on the EU

RoHS and REACH frameworks to analyze trade and environmental impacts on Malaysia and Vietnam.

Part III explores whether the green growth, low carbon development strategy can effectively spread beyond the East Asian region. In Chapter 10, Nikita Suslov examines the case of the energy-abundant emerging economy of Russia to explore why policy, institutions, and the performance of renewable energy are disappointing despite having such high potential. Chapter 11 summarizes the major findings of the chapters in terms of progress, achievements, and remaining challenges; it discusses future prospects and barriers to advancing green growth and low carbon development toward systemic transformation and widespread adoption. The chapter also examines the inherent limitations of this strategy and shares the experiences and lessons that other countries could learn from it.

Note

1   Guangzhou city and Hubei province started their pilot emissions trading scheme in 2014.

References

Barbier, E. B. (2010), *A Global Green New Deal: Rethinking the Economic Recovery*, Cambridge: Cambridge University Press.

Bell, M. (2012), "International technology transfer, innovation capacities and sustainable directions of development," in Ockwell, D. G. and Mallett, A. (eds.), *Low-Carbon Technology Transfer: From Rhetoric to Reality*, Oxon: Routledge, 20–47.

Chung, R. K. (2010), "Prospects for environmental sustainability in Asia and Pacific," in Chung, R. K. and Quah, E. (eds.), *Pursuing Green Growth in Asia and the Pacific*, Singapore: Cengage Learning, 1–6.

Department of Business Innovation and Skills, UK (2013), *Low Carbon Environmental Goods and Services (LCEGS) Report for 2011/12*, www.gov.uk/government/uploads/system/uploads/attachment_data/file/224068/bis-13-p143-low-carbon-and-environmental-goods-and-services-report-2011–12.pdf (last accessed on November 10, 2014).

Dodds, F., Laguna-Celis, J., and Thompson, L. (2014), *From Rio+20 to a New Development Agenda: Building a Bridge to a Sustainable Future*, Oxon: Routledge.

Duffield, J. S. (2014), "South Korea's national energy plan six years on," *Asian Politics and Policy* 6 (3): 433–454.

Ikuma, H. and Wang, T. (2010), *China's Environmental Cities: China's Strategy on Environmental Industry and Eco-City Business*, Tokyo: Nikkan Kogyo Shinbunsha (in Japanese).

Lin, J.-X. et al. (2014), "Policy target, feed-in-tariff and technological progress of PV in Taiwan," *Renewable and Sustainable Energy Reviews* 39: 628–639.

Millennium Ecosystem Assessment (2005), *Ecosystems and Human Well-being: General Synthesis*. www.millenniumassessment.org/documents/document.356.aspx. pdf (last accessed on November 10, 2014).

Mitchell T. and Maxwell S. (2010), "Defining climate compatible development," *Climate & Development Knowledge Network ODI Policy Brief November 2010*. http://cdkn.org/wp content/uploads/2012/10/CDKN CCD Planning_english. pdf (last accessed on January 20, 2015).

Mori, A. (2011), "Overcoming barriers to effective environmental aid: A comparison between Japan, Germany, Denmark, and the World Bank," *Journal of Environment and Development* 20(1): 3–26.

Mori, A. and Hayashi, T. (2012), "Transboundary environmental pollution and cooperation between Japan and China: An historical review," in Ueta, K. (ed.), *CDM and Sustainable Development: China and Japan*, Hong Kong University Press, 1–22.

Oberheitmann, A. and Ruan, X. (2013), "Low carbon city planning in China," in Urban, F. and Nordensvärd, J. (eds.), *Low Carbon Development: Key Issues*, Oxon: Routledge, 270–283.

OECD (2011), *Towards Green Growth: Monitoring Progress: OECD Indicators*, Paris: OECD Publishing. http://dx.doi.org/10.1787/9789264111356-en (last accessed on July 21, 2014).

Stern, N. (2007), *The Economics of Climate Change: The Stern Review*, Cambridge: Cambridge University Press.

UNESCAP (2008), *Greening Growth in Asia and the Pacific*, Bangkok: ESCAP.

United Nations Environmental Programme (UNEP) (2011), *Towards a Green Economy: Pathways to Sustainable Development and Poverty Eradication*, New York: United Nations Environmental Programme.

Urban, F. (2014) *Low Carbon Transitions for Developing Countries*, London: Routledge.

Urban, F. and Nordensvärd, J. (2013), "Low carbon development: Origins, concepts and key issues," in Urban, F. and Nordensvärd, J. (eds.), *Low Carbon Development: Key Issues*, Oxon: Routledge, 3–22.

Verbong, G.P.J. and Geels, F.W. (2010), "Exploring sustainability transitions in the electricity sector with socio-technical pathways," *Technological Forecasting & Social Change* 77: 1214–1221.

World Resource Institute (WRI) (2005), *Navigating the Numbers: Greenhouse Gas Data and International Climate Policy* [Chapter on cumulative emissions]. http://pdf.wri.org/navigating_numbers_chapter6.pdf (last accessed on August 2 2013).

Zadek, S. (2013), "Beyond climate finance: From accountability to productivity in addressing the climate challenge," in Haites, E. (ed.), *International Climate Finance*, Oxon: Routledge, 194–220.

Part I
Energy transition

1 Renewable energy toward green growth

Jinsoo Song

Introduction

Energy remains the key driver of social and economic development at national and international level. The energy demand is growing rapidly. To meet such increasing demand without damaging environment, the share of renewable energy should be significantly increased.

It is very fortunate that many developing countries in Asia and Africa have abundant resources of solar energy, as well as low-cost desert and arid land. Wider utilization of renewable energy should provide the foundation for not only reliable energy supply, but also, it may bring renaissance to the development of energy in developing countries. Furthermore, it can significantly contribute to enhancing the social and economic development of these countries.

Renewable energy is becoming more important in Korea with rapidly changing domestic business environment due to the frequent fluctuation of international petroleum price and UN framework convention on climate change.

Though Korea has started to focus on renewable energy industry later than other advanced countries, it is expected that the industry would be a national growth engine in the near future as the Korean government has made maximum efforts to support technological development and deployment of renewable energy in order to realize the green growth.

Significant technology advances and dramatic cost reductions have been achieved in renewable energy over the last decade in Korea. It is clear that supporting high-level research and facilitating exchange of information and experiences are crucial. And if renewable energy technologies are to be continually expanded, its costs would be lowered. Technology cost reduction can be realized through the active collaboration of all stakeholders on local, regional, and global level.

Status of renewable energy in Korea

Because of rapid economic growth accelerated by the heavy and chemical industries, Korea's energy consumption has increased rapidly since the mid-1970s. Total primary energy consumption (TPES), which stood at 43.9 million tons of oil equivalent (toe) in 1980, increased more than sixfold to 275.7 million toe in 2011. Thus, Korea became the 10th largest energy consuming country in the world. Energy consumption per capita in Korea also increased rapidly from 1.1 toe in 1980 to 5.1 toe in 2011. But Korea energy resources are limited to low-quality anthracite with small amount, which accounted for less than 1 percent of total primary energy supply. With poor domestic energy resources, Korea has to import almost all the energy required. The dependency on imported energy was 96.4 percent in 2011, and the cost of energy import amounted to US$ 1,725 billion, which accounted for 32.9 percent of total inbound shipments.

Korea's oil demand has been growing rapidly since 1970s, except during the two oil crises in 1973 and 1979. Coal demand also has been increasing annually at an average rate of 5.2 percent for the past 30 years, due to the large amount of industrial use including power generation. But the main use of domestic anthracite has been shifted dramatically from residential sector to industrial sector. Natural gas has been imported from 1986 in the form of LNG, and it accounted for 17% of the primary energy consumption in 2011.

Energy conservation and efficiency policies for reducing energy consumption aim at all components of energy system ranging from primary energy production to end-use. In public procurement, the government gives preference to commodities produced using clean energy technology. Despite nationwide efforts by the government to encourage energy conservation and energy efficiency, increasing demand of energy is expected to persist in the future due to the rapid growth of national economy.

At the end of 2012, the amount of new and renewable energy (NRE) supply was 8,851 thousand toe, which comprises 3.18 percent of the total primary energy consumption, 278,698 thousand toe. Of the total supply of NRE, waste utilization makes up 67.7 percent, followed by hydro power at 9.2 percent, and other types of renewable energy at 23.1 percent. NRE power generation also has increased rapidly, photovoltaic (PV) and wind power in particular. With regard to PV, power generation has increased nearly 30 times, from 31,022

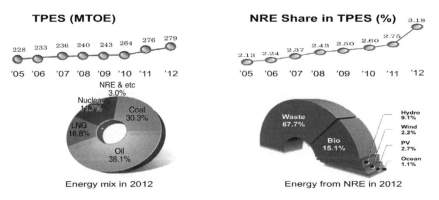

Figure 1.1 Energy consumption in Korea, KEMCO (2013)

Mwh in 2006 to 917,198 Mwh in 2011, whereas for wind, it increased from 238,911 Mwh to 862,884 Mwh. Fuel cell appeared as an electricity source in 2006, and its output in 2010 was almost 44 times higher than that of 2006, reaching 294,621 Mwh. Total NRE power generation accounted for 17,345 GWh, which is about 1.24% of total 501,527 Gwh of electricity generated in 2011.

According to the statistics of the OECD, the annual average growth rate of renewable energy at 6.8% in Korea was 14th among OECD countries during the 2008–2011, but in 2011, the penetration rate of 1.6% was ranked the lowest among the OECD countries. The average of technical standard is 86.2% compared to European countries; in addition, it is about 10% lower than Japan and about 5% higher than China. It must invigorate the system export-oriented business model to overcome the gap between these technologies and price competitiveness and weakness of domestic foundation market. Especially, in order to improve the market share of renewable energy, it must be performed not only through strengthening of price competitiveness and technological development, but also implementation of new big projects such as the Super Grid in Northeast Asia for the expansion of application areas and development of new utilization technologies.

The third basic plan for NRE technology development and deployment established in December 2008, which handles Korea's medium-long term target for NRE development and deployment, provides action plans and basic strategies. It aims at facilitating the NRE industries into a new growth engine for the Korean economy.

The background of basic plan is as follows:

1) NRE is classified as 11 fields of new energy technologies and renewable energy resources such as hydrogen, fuel cell, clean coal, PV, wind, solar-thermal, bio-energy, geothermal, waste and hydro, and suggests supply goals with concrete standards to meet international trends and domestic goals.
2) The fundamental direction of the plan is to classify renewable energy sources into deployment-oriented groups: wind, bio-energy, waste, and geothermal.
3) R&D-oriented group includes PV, hydrogen, and fuel cell.
4) Responding to the climate change and exhaustion of fossil fuels.

According to the business-as-usual (BAU) scenario of the basic plan, the NRE share of primary energy supply will account for 3.6% in 2015, 4.2% in 2020, and 5.7% in 2030, and by the target scenario, the NRE share of primary energy supply will account for 4.3% in 2015, 6.1% in 2020, and 11% in 2030.

Achievement of renewable energy in each area from 2007 to 2011 has increased sharply. The number of manufacturing companies in the NRE industries in Korea has increased from 100 in 2007 to 224 in 2011. It means that the increase was 224% with an annual growth rate of 45%.

The number of employees in the NRE industries has increased from 3,691 in 2007 to 17,161 in 2011, that is, 4.6 times with the annual growth rate of 92%. As PV and wind power industries are expected to become a core growth

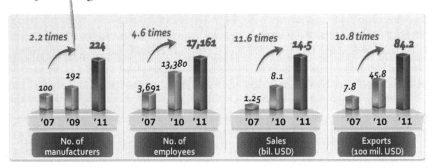

Figure 1.2 Achievement of NRE in Korea, Nam (2013)

engine in the future, the effect on employment will also be significant in these fields.

The sales of the NRE industries have increased 14.5 times from 2007 to 2011, that is from 1.25 billion US$ to 14.5 billion US$, whereas the export sales have increased 79.5 times, from 0.78 billion US$ in 2007 to 8.42 billion US$ in 2011.

As an effort to improve the condition of energy supply and demand and to promote the development of regional economies by supplying region-specific NRE friendly to the environment, the government has been promoting regional deployment subsidy program designed to support various projects carried out by local governments.

The government provides subsidy for NRE facility users to accelerate NRE deployment. The objective of the subsidy program is to create an initial market for new technologies and systems developed domestically, and to establish and activate the deployment infrastructure for technology and equipment commercialization. These subsidies are classified into two categories: the test-period deployment subsidy and the general deployment subsidy. The government provides the subsidy up to 50% of installation cost for commercialization of these systems.

International cooperation with Northeast Asian countries

Renewable energy is currently considered an effective mean for the climate change protection as well as a major driving force for sustainable economic growth. Recognizing such importance of renewable energy, the Korean government has been involved in a variety of international cooperation activities with international organization and various overseas counterparts.

The government has maintained close relations with its counterpart countries, mainly organizations from China, Japan and Mongolia, to exchange information and develop collaborative programs. In order to promote cooperative programs, joint seminars, business matchmaking, cooperation agreements, and to carry out joint research projects development, intergovernmental collaboration committees are organized. We cooperate with Japan, China, Germany, Spain, Algeria, Italy, Belgium, Chile, UAE, etc.

Many joint seminars have been organized to build the relations with those countries by exchanging current key policies and technological information in various areas such as PV, wind energy, solar-thermal and biomass. With regard to follow-up actions for these partnerships, this would be a great opportunity to identify beneficial areas in the field of NRE.

To construct the Super Grid in the Gobi Desert, international cooperation and the establishment of cooperation network among Northeast Asian countries should be promoted. However, Northeast Asian countries show many differences in the electricity frequency and transmission voltage, as well as power consumption and the capacity of power generation. Because of the poor power status and the size of the economy, it would be required to supply electricity from Gobi Desert to each country by HVDC transmission.

The historical background of international cooperation on renewable energy begins in 1995. Since 1995, Korea–Japan and Korea–China have been holding a joint seminar on renewable energy among Northeast Asian countries. A joint forum on renewable energy was held in Seoul, and the International RE Conference & Exhibition took place in Busan in 2003. Also, AFORE (Asia–Pacific Forum on RE) and GPVC (Global Photovoltaic Conference) were held in 2011. Furthermore, the NE Asia Consortium for Super Grid in the Gobi Desert was launched in 2012. AFORE is a regular event that began in 2008, and the main topics of the forum are renewable energy in terms of policy and strategy, and technology toward low carbon sustainable society.

Symposium on Super Grid was held in 2012. Korea, China, Japan and Mongolia discussed to establish a consortium for Super Grid in Northeast Asia and signed agreements at this symposium.

During the international joint workshop on Super Grid, a consortium and a working group were formed, with representatives from each of the four countries

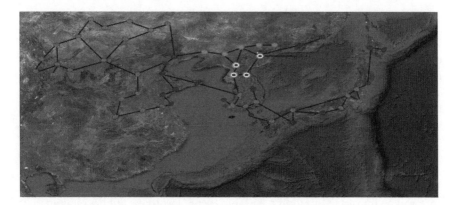

Figure 1.3 Concept of super grid in Northeast Asia, Song (2012)

in March 2013, and ADB financial support proposal was completed at round-table discussion for Asian Super Grid held in Seoul in May 2013.

The consortium will have a steering committee consisted of delegates from member countries, and a working group will be consisted of representative experts for each technical area from member countries and relevant international institutions.

For the promotion of Super Grid, Korea is running a demonstration test through operating supervisory control system with IT technology. China constructed Super Grid on the basis of demonstration experiences of large-scale PV, wind farm, HVDC, etc., whereas Japan developed a proposal of business model based on mega solar project including Asia Super Grid Plan after Fukushima nuclear disaster. Mongolia established monitoring centers at the Super Grid planned area to measure and collect weather data.

The main concept of Super Grid is related electricity transmission system, based on HVDC, designed to facilitate large-scale sustainable power generation in desert area for transmission to the center area of consumption. The participating countries are Korea, China, Japan and Mongolia.

The core technologies of Super Grid are (1) large scale RE power generation in the Gobi Desert; (2) IT, WAMS, ESS, HVDC; and (3) electricity transmission. Expected effects of Super Grid through the international cooperation in the Northeast Asian countries are technical benefits, economic benefits, social benefits, and environmental benefits. And key challenges could be (1) the consensus among participating countries and system sustainability; (2) developing implementation road map with action plan with member countries; (3) and developing managing rules and establishing organizations needed.

The VLS-PV systems should play an important role, as well as wind farms for clean and safe power generation. At present, a practical project for the "Super Grid in the Gobi Desert" has been proposed to raise funds for a feasibility study, which will carry out site selection, analysis of weather and electrical condition, and basic design for demonstration site in the next stage.

Conclusion

In the near future, renewable energy should become an economically viable option to meet the electricity needs of communities in remote or mountainous regions around the world where conventional power plants cannot be built. The rate of deployment of renewable energy is greatly influenced by the perception of general public and utilities, local, national and international policies, as well as the availability of suitable standards and codes to govern it.

In long-term period, with a solid strategy for building of the Super Grid in desert area, further expansion of large-scale renewable power generation can satisfy the increasing energy demand of the Northeast Asia in a sustainable way. In addition, diffusion of the various kinds of high-tech knowledge and experience will be transferred to local renewable energy institutes, utilities, and energy companies to keep track of worldwide technology developments, technology exchange between universities, and scientific institutes in Northeast Asian countries.

To realize our dream, we should try to build consensus with convergence, integration, and harmonization based on neighborhood.

References

KEMCO (2013), *Statistics of New & Renewable Energy, Yearbook of Korea Energy Management Corporation (KEMCO)*, December 2013.

Nam, G. (2013), Achievement of New & Renewable Energy in Korea, 4th International Asia Pacific Forum on Renewable Energy, Yeasu, Korea, November 2013.

Song, J. (2012), Super Grid in NE Asia, International Conference on RE & Grid Integration in NE Asia, Ulaanbaatar, Mongolia, November 2012.

2 Renewable energy and regional economies

Cases in Hokkaido, Japan

Fumikazu Yoshida and Haruyo Yoshida

Renewable energy and regional economies

Characteristics of renewable energy

The power derived from renewable sources of energy enhances rates of energy self-sufficiency and helps to combat global warming through the development and utilization of such local resources of natural energy as wind power, solar power, biomass, geothermal energy and small-scale hydropower. Its outstanding basic characteristics include the elimination of the need for fossil fuels, the absence of waste, and low CO_2 emissions. We are therefore now turning our attention to the idea of sustainable energy as an important resource that can work in tandem with the concept of energy conservation as well as acting as an alternative to nuclear power. On the other hand, renewable energy has certain disadvantages: low energy density, sparse distribution over wide areas and susceptibility to changes in climate. Its widespread usage will therefore require the development of new technologies, a solid infrastructure and clearly understood institutional frameworks.

Relationships between renewable energy and regional economies

Many of the areas with high renewable energy potential are sparsely populated: such places as farmland and fishery villages, rather than urban districts. As a result, the self-supply of energy can become a significant means of helping to prevent income outflow, though this alone is not sufficient as an objective for the development of renewable energy projects. Since the end of the country's period of rapid economic growth, all regions of Japan have faced the issues of population drain, ageing and industrial decline, and the opportunities provided by local resources of renewable energy must be used to help to address these issues.

Yet if, in the current situation, a large business operator outside the region participates in a renewable energy project and earns proceeds from the sale of electricity under a feed-in tariff (referred to here as "FIT") scheme, both the energy produced and the financial rewards go to urban areas with little return to the local community. Yet, although the manufacturers of the necessary equipment are not located in the countryside and such projects have a minimal effect in terms of increased job opportunities, local residents and governments can participate in projects implemented by outside businesses through stock ownership, while the electricity and heat produced can be provided to the local community at affordable prices. It is also possible to launch an energy-related business in the local community, while the local government as well as agricultural consortiums, consumer and/or forest cooperatives, and other organizations can link such businesses to their own in a subsidiary capacity. It is imperative to commercialize renewable energy projects so that locally produced energy is at least partially used to promote the well-being of the region and to improve the living conditions of local residents.

People used to view the many energy resources in the countryside as surplus to requirements or as obstacles to everyday life and industry, and such resources were wastefully disposed of. Local governments, businesses and organizations, which are highly familiar with their own regions, should now use their experience and knowledge to provide leadership in the development of funding mechanisms in which local residents can participate. And when a project is launched, we shall need to educate the local people so as to foster the development of individuals capable of improving technologies to suit local conditions in collaboration with the manufacturers of the energy-producing equipment. Above all, it is necessary to envision the future of the local community in the light of the fact that energy is essential for daily living and industrial activity.

Renewable energy business models and evaluation indicators

The experiences of Denmark, Germany and other countries, as well as Hokkaido's own efforts and plans, offer a variety of business models.

Today, business models involving large commercial operators outside the region feature the use of abundant capital, technology and manpower, and therefore play a major role in the promotion of renewable energy. However, the electricity generated and the proceeds from its sale flow out of the region; little profit is returned to the local community, which receives only fixed asset taxes and certain other forms of income. The Danish model for wind power generation serves as a useful reference in helping us to address this situation, as it involves the input of locals from the planning phase onwards and stresses the return of profits to the local community with such measures as mandatory local stock ownership and employment.

In Hokkaido, local governments undertake two types of renewable energy project. One incorporates direct management by the municipality in question (as seen in the initiatives taken by the towns of Tomamae, Suttsu and Setana), while the other involves management by quasi-public corporations (such as those run by the towns of Horonobe and Esashi). In these business models, the management capability of local governments is tested in fields such as planning and fund-raising (e.g., the securement of subsidies). The basic objective is to sell electricity, but the related profits remain in the hands of the local communities. The production of energy from biogas and similar projects contributes to the promotion of local industry and the well-being of the local residents.

One other business model allows local private businesses as well as agricultural, fishery and/or consumer cooperatives and other organizations to produce energy in such forms as electricity and heat in order to earn income via subsidiary businesses or for self-use. Yet, while business operators in Denmark and Germany who have located installations on farmland, in harbors and in other areas, are able to develop their commercial activities through the use of bank loans and other sources of financing, such businesses in Japan require capital investment subsidies and other support measures.

A further business model involves the resident-funded construction and operation of wind power plants or large-scale solar (mega-solar) power plants and the sharing of related profits, as popularly exemplified by the Hokkaido Green Fund. Such initiatives help to connect urban and rural areas.

In such ways, a variety of commercial operators are developing renewable forms of energy business on a regional basis, and it is from a regional perspective that the sections below examine the evaluation indicators for these business models. When local residents participate in the development and utilization of local energy resources, the basic premise of profit return to the local community is essential. This requires consideration of how best to use the energy that is produced, how to increase the number of local job opportunities, and how to enhance people's quality of life. In this regard, we can consider six evaluation indicators.

The first is the value of the energy produced and its contribution to the regional economy (e.g., value creation, employment and income); the second involves aspects of business management (e.g., fund-raising and profit securement); the third concerns the improvement in the local residents' quality of life on the basis of their participation in the project; the fourth has to do with the leadership provided by local governments and other bodies as well as levels of coordination among the parties in question; the fifth involves environmental conservation measures, such as those introduced to address global warming, noise and bird strikes; and the sixth deals with transparency and the public disclosure of essential information.

We need to consider these six indicators in the evaluation of projects concerning renewable energy and regional economies.

Present situation of the Feed-in Tariff (FIT) scheme and related issues

Significance of the FIT scheme

Because of the high initial installation costs that it involves, renewable energy is less competitive than types of conventional energy. Accordingly, it is necessary to foster the development of renewable energy by specifying the purchase price/period and setting a long-term popularization target. To this end, loans for renewable energy business are guaranteed under the FIT scheme for renewable energy. The purchase price and period are adjusted in accordance with the extent to which outlets of renewable energy will be disseminated and the resulting reduction in the cost of power generation. In relation to this, an institutional framework for investment in renewable energy business needs to be established to accommodate the involvement of private companies and local governments/residents.

The potential for renewable electricity cannot be fulfilled without a guaranteed connection or a priority connection to the grid. Because of just such a lack of a grid infrastructure, wind turbine construction in Hokkaido, in particular, has not progressed over the past decade despite the high potential for wind power generation in the northern region. And as the generation of wind and solar power depends on weather conditions, we must pay special attention to the development of provisions for back-up power adjustments and the securement of stable power supplies.

Because of Japan's small renewable energy market, the lack of benefits from the mass production of equipment, the high unit prices for equipment, and a resulting lack of renewable energy dissemination, the country has remained locked in a vicious cycle. We must now seize the initiative to create a virtuous circle by guaranteeing the viability of renewable energy businesses and by promoting related investment under the FIT scheme in order to promote as widely as possible the use of renewable energy and lower its procurement prices. The authors of this chapter hope that Japan's equipment manufacturers will take this opportunity, on the basis of feedback from an increasing number of renewable energy suppliers, to help make the extent of Japan's renewable energy resources internationally competitive. Above all, such manufacturers must establish a packaged service system that covers every need from repair to maintenance in order to guarantee the continued operation of power generation plants after their construction.

Framework conditions and establishment of numerical targets

The development and utilization of renewable energy in Japan can be traced back to the Sunshine Project (an R&D initiative that was related to new energy concepts) established after the 1973 oil crisis, a project that resulted in progress with the development and utilization of solar power generation. In fiscal 2003, following the reform and liberalization of the electricity market around 2000, the government introduced the RPS (Renewable Portfolio Standard) scheme (based on the Act on Special Measures Concerning New Energy Use by Operators of Electric Utilities). The scheme obliges electric utility companies to use a certain amount of electricity generated from sources of renewable energy. Although this scheme doubled the amount of electricity generated in this way, the overall total was still small, and the measure did not result in the full-scale adoption of renewable energy because utility companies were obliged to purchase only small amounts (as little as 2 percent of all electricity sold) and purchase prices were low (7–11 JPY/kWh). In 2004, Germany overtook Japan in terms of installed solar panel capacity, prompting the Japanese government to introduce the Excess Electricity Purchasing Scheme for residential solar power generation systems in fiscal 2009. This measure supported the introduction of a FIT scheme and dramatically boosted the adoption of household solar power generation systems.

As a result of the 2011 Fukushima nuclear disaster, the government at the time (The Democratic Party of Japan) officially launched a FIT scheme for renewable energy in July 2012, which promoted the introduction of renewable energy centering on solar power. Yet since December, 2012, when the Liberal Democratic Party returned to power, nothing more has been done to establish the numerical targets for renewable energy that had been proposed by the previous administration of the Democratic Party of Japan when it adopted the Innovative Energy and Environmental Strategy in September 2012. This proposed an increasing renewable electricity output by a factor of more than three by 2030 as compared to the 2010 level (300,000 million kWh; more than an eightfold increase if hydropower generation is excluded). The full-scale expansion of renewable energy requires numerical targets.

Purchase price and period of procurement

Under Japan's renewable energy FIT scheme, which was based on the Act on the Promotion of the Use of Non-fossil Energy Sources and Effective Use of Fossil Energy Source Materials by Energy Suppliers (and the Act on Special Measures Concerning the Procurement of Renewable Energy by Electric Utilities), was launched in July, 2012, electric utility companies are obliged to purchase electricity generated from renewable energy when asked to do so by renewable-energy suppliers (thereby promoting a priority connection to the grid). Such companies are also obliged to make these purchases for a government-specified price and period (referred to as purchase at fixed feed-in tariffs). This allows renewable energy suppliers to sell their product at an initially set price for a certain period of time. As technological advances and market competition will lower the market price of electricity and power plant construction, so, in the future, operational costs will also decline, while the procurement price for power suppliers entering the power generation market will be reviewed annually.

The installed capacity of renewable energy facilities certified under the FIT scheme was to be 21 million kW by March 2013, and the total installed capacity of renewable energy facilities that were due to begin operation by this time would amount to 2.08 million kW. While the effects of the FIT scheme are clearly seen in comparison with cumulative installation completed by 2011, which amounted to approximately 20 million kW, solar power accounted for an overwhelming proportion (95 percent) of the newly installed capacity. This is attributed to the ease of solar panel installation on the rooftops of houses and corporate buildings and the relatively simple installation of large-scale solar power (mega-solar) set-ups on vast and inexpensive areas of land with abundant sunshine. A prime example of this is seen in plans to locate mega-solar power installations in Hokkaido, which, as of November 2012, accounted for approximately 27 percent of the nation's applications for generation installation certification, and while many Japanese manufacturers make mega-solar panels, about two thirds of the scheduled installation subcontractors are located outside Hokkaido. If certified plans are implemented by 2014, total investment in the construction of solar power generation systems is expected by this time to be 167 billion JPY (510,000 kW x 325,000 JPY), with power suppliers receiving an estimated annual income of 21.2 billion JPY (based on an operating rate of 12 percent) (Hokkaido Bureau of Ministry of Economy and Industry, 2012). The local Hokkaido communities, however, will not benefit from these developments. Non-residential solar power systems are particularly problematic. Despite the issuance of certification to become valid on May 31, 2013, the operation of as much as 17.71 million kW of installed capacity nationwide had not been initiated as of August 2013. Some economists have pointed out that such solar power systems have been used as a means of speculation that has targeted an extraordinary procurement price of 42 JPY/kWh over a procurement period of 20 years.

Guaranteed priority connection to the grid

Under Japan's FIT scheme, electric utility companies may refuse to connect renewable energy sources to the grid if there is a likelihood of detriment to the smooth supply of electricity (Article 5, Paragraph [1] of the Act on Special Measures Concerning the Procurement of Renewable Energy by Electric Utilities). There are two possible scenarios for a refusal to connect sources to the grid. One concerns the issue of grid connection with the power network viewed as a whole. The fluctuating supply of energy generation from wind or solar power sources leads to a lack of short-term frequency regulation capacity. The reduction of the thermal power generation output that is meant to enable electricity generated from wind power sources to be received at night causes maximum output to decrease during the day. If inclement weather prevents wind power generation the following day, there will be a shortage at peak demand times, resulting in an insufficient power margin able to reduce the output of a power system in an orderly way. This then results in insufficient coordination capability for the electric utility company's entire service area. In Hokkaido, as a result of this weakness, the connection of solar power generation installations to the grid is restricted. The other possible scenario for a refusal to connect has to do with local issues regarding the connection points. Problems such as excess voltage, reverse power flow and excess thermal capacity have prompted power suppliers to change connection points, thereby placing an additional burden on them. Unlike the practice in Germany and other countries,

Japanese regulations do not oblige electric utility companies to reinforce their power systems even if there is insufficient connection point capacity. Accordingly, such companies may refuse grid connection for these reasons. Consequently, in fiscal 2013, the government allocated a budget of 25 billion JPY for grid improvement for areas where the introduction of wind power generation has not progressed due to low levels of electricity demand and supply and less-robust grids (particularly areas of northern Hokkaido), while it set up specific-purpose companies for grid development and management. Also under way is a project to verify the feasibility of using large-scale storage batteries for the stabilization of the electric system.

Another issue that affects the priority connection of renewable energy sources relates to the conditions for receiving electricity generated from sources of mega-solar power. The Hokkaido Electric Power Company has received 87 grid connection applications (1.56 million kW, as of March 31, 2013) that require high-voltage connection for large-scale solar power installations with an output of 2,000 kW or more. The figure is equivalent to around four times the current connection capacity of 400,000 kW and is premised on the operation of the company's three nuclear power generation units. This means that Hokkaido Electric Power's grid connection slot for electricity generated from wind power sources, which is expected to grow in the future, will be used up by electricity generated through the use of large-scale solar power systems.

In response to this situation, the Agency for Natural Resources and Energy announced three steps with regard to the grid connection of large-scale solar power generation installations in Hokkaido (April 17, 2013). First, the conditions for grid connection will be changed in certain areas to promote the expansion of connection capacity (allowing exemption from the provisions obliging utility companies that ask renewable power producers to restrain output for a period exceeding 30 days per year to compensate for the loss). Second, large-scale storage batteries will be introduced at electricity grid substations (the first time that this has been done anywhere in the world) to allow the receipt of more renewable power. Third, broad inter-area operation will be expanded in line with electricity system reform policy. Furthermore, the revision of a ministerial ordinance in July 2013 guaranteed the right of small power suppliers to connect their mid-sized installations with an output of 500 kW or more and under 2,000 kW to the grid of Hokkaido Electric Power Company. These steps are expected to encourage local small and medium-sized enterprises to enter the power generation market.

We can now identify, in terms of the status of FIT implementation as outlined above, a number of challenges when viewed from the perspective of Hokkaido's economy. Although the purchase price and period for the procurement of renewable energy-generated electricity are guaranteed, purchase per se is not virtually guaranteed. The existing electricity infrastructure and systems are not designed to accommodate such types of electricity. Accordingly, there is virtually no prospect, even after the implementation of FIT, that Hokkaido's wind power generation business will grow, despite the high expectations placed upon Hokkaido in this regard, for only limited amounts of local capital are involved in the mega-solar business, which has rapidly expanded following the implementation of FIT, and in the related construction work. If this situation continues, Hokkaido's role is likely to amount to little more than simply a provider of land. Consequently, the true worth of Japan's much-awaited FIT scheme faces some tough testing.

Renewable energy potential in Hokkaido and related developments

Hokkaido's abundant and diverse potential

According to the Study of the Potential for the Introduction of Renewable Energy by Region, issued by the Japanese Ministry of the Environment (2011), Hokkaido has a generation capacity of 564.06 million kW, representing a quarter of Japan's total capacity. In particular, the region accounts for half the capacity of the country's onshore wind power generation and a quarter of its offshore wind power generation capacity.

A close look at Hokkaido's renewable energy potential shows that the estimated annual output with wind turbines installed at all existing and potential wind farms in Hokkaido (with a wind speed of at least 5.5 m/s on land) would cover almost all of the region's electricity needs even if only 10 percent of wind power generation potential is used.

A much closer look at Hokkaido's field- and region-specific renewable energy potential indicates a high capacity for wind power generation in the areas of Hiyama, Soya and Rumoi. In terms of annual average wind speeds, Ishikari, Shiribeshi and Oshima are also rich in areas suitable for wind power generation (at least 3.5 m/s). Areas with high potential for solar power generation are Iburi, Hidaka, Okhotsk, Tokachi, Kushiro and Nemuro, where the average solar radiation level is high (3.77–4.07 kWh/m^2). Areas with abundant biomass resources are Okhotsk (woody biomass and livestock manure), Tokachi (woody biomass and livestock manure), Kamikawa (woody biomass), Kushiro (woody biomass and livestock manure), Sorachi (woody biomass) and Ishikari (food waste).

If we view Hokkaido's renewable resources in this way, we can see that the region's overall energy potential is not only abundant but also diverse, with different available energy resources in different districts.

Background to renewable energy introduction

A look at the circumstances leading up to the introduction of renewable energy in Hokkaido before the implementation of FIT shows that installation subsidies from the New Energy and Industrial Technology Development

Organization (NEDO) and other organizations played a central role in the promotion of wind power, solar power and the use of biomass. Although the RPS scheme and the Excess Electricity Purchasing Scheme were also in place, they were not able to guarantee full-scale dissemination and the ongoing operation of the sustainable energy power generation systems until FIT had been implemented.

For the generation of wind power, projects subsidized by NEDO played a major role. From 1999, NEDO implemented the Support Project for New Energy Business Enterprises, the Project for Promoting the Local Introduction of New Energy and other initiatives, while it also subsidized a variety of wind power generation projects run by local governments and private enterprises during the initial phase of the introduction of wind power generation. We give below examples of such implementation in Hokkaido.

Wind power installations operated by local governments include: 3 turbines at Tomamae Yuhigaoka Wind Farm owned by Tomamae Town (1998–2000); 3 turbines at Kotobuki No Miyako Wind Farm (2002–2003) and 5 turbines at Futa Wind Farm (2005–2007) both owned by Suttsu Town; 28 turbines at Esashi Wind Power Plant (2000–2001); 28 turbines at Otonrui Wind Farm owned by Horonobe Town (2000–2001); 3 turbines owned by Wakkanai City Government's Water Service Department (1999–2000); and 2 offshore turbines owned by Setana Town (2002–2004). Those operated by private enterprises include 19 turbines owned by Dream-Up Tomamae Co., Ltd. (a subsidiary of Electric Power Development Co., Ltd.) (2000–2001); 20 turbines operated by Eurus Energy Tomamae (1999–2000); 4 turbines owned by Eurus Energy Hamatonbetsu (2000–2001, 2005); and 3 turbines owned by Hokkaido Green Fund in Ishikari City (2004, 2006–2007).

NEDO subsidies covered approximately half the initial equipment costs for all the above installations, and the remaining costs and equipment maintenance/operation expenses became the responsibility of the relevant local governments and private enterprises.

NEDO subsidies were also used to install solar power generators at schools and other public facilities.

In addition to NEDO funding, subsidies from Projects for the Comprehensive Development of Hilly and Mountainous Areas and other initiatives funded by the Ministry of Agriculture, Forestry and Fisheries and the Hokkaido Government were used for the construction of biomass and biogas plants.

As for the electricity purchases made by the Hokkaido Electric Power Company under the RPS scheme, the reduced unit purchase price and the restricted purchase amounts introduced after the target had been met through the use of electricity from new energy sources placed a strain on the management of the renewable energy businesses.

Challenges from the countryside

Wind power generation

Present situation and related problems

Amongst the regions of Japan, Hokkaido provides the country's largest potential opportunities for harnessing wind power. Areas with particularly favorable conditions are the coast of the Sea of Japan, Cape Soya and the Nemuro Peninsula, all of which are characterized by strong onshore winds and heavy snowfall in winter (Figure 2.1). In addition to the harsh winter conditions, seasonal winds unique to these areas hinder agriculture and fisheries. Nevertheless, these winds, which have long caused problems for local residents, have been creatively leveraged for the commercialization of wind power generation. Around 2000, local governments, major electric utility companies, trading firms and other organizations all made forays into the wind power generation sector, catapulting this northern region to the forefront of the field of wind power generation in Japan. Yet today, however, Hokkaido ranks second to Aomori Prefecture in terms of the total output of power generation.

A look at the status of installations shows that approximately 70 percent of the 52 wind power plants in Hokkaido were installed by private companies, the remainder by local governments. A number of wind farms operated by electric utility companies and town offices (including quasi-public corporations) are

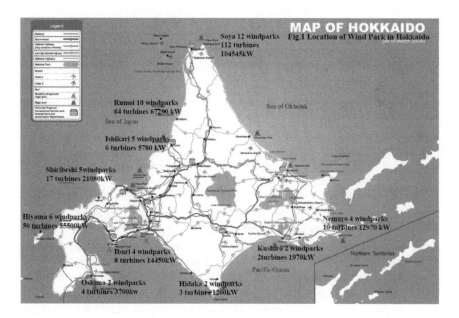

Figure 2.1 Locations of wind farms in Hokkaido

located in Wakkanai City, which is home to the most favorably located Cape Soya, the most northern point in the Japanese archipelago, and in the Sea of Japan coastal towns of Horonobe, Tomamae, Suttsu, Setana and Esashi. On the Pacific coast, wind farms are concentrated around Nemuro, Date and neighboring municipalities. A significant number of wind turbines have been installed over the years, but many are small and old. In fact, the number of installations has not increased since around 2005. One of the causes for this sluggish wind power market is that northern Hokkaido, despite its great wind power potential, has a low population density and the local residents are mainly engaged in agriculture, forestry and fisheries. Another reason is that the grid connecting the region with electricity-hungry urban areas is not robust and lacks the full capacity to handle wind power-generated electricity. Such problems have been left unresolved for nearly 15 years, despite the inauguration of the full-scale wind power generation business and a growing awareness that the amount of wind power that could be produced would far exceed demand.

Further factors behind Hokkaido's stagnant wind power generation scene include low electricity prices under the RPS scheme, and the prevalence of problems with and the maintenance needed for foreign-made wind turbines during the early phase of introduction, which placed a heavy burden on the management of the companies that supplied the wind power machinery. As wind turbines installed in around 2000 are already over 10 years old and technological advances in wind power generation have been remarkable, now is the time to replace these units with new ones featuring enhanced efficiency and a capacity based on repowering. We need to address this task at once: there is little time to lose.

According to a report issued by the Hokkaido Industrial Safety and Inspection Department entitled The Present Situation and Problems of Wind Power Generation in Hokkaido (Hokkaido Bureau of Ministry of Economy and Industry, 2012: 28), current issues regarding the reliability of installations include a range of problems and the difficulties faced in obtaining foreign-made wind turbine parts. In terms of the operation and maintenance of foreign-made installations when they were first introduced, the report points out such common problems as manufacturer responses (e.g., current manufacturers' lack of understanding of old manufacturers' models and the time-consuming process of parts supply), high operation and maintenance costs (e.g., due to overseas procurement) and the complex operation and maintenance systems (e.g., manpower shortages and a lack of repair companies). These issues clearly indicate that we need to manufacture our wind turbines here in Japan.

On the other hand, the Muroran Plant of the Japan Steel Works, Ltd. (a wind turbine manufacturer) is located in Hokkaido, and it is therefore in a better position to meet regional needs on the basis of feedback from local users. Although there is indirect demand for the output of local machine manufacturers, while local maintenance services companies have also been founded, it is nonetheless necessary to set up systems to ensure that local demand is adequately met. Japanese manufacturers should learn from Vestas Wind Systems A/S in

Denmark and Enercon GmbH in Germany. These globally leading wind turbine manufacturers work constantly to improve their products and establish maintenance systems based on feedback from domestic users.

Since the implementation of the FIT scheme, over 90 percent of all related investment has been directed towards the generating of solar power, for despite being seen as the most viable source of renewable energy, wind power generation faces immense challenges. These include the following: (1) the time and cost involved in conducting installation-related surveys and environmental impact assessments; (2) building standards requiring levels of earthquake resistance as stringent as those for general buildings; and (3) difficulties in coordination with electric utility companies due to grid shortages. If the national government hopes to overcome these challenges, it needs to establish clear and achievable goals for the promotion of renewable energy use and steadily improve conditions to this end. And in all this, we have to keep in mind that the use of renewable energy cannot be promoted without the development of various infrastructural elements that are necessarily required for purchasing electricity in addition to guaranteeing purchase prices under the FIT scheme.

Tomamae town – a Pioneer in Japanese wind power generation

Between 1998 and 2000, a total of 42 wind turbines (total output 52,800 kW) were erected in Tomamae Town. Out of these turbines, the town owns three, and they are located on a hill that offers a grandstand view of the sunset over the Sea of Japan. Of the remaining 39, which are located on a municipal coastal plain, 20 are owned by the organization today known as Eurus Energy, and 19 are owned by a subsidiary of the Electric Power Development Co. When the turbines began operation, they were Japan's first fully fledged wind farms, and over the past 15 years, they have operated relatively problem-free. This pioneering experience has helped to clarify the issues that specifically affect the operations of wind farms and has highlighted some unexpected problems in the field.

The first issue relates to wind condition surveys. Although the original surveys anticipated that the municipally run wind turbine utilization ratio would be 30 percent, the actual figure turned out to be around 20 percent. The area's topography may weaken winds in summer, and other factors such as wind blowing up from the sea below the cliffs and the influence of neighboring wind turbines may hinder efficiency. These problems highlighted the importance of pre-installation survey.

The second issue is an unexpectedly large number of problems connected with the facilities themselves. As the generators are located at great heights, all the repair and maintenance work involves extra expenditure on crane operations and similar necessary maneuvers. The surveys also highlighted the superiority of gearless wind turbines, which are multipolar and eliminate the need for noisy, issue-prone gearboxes.

The third problem is the unexpectedly large number of bird strikes (far exceeding the pre-installation survey estimates), particularly in the case of coastal wind turbines. The results of ongoing surveys in this regard will be reflected in the positioning of future installations.

When we look at the local economy and conditions of employment, we find that the installation of the 42 wind turbines created nine new jobs and that any future increases in the number and size of wind turbines may further boost opportunities for year-round employment. The town government considers local consumption of energy generated from the municipally run wind turbines in addition to the sale of electricity created in order to reduce energy purchase costs flowing from the town a means to promote the establishment of new businesses to provide more local jobs. Specifically, the Tomamae Town government plans to produce hydrogen fuel by using wind power-generated electricity so as to supply energy to cogeneration facilities and fuel-cell vehicles.

Wind power generation by Suttsu Town to address a budget crunch

Suttsu Town is also located along the Sea of Japan coast at the base of the Oshima Peninsula. From spring to summer, the town is constantly buffeted by strong eastern winds blowing from the direction of Kuromatsunai Town and the Pacific town of Oshamambe (also known as Suttsu-Dashikaze) and by western winds in winter. These hinder agriculture and fishery. To strengthen the town's finances, the Suttsu Town government formulated the idea of making use of these winds creatively and to this end developed a municipal project to harness winds for power generation. In 1989, as the prime mover among local governments, Suttsu installed five Yamaha two-bladed wind turbines (82 kW) to provide electricity to the local junior high school, but because of a lack of preliminary surveying, the utilization rate was disappointingly low. Against this backdrop, the town investigated the feasibility of wind power generation and invested five million yen in the installation of an Enercon wind turbine (230 kW) near Yubetsu No Yu municipal spa facility under a subsidy project for comprehensive development towards the revitalization of rural areas in hilly and mountainous regions. The wind turbine produced good enough results for the town government to envisage its potential commercialization. To erect wind turbines, which require large initial investment, the town government juggled its finances and developed the project step by step using subsidies from NEDO and elsewhere. In 2003, three Enercon wind turbines (600 kW) came into operation, and extra turbines were added in 2007 and 2011. The town now has 10 wind turbines with a total output of 16,350 kW. Solid results are achieved with a facility operation ratio of 97 percent and a facility utilization ratio of 26.5 percent.

In terms of management, the Suttsu Town government invested 4.6 billion JPY in installations and a similar amount over a period of nine years from 2003. Commercial income comes from electric utility bonds (2.1 billion JPY) and electricity sales (1.3 billion JPY), while expenditure includes wind power generation business expenses (3.1 billion JPY), the balance carried forward in the general account (500 million JPY), and long-term interest expenses (540 million JPY). In 2009, revenue from electricity sales was nearly 300 million JPY, although the figure varies annually. The implementation of the FIT scheme is expected to increase revenue to about 370 million JPY per year.

The main factor behind the great success of Suttsu's wind power generation project was the clear goal of strengthening the town's tight finances through the commercial income raised by the turbines' operation. Another factor was adequate examination of the project's commercial feasibility. If the town government had simply invited wind power suppliers from outside the town to build wind farms in Suttsu, it would not have been able to secure enough income because it would have been unable to depend on revenue from fixed-asset taxes whose amount decreases over time, while the amount of local allocation tax also decreases. Today, approximately 8 million JPY of the annual commercial revenue of 200 million JPY is transferred to the general account and used for purposes such as the promotion of local industries (e.g., measures taken against rocky-shore denudation in order to support fisheries).

Another factor behind the initiative's success in terms of its commercial feasibility was the introduction of costly but reliable wind turbines manufactured by Enercon in Germany on the advice of Hokkaido Electric Power Company, which has itself become interested in wind power generation. Enercon's gearless wind turbines are known to be relatively problem-free and easy to maintain. The German company provides maintenance services in collaboration with Hitachi, Ltd., Japan. Apart from the initial Yamaha wind turbines, Suttsu has consistently used the Enercon type, and these have supported the smooth operation of its wind farms. Lastly, as the town government gradually expanded its wind farms, it tenaciously negotiated with Hokkaido Electric Power Company and, against the recent backdrop of restricted grid connections, had to introduce storage batteries when it added two turbines in 2011. In future work, Suttsu will seek to ensure priority connection and further expand its wind generation business through grid reinforcement.

Setana Town – the home of Japan's first offshore wind farm

The municipal wind power generation project run by Setana Town in southern Hokkaido began in conjunction with a canceled project to utilize deep ocean water for energy, and ultimately, it resulted in the construction of Japan's first offshore wind farm. Built near the port's eastern outer breakwater, the site has an average wind speed of 10 meters per second and a high average facility utilization ratio of 34 percent. It is well known as Japan's only offshore wind farm and is a popular tourist attraction. Although the wind turbines do not generate noise or cause other problems, maintenance work is intensive owing to their site that is located at a 10-minute boat ride from the port.

Total construction expenditure amounted to 690 million JPY, including the cost of two wind turbines (600 kW) manufactured by Vestas Wind Systems A/S, Denmark, while the foundation work cost twice as much as the turbines – 200 million JPY. Of this amount, 310 million JPY was subsidized by NEDO and the rest was covered by bond issuance. Annual expenditure includes

34 million JPY on bond redemption, 1.1 million JPY on repairs, 3.7 million JPY on maintenance commission fees and 2.1 million JPY on non-life insurance premiums (for such natural hazards as lightning strikes). For fiscal 2010, the wind farm posted a loss of 10 million JPY against 33 million JPY of revenue from electricity sales. The contract between Setana and Hokkaido Electric Power Company entered into under the RPS scheme guaranteed that the latter would purchase electricity at about 10 JPY/kWh for 17 years after commencement of operations in 2004. With the introduction of the FIT scheme, however, the purchase price increased to 17–18 JPY/kWh, which eliminated most of the deficit. Yet since the scheme does not have a feed-in tariff for offshore wind power, the operators have had to use a tariff as low as that applied for onshore wind power. Like Suttsu, Setana not only has strong easterly winds in winter but from spring to summer as well (these are known as Yamase winds). As the town is an ideal place for wind power generation, Setana's administrators hope that in the future private companies will also enter the field.

Hokkaido green fund – a pioneering force in Japan's community wind turbine field

While local governments and private businesses were constructing wind farms, the Hokkaido Green Fund was working to build publicly funded wind farms as a measure to fight global warming without needing to rely on nuclear power generation. As a first step, the Green Fund established the power supplier Hamatonbetsu Community Wind Power Co., Ltd. with money from the Fund to build Hamakaze-chan ("little beach wind") – Japan's first publicly funded wind power plant – in Hamatonbetsu Town. The company raised funds to cover 80 percent of the total cost (including the 200 million JPY or so required to erect a wind turbine) by concluding an anonymous association contract with 217 residents on condition that power generation profits would be shared between the investors. The company also served as a conduit for loans from financial institutions and further concluded a contract with Hokkaido Electric Power Company to sell electricity. Hamakaze-chan was built earlier than many other community wind turbines in Hokkaido, and since it was blessed with high electricity prices, few problems, and favorable wind conditions, making its operation smooth. It has served as a model for subsequent community wind turbines, and the Hokkaido Green Fund alone has financed the installation of 14 community wind turbines involving a total of 4,000 investors. Yet because Hokkaido's electricity supply situation is complex, as our previous discussion has shown, any related business deployment has been significantly restricted.

Solar power generation

Although, because of its cold and snowy winter climate, Hokkaido has previously been thought of as unfit for solar power generation, some areas along the Pacific coast, the central region of Tokachi, and several other regions have long hours of sunshine. Since semiconductors are used in solar panels, Hokkaido's cool refreshing summers in fact make the region highly suitable for solar power generation as the implementation of NEDO's Wakkanai Mega-Solar Project (currently under the management of Wakkanai City) has shown. This research initiative was run from 2006 to 2011 with 28,500 solar panels (five types) installed on frames at three different tilt angles on a vast 14-ha site, producing a total output of 5 MW. A variety of data on the mega-solar power system was obtained under harsh natural conditions of snowfall, low temperatures and strong winds. Sodium–sulfur (NaS) batteries (1.5 MW) were also installed to support grid stabilization experiments. This was the beginning of mega-solar power generation in Hokkaido. In 2011, Hokkaido Electric Power Company established the Date Solar Power Plant (output 1 MW) next to a thermal power plant. As we have already mentioned, the availability of vast areas of inexpensive land in Hokkaido has led to the construction of an increasing number of mega-solar power generation systems in the region following the implementation of the FIT scheme.

The individuals who own solar panels are both the energy producers and the consumers, thus providing the opportunity to realize a decentralized energy system. Yet when outside business operators build mega-solar power systems, the focus so far has been solely on the area of available land, low land prices and the hours of sunshine; little consideration has been given, or is being given, to local job creation.

Mega-solar power systems of the Hamanaka Agricultural Cooperative

The Hamanaka Agricultural Cooperative (also known as JA Hamanaka) is located in eastern Hokkaido and has attracted much attention for its community solar power generation initiative. JA Hamanaka has a unique inspection system and supplies high-quality milk to Häagen-Dazs for the production of ice cream. The cooperative has set up environmentally friendly dairy farming as the central pillar of its policy, and in order to change the current status of dairy farming, which causes environmental pollution owing to deforestation, livestock waste pollution and CO_2 emissions from fossil fuel combustion produced by agricultural machinery, it promotes tree planting, biogas utilization and other green activities. As part of these green initiatives, the agricultural cooperative installed Kyocera Corporation solar modules at 105 dairy farms and related facilities (10 kW each) using a subsidy system available until fiscal 2010. These farms and facilities collectively form a mega-solar power system. In fiscal 2011, 50 percent of the electricity generated was consumed in-house, and the remaining half was sold to the local electric utility company. Individual households made additional energy-saving efforts, and on average, reduced electricity consumption by 15 percent. Annual output fluctuations are small, and the influence of fog, which is common in the region, is also minimal. Even with an electricity purchase price from fiscal 2010 of 24 JPY/kWh (before the FIT scheme started), the Cooperative expects to recoup the initial investment after subsidy deduction within six or seven years. When farms install solar panels, each farm household can save approximately 200,000 JPY a year on electricity. JA Hamanaka not only supports the management of its member farms but also seeks to enhance the brand power of locally produced milk by publicizing the Cooperative's efforts and achievements as the world's first dairy farms to use natural energy generated from mega-solar power installations.

Livestock biogas and woody biomass

While *livestock biogas* is the name for methane produced by fermenting the main feedstock of animal manure mixed with other types of organic waste, such as feed and food processing residues, *woody biomass* is the name given to resources such as timber from forest thinning as well as wood chips and the residue from sawmills. When these two gases are used as fuel in cogeneration facilities, they produce electricity and heat. Livestock biogas and woody biomass are both derivatives of resource recycling chains common in agriculture and forestry. Although supplies are not inexhaustible, as long as raw materials are available, they provide a stable supply of energy unaffected by weather and other conditions. In some cases, gas and wood chips can be stored to supply energy as necessary. Although they are categorized as renewable energy sources and are expected to play a supplementary role to other renewable energy sources, livestock biogas and woody biomass have characteristics different from those of wind and solar power. In fact, livestock biogas is an important pillar of the renewable energy policies of Denmark and Germany, where dairy farming thrives. Woody biomass is also important in Austria, where forestry is a vibrant industry.

Livestock biogas utilization

Although as the scale of farm operations expands within Japan's dairy farming industry and the livestock industry in general, we can expect biogas plants (at which heat and electricity are produced from biogas) to become more widespread, in fact the number of successfully run biogas plants is currently low both in Hokkaido and in Japan as a whole. The objective of operating such plants is not only to produce energy, but also to help to prevent environmental deterioration by supporting the appropriate treatment of livestock waste and the recycling of by-product liquid manure as a high-quality fertilizer. Consequently, the operation of multi-purpose biogas plants requires unique skills and wide experience.

THE CENTRALIZED BIOGAS PLANT OF SHIKAOI TOWN (TOKACHI REGION)

Shikaoi Town, located in the Tokachi region, is home to 5,600 people and 29,000 dairy and beef cattle. If all the manure from these animals were to be treated at the local biogas plant, the electricity produced would power the entire town. As the numbers of dairy/stock farmers and crop farmers are almost the same, the liquid fertilizer produced at the plant could also be consumed entirely within the town.

The biogas plant of the Hokkaido Shikaoi Environmental Preservation Center produces electricity and heat from two cogeneration units (108 kW and 200 kW) that generate biogas by treating dairy cattle manure from 11 dairy farms, which is approximately a tenth of all the livestock manure produced in the town. Since the commencement of its operation in 2007, the facility – one of Japan's largest centralized biogas plants – has operated reliably. The origins of its construction can be traced back to local objections to offensive odors from compost applied to dairy farms near the town center, and because of complaints from nearby residents, some dairy farmers even decided to give up farming altogether. The town government also had to consider the likely feelings of the large numbers of tourists visiting Lake Shikaribetsu, located within the town's territory. Since the local government needed to involve all dairy farmers living near the town center in order to solve the problem, it proposed the construction of a centralized biogas plant. In the building of the plant, collaboration and role sharing based on consensus among farmers and various other stakeholders were important. In order to raise funds , the town government worked to secure the input of local financial institutions by basing their fundamental expenditure on subsidies from national and prefectural government bodies, while promoting the plan in close cooperation with the plant manufacturers involved in the preliminary survey and specification design phases. Another factor behind the successful operation of the plant is the roles played by the plant manager, who formulated solutions to a range of potential operational issues identified in advance in collaboration with the plant manufacturer. It is also significant that the plant manager worked on capacity building by accumulating a wide range of knowledge and experience with regard to the plant's operation.

On the financial front, the total cost (which included the construction of the plant/ancillary facilities and the purchase of feedstock transportation vehicles) was 996 million JPY. Agricultural subsidies from national and prefectural government bodies covered more than 90 percent of these costs, while the rest was borne by the town government. A look at the operating balance of the plant until 2012 shows that more than 80 percent of the plant's income came from waste treatment and sales of recycled liquid fertilizer, and that installation repairs accounted for more than half of all expenditure. Other unavoidable expenses for the centralized plant include the cost of fuel for the feedstock transportation vehicles and the drivers' wages. Although initially only about 10 percent of income was profit, this figure is expected to increase significantly because proceeds from electricity sales will rise in relation to the plant's designation as a FIT-certified facility in fiscal 2013. However, even if the town government manages to make ongoing profits, future reconstruction of the plan will be difficult without agricultural subsidies. There are for two reasons for this: first, many plant facilities and vehicles were imported from Europe, and were expensive. Second, no income has been derived from heat generated along with electricity at the plant because part of it is consumed only in-house. Similar facilities in Denmark generate almost identical proceeds from electricity and heat sales. As producing electricity and heat at biogas plants is costly, it is important to utilize the products efficiently. In particular, we must find effective ways to use heat if we hope to support the proliferation of biogas plants throughout Japan. Lastly, the biogas plant performs the significant public welfare function of protecting the local environment and local agriculture, although these benefits are not shown in the operating balance sheet. Such functions include the prevention of offensive odors, the provision of high-quality organic fertilizer to crop farmers, and the reduction of CO_2 emissions within the town's boundaries. In this regard, the use of agricultural subsidies for biogas plants can be seen as a significant policy measure for rural revitalization.

INDIVIDUAL BIOGAS PLANT AT SUZUKI FARM IN SHIHORO TOWN

Dairy farming also thrives in Shihoro (a town adjacent to Shikaoi), where efforts to promote the operation of individual biogas plants are currently under way. Suzuki Farm, like its neighbors, engages in large-scale dairy farming with three family members and three additional workers raising approximately 400 dairy cattle. The farm uses state-of-the-art technology for mechanization and labor reduction in farming tasks ranging from daily milking to the nursing of calves. In accord with its management policy, the farm built a biogas plant in conjunction with the town's verification testing of such plants. While centralized plants require much labor, manure collection for individual plants does not; manure falls through the slotted floor of a free-stall barn into an underground gutter the leads to a 5-meter-deep fermenter. A Yanmar Company micro gas engine (25 kW) then converts the resultant biogas into electricity and heat. The plant produces 210,000 kWh of electricity annually, most of which is consumed in-house, while the remaining 50,000 kWh is sold to Hokkaido Electric Power Company. The generated heat warms water to 75–80°C for use in the barn, while the by-product liquid fertilizer is applied to the farm's 66 hectares of fields and is also sold for 300 JPY/ton (including the application fee) to farmers who provide wheat straw for bedding and grow silage corn on commission. Suzuki Farm uses no imported feed. The factors that lie behind the success of the individual biogas plant include stable procurement of feedstock due to large-scale farm management and the utilization of the heat generated and the by-product liquid fertilizer. Since the plant commenced operations in 2004, Suzuki Farm has also collaborated with local agricultural machine manufacturers to improve its technical facilities (e.g., upgrading the power generators and improving the design of the fermenter), and has through these activities gained a wealth of experience.

Woody biomass

Owing to prolonged sluggishness in the domestic forest industry, even Hokkaido, which abounds in forests, provides few examples of the utilization of woody biomass. Tsubetsu is a mountain town dependent on forestry located inland across a mountain pass from Kitami City on the Sea of Okhotsk coast. In Tsubetsu, 300-worker sawmills operated by the Tsubetsu Veneer Cooperative Association and the affiliated company Marutama Industry Co., Ltd. produce veneer and plywood from local Sakhalin firs and Japanese larches, which are deemed to be unfit for plywood. Approximately 40 percent of the logs collected from within a 100-kilometer radius end up as waste. In 2007, the Association introduced a large boiler (capacity 70 tons) and 4,700-kW cogeneration facilities (2.1 billion JPY; subsidy ratio 25 percent) to dispose of sawmill residues and generate heat and electricity for in-house consumption, thereby cutting heavy oil consumption by 30,000 kl a year. The Association also sells 400 kW of surplus electricity a year to Hokkaido Electric Power Company – almost enough to power every household in Tsubetsu. The heat generated is used throughout the year for steaming and drying of lumber in the veneer production process, but a 20-ton portion of the 70-ton boiler remains unused. Although this idle capacity could be used for district heating, such a system would require additional woody biomass fuel and dedicated installations such as heating pipelines. In any case, Tsubetsu provides a valuable case study of a successful example showing that turning waste that is difficult to dispose of into an energy resource provides local jobs and helps to achieve energy self-sufficiency.

With a population of 3,600, Shimokawa in northern Hokkaido is another forestry town where afforested land accounts for 88 percent of the district, and the town government and the local forestry cooperative work together closely to achieve sustainable and cyclical forest management. To this end, they seek a stable economic foundation and secure employment based on the management of municipal forests that have been sold off by the national government. Such efforts include promotion of woody biomass for utilization as energy in combination with the comprehensive adoption of forest resources (e.g., timber from forest thinning). Forest residues, trees that cause obstacles along rivers, willow trees that have been grown as energy resources and other materials are processed to make wood chips for use as biomass boiler fuel along with laminated wood waste and other sawmill residues. The fuel is used in district heating for the town office and neighboring public facilities. Woody biomass cogeneration facilities have also been introduced for collective housing units in the Ichinohashi Area (population 150) to help support the graying population. By expanding these efforts and utilizing a small, distributed biomass energy production system, the town government aims by fiscal 2018 to achieve 100 percent energy self-sufficiency in order to ensure a stable energy supply to the local community. This will also boost local circulation of the economy and prevent money spent on energy from flowing out of the town. These are important issues facing all regions of Japan today. Specific plans under consideration include the development of district heat supply systems by introducing biogas boilers in areas near elementary and junior high schools and the introduction of cogeneration systems in private sawmills. Implementation of these plans will require the involvement of more local residents. With 80 percent of households living within a kilometer of the town office, Shimokawa is in an advantageous position to promote district heating and it is therefore expected to play a pioneering role in the field.

Geothermal Heat

Geothermal development – renewable energy and nature protection issues

Japan has one of the world's largest resources of geothermal energy. To promote the use of geothermal heat, whose adoption in the country has been slow when we consider its abundant availability, the electricity purchase price under the FIT scheme was set at 27.3 JPY/kWh. The main issue we face here is how to strike a balance with nature conservation efforts in cases where such resources are located in national parks. As an example of this potential conflict of interests, this section of our chapter details the current status of geothermal resource development in the Shiramizusawa area of Sounkyo in Hokkaido's Daisetsuzan National Park. Kamikawa Town, in which Shiramizusawa is located, has a long history of geothermal development stretching back to the 1960s. A survey to support the expansion of hot spring sources in Sounkyo Hot Spring Resort prompted the Hokkaido Underground Resources Investigation Institute to conduct an eight-year-long official survey starting in 1965, which resulted in the confirmation that a powerful geothermal heat source was present in the Shiramizusawa area. However, a memorandum of understanding concluded in 1972 between the Environmental Agency and the Ministry of International Trade and Industry limited geothermal power generation development in national parks to six locations in Japan, and Shiramizusawa was not among them. In 1988, the town government developed the Daisetsu Enetopia Program to promote the use of hot water for purposes other than electricity generation, but the initiative was suspended in 1996 due to water rights issues. We see here therefore that geothermal power generation has a long history rather than being a recent concept, and that its utilization as a renewable energy source will not be straightforward.

The fundamental problem is the national government's failure to establish clear basic policies regarding (1) landscape protection and environmental conservation in national parks and (2) the utilization of geothermal heat as a renewable energy source. Even within Japan's Ministry of the Environment, there is insufficient coordination between the Nature Conservation Bureau (which is in charge of national park administration) and the Global Environment Bureau (which is responsible for policy measures against global warming). Unlike the Germany administration's stance on this issue, Japan's Ministry of the Environment does not assume responsibility for the development of renewable energy sources, and a year after the Fukushima nuclear disaster of March 11, 2011, the Ministry of the Environment eased restrictions on geothermal power development in national and quasi-national parks, albeit with certain conditions. According to a Ministry directive titled

Regarding the Handling of Geothermal Development in National and Quasi-national Parks, geothermal development was not in principle permitted in Special Protection Zones or in Class I Special Zones. For Class II and Class III Special Zones, permission for geothermal development with certain conditions was to be determined on a case-by-case basis. These conditions included consensus building with stakeholders, the perceived contribution to local communities, information disclosure and the making use of expert opinion. Once the government decided to allow promising projects for the development of geothermal resources in Class II and Class III Special Zones, the Shiramizusawa area was seen as a suitable candidate site. Local stakeholders held discussions under the leadership of the town government, and a prospective business partner (Marubeni Corporation) began a survey. The plan involved an environmental impact assessment based on the results of the first-phase survey. Since geothermal development projects are considered too costly and risky for community-funded investment, and take as long as 10 years or so to progress from survey initiation to power-plant construction, a local hot spring inn association published its intention to oppose any such development if it would be likely to cause the depletion of existing hot spring water. In this regard, the association requested the implementation of a survey, arguing that clarification of the local hot spring mechanism would serve as useful reference (Third Meeting of the Research Association for Geothermal Resources in Shiramizusawa and Other Areas in the Sounkyo Hot Spring Resort of Kamikawa Town, February 26, 2013). Meanwhile, nature conservation groups also insisted that geothermal development would inevitably affect the natural environment and damage the extensive biodiversity of Daisetsuzan National Park, and that natural parks should be ruled out as geothermal power generation sites rather than being the subject of discussions on the feasibility of related monitoring (Nature Conservation Society of Mt. Daisetsu and Ishikari; Symposium on Geothermal Power Generation, April 20, 2013).

Nevertheless, today, 10 of Japan's 18 active geothermal power plants are located in national or quasi-national parks. Hokkaido Electric Power Company runs a geothermal power plant in Hokkaido's southern Mori Town area, but this is not a national park. The issue of striking a balance between renewable energy promotion and environmental conservation applies not only to geothermal development but also to wind power generation. The sustainable utilization of renewable energy and the prevention of environmental degradation resulting from the development of renewable energy projects are major issues that we must think about now rather than leave them to be dealt with in the years ahead.

Conclusion

This chapter has examined the requirements necessary for expanding the usage of renewable energy and the related issues that have to be dealt with from the viewpoint of regional economies, based on surveys conducted in

Hokkaido before and after the introduction of the FIT scheme. Lessons learned in Hokkaido, which has been at the forefront of renewable energy deployment for over 15 years, highlight the following as important factors in such expansion: (1) improvement of the conditions for establishing institutional frameworks, including FIT, under the initiative of the national government; (2) clarification with regard to the positioning and prospects of renewable energy within the government's energy policy (as premises for conditions); and (3) numerical targets for the introduction of expanded renewable energy resources. The situation as it now appears since the introduction of the FIT scheme suggests that the operational conditions of FIT need to be improved. To ensure balanced utilization of local renewable energy resources by category, there is an urgent need to ensure flexibility in purchase prices/periods, to develop a related infrastructure (e.g., grid expansion to realize the principles of priority connection) and to examine the separation of power generation and transmission. In conjunction with these domestic measures to promote renewable energy, it is necessary to foster the development of manufacturing industry to match international competitiveness in related installation products, storage batteries for new electricity system operation and other products. There is also a need to expand the electricity-focused FIT scheme to utilize energy resources more comprehensively and additionally to institute appropriate planning to promote district heating and energy co-generation.

However, these government-led measures only support the initiatives of local governments, businesses and local residents. In this regard, it is necessary to establish a structure to implement projects based on discussions and fund-raising efforts within local communities. Kanzo Uchimura (a member in 1880 of the second graduating class at Sapporo Agricultural College) once gave a lecture on Denmark's efforts to rehabilitate itself after the Second Schleswig War of 1864 (published in Talk of the Largest Relic – Denmark Country to Posterity, 1911, Iwanami Bunko). According to Uchimura, the country overcame the crisis that stemmed from losing territory as a result of defeat in the war against Prussia by redeveloping national land through efforts such as providing education for people and promoting afforestation and/or agriculture. In so doing, the nation cultivated a tradition of democracy as people made decisions based on mutual discussion. Uchimura also mentioned renewable energy forms, such as solar and wind power, and proposed local exploration of resources. Today, Denmark's renewable energy technology and welfare systems are relatively advanced, and an important lesson to be learned from Denmark's experience is that crisis gives rise to opportunity. The potential for opening roads to a brighter future for Japan lies in the application of efforts from the ground up that will enable us to take advantage of the current power crisis and so pave the way towards more efficient energy conservation and the use of renewable energy sources for regional revitalization.

References

Hokkaido Bureau of Ministry of Economy and Industry (2012), *The Status and Problems of Wind Turbine Generator Systems in Hokkaido – The Research in the Operations and Maintenances*. Sapporo, Japan: Hokkaido Bureau of Ministry of Economy and Industry.

Hokkaido Prefectural Government (2011), *The Survey of Potential Renewable Energy in Hokkaido*. www.hkd.meti.go.jp/hokpk/renrakukai13/data4_2.pdf (last accessed on January 22, 2015).

Japanese Ministry of Environment (2011), *The Survey of Potential Renewable Energy in Japan*. www.env.go.jp/press/press.php?serial=13696, Hokkaido (last accessed on January 22, 2015).

Nature Conservation Society of Mt. Daisetsu and Ishikari (2013); *Symposium on Geothermal Power Generation*, April 20, 2013.

3 Japan's energy policy in the aftermath of the Fukushima nuclear disaster

Has anything really changed?

Kazuhiro Ueta

Introduction

A severe nuclear accident at the Fukushima Daiichi Nuclear Power Station of Tokyo Electric Power touched off a fundamental review of Japan's energy policy.

The incident prompted then-prime minister Naoto Kan to overhaul the Strategic Energy Plan (2010), directing his cabinet to rewrite the plan and chart a new course for the nation toward a nuclear-free future. Among the central features of the Strategic Energy Plan was a call for a substantial increase in nuclear power generation by 2030, an idea that was stripped of any semblance of reality by the Fukushima meltdowns. The situation clearly called for a fundamental review of Japan's energy policy. In the circumstances, Mr. Kan simply did what any reasonable person would have done.

Responsibility for policy specifics was assigned to the Energy and Environment Council, a ministerial committee established to support government officials as they set about formulating (1) short-, medium- and long-term energy and environmental strategies to rectify imbalances among and vulnerabilities within the nation's energy systems and (2) domestic policy measures in preparation for a coordinated national response to global warming, intended for implementation in 2013 and beyond. The Minister of State for National Policy was appointed as council chair, and the Ministers of the Environment and the Minister of Economy, Trade and Industry were appointed as vice chairs. In June 2011 and at the behest of Mr. Kan, the committee was established within the National Policy Unit of the Cabinet Secretariat. This demonstrated an intent to thoroughly revamp the nation's energy policy.

Below, we review the debates over revisions to Japan's energy policy and discuss how that policy has or has not changed in the aftermath of the Fukushima accident (Ueta, 2013).

Energy policy: a review of content and formulation

The Energy and Environment Council took various approaches in response to their directive.

First, in October 2011, the council established a cost review committee. Before the Fukushima disaster, proponents of nuclear power would typically argue their case by citing (1) the lack of CO_2 emissions from nuclear power plants, (2) the putative safety of such facilities, and (3) the lower cost of nuclear power relative to other sources of energy. The Fukushima meltdowns, however, demonstrated that this claimed economy failed to account for substantial social costs. Hence, the cost review committee was established to standardize the approach to estimate the cost of power generation and apply that approach to nuclear and other power sources to provide policymakers with data for objective comparison.

Similarly, the Electricity Supply–Demand Review Committee was established in March 2012. The electricity supply-and-demand situation was expected to be particularly severe in the summer of 2012, and this committee was tasked with preparing for this prediction by measures such as setting energy conservation targets for utilities around the country.

Furthermore, with regards to energy and environmental strategy, the council organized public town hall debates, presenting the people of Japan with three options to discuss and consider for eventual inclusion within the Innovative Strategy for Energy and the Environment. In examining the process for formulating this strategy, we touch on several key points below.

The process of formulating energy strategy was itself subject to change

We note that in its approach to the issue, the Energy and Environmental Council concerned itself with both the content of energy policy and the process by which it is formulated.

This division of energy policymaking into content and process reveals two factors that we believe are indispensable for making fundamental changes in energy policy. First, it highlights the degree to which policymaking follows democratic principles. Second, it underscores the importance of changing the policymaking process as part of changing policy content.

The Energy and Environmental Council's attempts to change the energy policymaking process are particularly notable for the following three reasons.

First, the council's call for a unified strategic approach brings together the areas of basic energy policy, nuclear energy policy, and global warming policy. Conventionally, these are treated as three separate domains, each covered by its own legal framework and under the purview of a different administrative body with each treated separately from the others. Here, the Energy and Environmental Council, while aware that it could do little about the divergent legal frameworks that straddle these three domains, nonetheless attempted to instill some order by creating a unified strategy for alternative energies and the environment. That is, through its call for strategic consistency, the council highlighted the need for stricter coherence among policies for energy, nuclear power, and global warming.

The establishment of the council was itself significant. This represented an effort to formulate a coherent strategy under political leadership, particularly in the council's attempt to centralize the policymaking process, which was previously scattered among various agencies, under the National Policy Unit, an entity within the Cabinet Secretariat. This made it feasible to formulate a coherent strategy at the administrative level by overseeing the governance of the policymaking process.

The third reason, and one that is particularly notable as the first such attempt in the long history of Japanese public policy formulation, is that democratic debate at town hall meetings was to be incorporated into the policymaking process. Subsequent events show that this was imperfectly accomplished, particularly with regards to debate-based popular opinion surveys and the conduction of public hearings, but these efforts nonetheless both demonstrated that it is possible to incorporate public debate within the decision-making process and highlighted the importance and unique role of "process" and "procedure" in public policy formulation.

Since a general election at the end of 2012, however, these three points have been fading from public view, not least because the new administration has paid them little heed. Even so, the series of measures advanced by the Energy and Environment Council is nonetheless important because it underscores the significance and potential of changing not just policy, but also the way in which policy is determined. In short, a social experiment was conducted on the process of public policymaking, and the people clearly remember its findings. It is an experiment worth reviewing, even after the fact, as an academic endeavor on policy theory.

The populace was to be presented with clear options

To assist in formulation of the Innovative Strategy for Energy and the Environment, the Energy and Environment Council called for the preparation of a variety of options within their three basic areas of responsibility: basic energy policy, nuclear energy policy, and global warming. These were to be presented to the public for discussion and debate.

The first set of options concerns basic energy policy. Here, the Fundamental Issues Subcommittee of the Advisory Committee for Natural Resources and Energy was established under the Basic Act on Energy Policy. In late 2012, the new administration recast the subcommittee as the Kihon Seisaku Bunkakai [Basic Policy Subcommittee]. This organization was directed by the Energy and Environment Council to determine the fundamental direction for a new Strategic Energy Plan, with one of its first assignments being to prepare a series of proposals on an optimal energy mix as a target for the year 2030, intended to serve as a framework for public debate.

The second set of options concerns nuclear energy policy. Here, the Japan Atomic Energy Commission, which was promoting its own review of the nuclear power policy platform, was assigned by the Energy and Environment Council the task of developing a variety of options for the nuclear fuel cycle, with concrete debate to be carried out within a technical subcommittee of the commission.

The third set of options concerns government responses to global warming, which, while not an energy issue in itself, is nonetheless inextricably linked to energy policy. Here, the Energy and Environment Council directed the Global Environmental Committee of the Central Environmental Council to prepare a set of options for a review of policy responses to global warming.

The debate was to be fair and impartial

However, observers were quick to point out that within the process of deliberating the various options presented by these assorted committees, preconditions for fairness and impartiality were not met, beginning with the composition of the committees themselves and the secretariats that oversaw them.

For instance, a participant in the first meeting of the Fundamental Issues Subcommittee had this to say about the composition and organizational structure of that subcommittee:

> The secretariat of the subcommittee is none other than the Agency for Natural Resources and Energy, home ground for the pro-nuclear cadre that gave us the Fukushima accident in the first place. It is just not right to conduct a fundamental review of the nation's basic energy policy under this secretariat while we have yet to see any clear assignment of responsibility for the disaster.

While it is certainly true that the Fukushima meltdowns did act as an impetus for this review, we must nonetheless note that the debate was being advanced without any reasonably thorough investigation into the cause of the accident nor any clear assignment of responsibility. The Japan Atomic Energy Commission, the Nuclear Safety Commission, the Agency for Natural Resources and Energy – these were the organizations leading the policy review, organizations within which no one was being held clearly responsible for anything.

A review of energy policy initiated in response to the Fukushima accident should be advanced under a clear understanding of the causes of the accident and the faults or omissions of the parties responsible for the accident. That almost goes without saying. We add to this the prospect that the parties responsible for Fukushima were to take a central role in reviewing the policies that led to it. One naturally suspects that the review will end up defending the policy choices for which those parties are themselves responsible. In this sense, we could say that this round of energy policy revision was essentially guaranteed to fail from the very start.

With regard to nuclear energy policy, an area long under the purview of the Japan Atomic Energy Commission, the preparation of options relating to the particularly pressing issue of the nuclear fuel cycle was entrusted to a technical subcommittee of the Commission. This subcommittee contained many members with links to the pro-nuclear camp, and similarly quite a few staffers within the secretariat happened to be employees seconded from electric utilities and other related parties. Such staffing issues were quickly pointed out as evidence that the preconditions for fair and impartial deliberation had not been met. Furthermore, the holding of private meetings among some members ahead of meetings of the full committee naturally raised suspicions of collusion to lead the deliberations to some predetermined conclusion.

Again, if we consider the Fukushima disaster as the impetus for policy review, then a precondition for a fair and impartial deliberation of related policymaking issues would be a good understanding of the cause of that accident and a clear assignment of responsibility for its occurrence. We cannot chart a clear direction for a review of energy policy without learning from the mistakes that were made at Fukushima. Yet, even by the time that these committees began putting together their policy options, neither the National Diet of Japan's Fukushima Nuclear Accident Independent Investigation Commission nor the Cabinet's Investigation Committee on the Accident at the Fukushima Nuclear Power Stations had released a report. Furthermore, although the Diet and Cabinet Office did eventually release their reports, to this day we have no clear consensus on how either party might someday put those contents to use to further a review of energy policy.

A second precondition for a fair and impartial deliberation is a shared understanding that for a review of energy policy to be successful, it must include a consideration of how that policy is formulated. As noted earlier, the Energy and Environment Council's mandate does point to a review of the decision-making process, but even with this our apprehensions are not fully allayed.

We elaborate on this a bit here. Reviews of energy policy have, to now, been advanced within a compartmentalized field of related issues (e.g., energy mix, nuclear fuel cycling, global warming) with options for each examined separately. Thus compartmentalized, the issues do require a degree of specialized knowledge to evaluate, and here we can understand the need for expert committees to adequately do so. What causes apprehension on this front, however, is that the composition of the committees, along with the way such deliberations are advanced, can and often does foment a bias that acts to the benefit of some special interest. Indeed, this might be seen as an inherent limitation of the committee system. Another related issue is that when a committee arrives at some conclusion that may benefit a special interest, that conclusion will often restrict the range of debate and the options presented at the next higher level of discussion.

It is also worthwhile to note that while it is important to have a degree of specialized knowledge when discussing basic energy policy, nuclear energy policy, and climate change as separate, distinct issues, it presumably is important to also have a degree of specialized knowledge when discussing them together, as a whole composed of interacting parts. Yet we see no forum for any such discussion, which means that the task of tying together energy policy and all the options they entail falls upon the Energy and Environment Council. The council is political by its nature: it is meant to play a central role in political decision-making. As it does so, it must predicate its decisions on suitably disclosed criteria that reflect the will of the people. The process of creating the criteria that will be used as the basis of decisions, however, is far from clear when viewed from the eyes of the people.

The Nuclear Regulation Authority and the assessment of nuclear power generation

Any review of energy policy must begin with some sort of assessment of nuclear power. In summer 2012, the Energy and Environment Council encouraged public debate about the general direction of energy policy, inviting citizens to assemble at town halls to consider three options (0%, 15%, and 20–25%) for the proportion of nuclear power within Japan's electricity generation mix in 2030.

In the town hall meetings, the debate usually came down to the question of what to do about nuclear power, demonstrating the high degree of public interest in this issue. Similarly, the round of general elections held at the end of 2012 centered on the nuclear issue in many forms, including "a nuclear-free society," "graduating from nuclear power," "no nukes," and "reducing our dependency on nuclear energy." Indeed, voters' attitudes toward nuclear power generally determined which of the various energy policy options they would support.

Attitudes toward nuclear power are expressed most strongly on the issue of whether to permit nuclear power plants to resume operations after a regulatory maintenance shutdown. The controversy came to a head in the summer of 2012, when the government permitted the restart of the Ooi reactor, the first rector to be shut down and restarted following the Fukushima meltdowns. Under a new set of regulations from the Nuclear Regulation Authority governing commercial nuclear power reactors, the issue of reactor restarts has once again come to the forefront.

The current administration, declaring that it will "restart those reactors that are confirmed to be safe by the Nuclear Regulation Authority," has made the resumption of nuclear power generation an integral element of its economic growth strategy. Needless to say, this raises the following question: can reactor restarts be justified on such grounds in the first place?

Reactor safety and the Nuclear Regulation Authority's new regulatory requirements

The primary determinant of one's stand on reactor startups is his or her underlying assessment of nuclear power plant safety. As mentioned above, the administration itself says that it will restart reactors "confirmed to be safe." In other words, if a reactor is not confirmed to be safe by the Nuclear Regulation

Authority, it will not be restarted. This naturally leads to the question of how we determine whether or not a reactor is safe.

What do we mean by "safe" in the context of nuclear power? Not even its most ardent proponent would argue that nuclear power is entirely free of hazards. There can be no assurance of absolute safety, no ironclad guarantee that no reactor will ever experience any kind of trouble whatsoever. Instead, we are asking whether the undeniable hazards of nuclear power can, through technology and regulation, be adequately mitigated, whether the risks it presents can be kept at a level acceptable and tolerable to society at large.

Thus, the question of nuclear safety comes down to technology and regulation. This naturally draws attention to the quality of standards prepared by the Nuclear Regulation Authority and the adequacy of the system that the regulatory agency uses to ensure nuclear operators comply with standards.

Thus, on nuclear safety there are several important questions. Who will be responsible for it? Who will assess it? How is that assessment to be done?

Obviously, power producers (electric utilities, typically) must shoulder responsibility for the safety of its power production business. Yet, in the aftermath of the Fukushima meltdowns, we saw some extremely sloppy management, particularly in regard to the handling of radioactive contaminated wastewater. We cannot simply let electric utilities handle things on their own.

The Fukushima meltdowns showed us that we have a serious problem with the system of nuclear power safety reviews. The Nuclear and Industrial Safety Agency had, of course, conducted safety inspections for the Fukushima Nuclear Power Plant many times before its eventual catastrophic failure. Note, however, that this agency is simply a unit within the pro-nuclear Ministry of Economy, Trade and Industry, a positioning that heightens the likelihood of safety reviews being twisted into something that promotes the interests of nuclear proponents. Furthermore, the agency already had a reputation for dry, pro-forma reviews. The agency has itself played a substantial role in the creation of the nuclear safety myth.

In principle, Japanese reactors run in 13-month cycles, between which they are temporarily shut down for maintenance and inspection. The Fukushima disaster, however, made it difficult for operators to restart their reactors after a scheduled maintenance and inspection shutdown, and so the units ended up going off line one by one, and not being allowed to resume operation until a new system for safety regulation and inspection could be put in place.

The government sprang into action, declaring that it will institute the world's highest level of nuclear safety standards and systems and, in support of that goal, introduced the Act for the Establishment of the Nuclear Regulation Authority, which became law on 20 June 2012. This was followed by the establishment of the Nuclear Regulation Agency as a regulatory body to implement and enforce the new law. The agency promulgated a new set of regulatory standards on 19 June 2013 for enforcement from July 8 of that year.

Reactions to the new standards were many and varied. On one hand, the electric utilities, eager to restart their reactors, complained that the standards were excessively strict and often lacked a scientific basis. Others pointed out that the standards were far short of the "world's highest level" touted by the administration. Still others voiced dissatisfaction that the new rules effectively gave the utilities a green light to resume reactor restarts.

Just what impact would the new standards have on attempts to restart idled nuclear power plants? Would the Nuclear Regulation Authority, backed by the standards, really be able to create a regulatory system capable of preventing any more severe nuclear accidents in the future?

The reconfiguration of regulatory standards

The Fukushima meltdowns did bring about a major shift in the conceptual approach to regulatory standards. Earlier, when the myth of nuclear safety still held some sway, regulatory standards were implicitly founded on the premise that a severe accident would not occur. After the meltdowns, this premise was revised because severe accidents can occur, and thus regulatory standards should be reconstructed accordingly. In addition to strengthening the extant standards so as to prevent severe accidents from occurring in the first place, new standards were added to cover responses to severe accidents and events such as terrorist attacks.

These included standards for coping with an intentional crashing of an airliner into a reactor building, for forestalling any widespread dispersion of radioactive substances, and for reinforcing containment vessels to make them more resistant to damage. With regards to boiling water reactors (i.e., those of the same type as the Fukushima Daiichi units), the installation of filtered vents was added as a precondition for permission to restart a reactor. Other requirements mandate additional backup power sources for each unit and an emergency control station capable of cooling down a reactor by remote control. This said, operators were given a five-year grace period in which to install such equipment.

Also bolstered were measures intended to strengthen resistance to earthquakes and tsunamis. Among the new preconditions for a restart is an estimation of a maximum hypothetical tsunami height and, taking that as a base height, the construction of a seawall capable of protecting the plant from it. Likewise, the construction of a reactor or other vital plant components above an active fault is now explicitly prohibited. That is, any nuclear power plant located on a fault will not be allowed to operate. Also, the criterion for what indicates an "active" fault was shifted from a seismic dormancy of 120,000–130,000 years to, in some cases, dormancy of 400,000 years.

From the above, the new standards appear stricter than the old. Furthermore, the standards are retroactive; they also apply to existing nuclear power plants. That is, an operator that wishes to restart a reactor must first bring the facility into full compliance with the new regulations. The amount of work entailed by this varies considerably from one reactor to another. Important to note here, though, is that the electric power companies can decide whether to implement these measures.

How does the utility make this decision? By what standards does it decide whether or not to spend the funds necessary to bring a reactor to compliance?

If the company is economically rational, it will make that decision after a balanced consideration of the cost of corrective actions and the value of the returns thus obtained, particularly the earnings to be generated in the future by that reactor should it be brought back online. For example, for some reactor, the expenses may be high and, because the reactor is already old, the potential for earnings within its remaining service life may not be enough to fully offset those expenses. In that case, a rational operator would forgo the expense and instead simply scrap the facility.

Various reactors will require various degrees of corrective action, and so the cost to achieve regulatory compliance will vary as well. The new standards, purportedly intended to ensure the safety of nuclear power plants, can, depending on the manner in which they are applied, actually end up encouraging operators to screen and potentially restart hazardous facilities because that would be the economically efficient choice.

Problems with the new standards

Furthermore, even the updated standards have a number of problematic areas that cannot be overlooked. In fact, they appear contrary to the stated purpose of the standards (i.e., to promote nuclear safety by preventing severe accidents).

The first such issue is that operators are given a grace period before fully compliance with the new standards is enforced. It does take time to put safety measures in place, and presumably those companies are happy to have it, but this nonetheless raises the question of how safety is to be ensured before the end of the grace period.

Second, although the operating life of a nuclear power plant is generally limited to 40 years, extension of up to 20 years beyond that are to be granted if the plant is found to meet the new standards after a detailed round of special inspections. It is hard to imagine how such extensions might further the supposed safety-promoting objective of the new standards.

Third, directives on plant site selection, contained within the old standards, are missing from the new directives. Such directives concern the suitability of locating a plant at some particular area, particularly as it concerns the vulnerability of the surrounding community to a nuclear incident or accident. The idea, of course, is to provide a degree of physical separation between the reactor and the people who live nearby, enough that local residents will not be in immediate danger of exposure should something go wrong. Such directives are missing from the new standards. It seems that stricter standards for reactor-side venting systems are intended to take their place. Note, however, that as pointed out by a capable engineer, Koichi Takitani, site selection rules based on principles learned from the Fukushima experience would make many existing plants ineligible for further operation (Takitani, 2013). Technology-based controls are certainly necessary to limit the threat, danger, and harm of widespread dispersion of radioactive contamination in the event of a nuclear power accident. So too are control on site selection.

Fourth, there is the issue of radiation exposure among people who work at nuclear power plants. With regards to Fukushima, here we cite high exposures among workers assigned to help clean up the mess and less-than-ideal monitoring of their cumulative exposures. Note too that it is necessary to shield workers from excessive exposure, not only as they respond to a serious accident at a damaged reactor, but also as they go about their daily tasks within a smoothly functioning facility. Such radiation exposure monitoring and management are given short shrift within the new standards. Some experts point out that cumulative radiation exposure can be surprisingly difficult to manage on even a daily work level (Japan Federation of Bar Associations, 2012). This handling of the working environment within a nuclear power plant also raises ethical questions, not least as pertains to the use of multiple layers of subcontractors.

Above we have listed various problems with the new regulatory standards. We see that just because a facility satisfies these standards does not mean that it can operate safely. To declare otherwise – to conclude that an electric power utility is safe because it is up to regulation – would run counter to efforts to ensure that risks are kept at a level acceptable and tolerable to society at large. Of course, operators must stand at the front line of nuclear safety, but it is also indispensable to have open lines of communication, with community participation and full disclosure. Essentially, what we need is a system of strategic environmental assessments, but power plants are exempted from this at present (Harashina, 2011).

One more point to keep in mind is the general feebleness of the organizational structure assigned with the task of assessing compliance with the new standards. Relative to the United States Nuclear Regulatory Commission, an independent entity, the investigative arm of the Nuclear Regulation Authority is conspicuously weak in terms of both quantity and quality of resources and regulatory tools. Further raising concerns is that despite the indisputable shortcomings of this unit, it seems to be under pressure to complete assessments quickly.

The final problem extends beyond the contents of new regulations or the regulatory system intended to enforce them. It pertains to the fundamental paradigm; specifically, the idea that if the new regulatory standards are satisfied, that alone is reason enough to permit a restart.

Conclusion

In this chapter, we center our discussion on the method by which energy policy is formulated within the context of recent nuclear safety regulations. Japanese energy policy is undergoing changes in the aftermath of the Fukushima disaster. Attempts are being made to reform energy policy, and indeed we do see some changes here and there. We also see plenty of new problems.

For future work, we plan to investigate the effects of a feed-in tariff. The post-Fukushima (July 2012) introduction of the feed-in tariff, an incentive structure that obligates utilities to buy renewable electricity at above market rates, has led to a major change in energy policy. Yet, although this initiative has brought about rapid and significant changes that continue to this day, it has also raised a number of issues, including a need to reinforce the power grid and a need for regulatory reform. We intend to discuss these points more fully in another paper.

References

Harashina, S. (2011), *Environmental Assessment* [Kankyo Assessment], Iwanami Shoten (in Japanese).

Japan Federation of Bar Associations, ed. (2012), *Investigation: NPP Labour Issues* [Kensho Genpatsu Roudo], Tokyo: Iwanami Booklet (in Japanese).

Takitani, K. (2013, 2 July), "New regulations do not protect against radiation exposure: removing the requirement for an assessment of site suitability" [Hibaku kara Mamoranai Shinkisei: Ricchi Tekigou-sei wo Hazusu], *Ekonomisuto*, 92–94 (in Japanese).

Ueta, K. (2013), *A Treatise on Greening Energy* [Midori no Enerugi Genron]. Tokyo: Iwanami Shoten (in Japanese).

4 Studies on the background to the expansion of wind power in China

Lei Wang and Fumikazu Yoshida

Introduction

The conservation of energy and the greater utilization of sources of renewable energy are the major approaches now being followed to solve the problem of climate change. As the country that emits more CO_2 than any other, China is trying to reduce its CO_2 emissions through the use of nuclear power, but mainly by energy conservation and the increasing share in the overall generation of power contributed by the resources of renewable energy. In 2011, the capacity of total installed power was shared out as follows: thermal power 72.5% (770 million kW), hydro power 21.8% (230 million kW), wind power 4.3% (4.5 million KW), while nuclear power accounted for only 1.2% (1.2 million kW) (The State Electricity Regulatory Commission [SERC], 2011). Between 2005 and 2010, China's wind power generation grew by 94.75%, and by the end of 2011, its installed capacity had reached 62.73GW, making it the world's greatest generator of wind-powered energy (The Global Wind Energy Council, 2001). This means that China is not only the country that emits the greatest quantity of CO_2, but at the same time is the country with the world's largest wind power installed capacity. It therefore becomes important to reveal the steps by which China has achieved this preeminent position.

Since 2005, the number of wind farms in China has increased rapidly, amounting in 2010 to 500 plants (Kang et al., 2012). By 2010, the building of wind farms had become a large-scale operation: 9,793 units with a 1.5M single unit capacity had been installed, occupying 77.6% of the new increasing installed capacity, along with 980 units with 2MW single unit capacity that occupied 10.4% of the new increasing installed capacity (Chinese Wind Energy Association [CWEA], 2005–2010). With the rapid expansion of wind power, the average price of 1kW per wind power plant had fallen by the end of 2010 to 3,500 yuan. There is no doubt that the reduction in the price of the wind power equipment has helped to expand the number of wind power plants. By 2011, China's wind power equipment suppliers had combined to form 29 companies, compared to 70 smaller companies in 2008(China Wind Power Development Report, 2012).

The Chinese state-owned enterprises have played a major role in the development of wind power. Although about 60 companies have now entered the wind

Table 4.1 The statistics of China's wind power installed capacity

Years	New grid-onnected installed capacity (MW)	Cumulative installed capacity (MW)	Growth rate (%)
1994 or earlier	Na	9.7	57.82
1994	12.9	22.6	132.99
1995	11.1	33.7	49.12
1996	23.3	57.0	69.14
1997	84.7	141.6	148.60
1998	71.9	213.5	50.78
1999	50.3	263.8	23.56
2000	77.3	341.1	29.30
2001	41.7	382.8	12.23
2002	65.7	448.6	17.16
2003	98.3	546.9	21.91
2004	215.9	762.7	39.48
2005	506.1	1,268.8	66.36
2006	1,399.4	2,668.2	110.29
2007	3,360.8	6,029.0	125.96
2008	6,143.7	12,172.7	101.90
2009	5,497.3	17,670.0	45.16
2010	13,640.0	31,310.0	77.19
2011	16,530.0	47,840.0	52.79

Source: (China Wind Power Development Report, 2012)

power market, this is a relatively small compared to the number of central state-owned enterprises (China Wind Power Development Report, 2012). China Guangdong Nuclear Power Company, China's largest nuclear power plant manufacturer, and the Shenhua Group, a coal-related company, are the two largest companies in the wind power plant business.

Most of the many prior studies on wind power promotion have stressed the importance of government policies for the promotion of China's wind power industry (Liu et al., 2002; Wang and Chen, 2010; Zhang, Yang, et al.,2009). Others evaluate the status of wind power penetration (Xu et al., 2010), the importance of equipment manufacturing (He and Chen, 2009), the promotion of renewable energy through the application of (Clean Development Mechanism) CDM (Wang and Chen, 2010). In addition, several studies have analyzed the challenges that the wind power has faced, such as the low quality of the turbines (Li, 2010; Liao et al., 2010; Yu et al., 2009), the mismatch between policy and regulations (Li, 2010; Yang et al., 2010). Furthermore, many studies have pointed out the weakness of the wind power generation system. For example, the disposal of generated wind power and the instability of output (Cyranoski, 2009; Han et al., 2009), the lack of a power grid infrastructure (Li, 2010; Liao et al., 2010; Liu and Kokko, 2010; Yu et al., 2009; Wang, 2010), as well as stagnation in the development of domestic manufacturing and the high costs of power generation (Han et al., 2009).

Previous studies have taught us that China has experienced a rapid expansion of wind power as an energy source, and that government policy has played, and is playing, an important role in the development of the wind power industry. The reduced cost of wind equipment and a clear target for the promotion of wind power are the two major incentives that have encouraged the implementation of wind power, while the "Renewable Energy Law" has in particular been evaluated highly (Horii, 2011). Yet these earlier studies have not analyzed the background to the rapid spread of wind power, nor have they made clear why the competitive bidding system that started in 2003 began so smoothly despite the low profits. And though these previous studies have pointed out that the CDM projects have been effective in promoting wind power, the analysis of the effects has been inadequate. Therefore, to explore the problems mentioned above, we focus in this chapter on the background to the rapid expansion of wind power. The layout of the chapter is as follows: we first analyze the background to the promotion of wind power promotion in the 1990s; second, we analyze the background to the promotion of wind power after 2000; finally, we summarize the characteristics of China's promotion of wind power.

The background to the attempts to implement wind power in the 1990s

Since China adopted the policy of reform and opening-up in 1978, the growth of China's gross domestic product (GDP) has been remarkable. In order to sustain its economic growth rate, the Chinese government's Seventh Five-Year Plan (1986–1990) laid out a plan to disseminate the power supply from thermal power, hydropower and nuclear power to other sources of energy (James and Clark, 1987). At that time, the government's position on attempts to expand such sources of renewable energy as wind power and biomass had not yet been made clear. Since the 1990s, however, the Chinese government has been focusing on the promotion of wind power. If we consider the energy supply, trends in the international energy market and China's power supply in the 1990s, we can point to three reasons for this. The first reason is the fear of a shortage in the energy supply, for despite being rich in the reserves of energy, especially coal, it is possible that China will not be able to meet its energy demands in the future (James and Clark, 1987). As we all know, the consumption of energy supports economic growth, and between 1978 and 1993, China's average GDP growth rate was 9.3%, its energy production growth rate was 3.7%, and its energy consumption growth rate was 4.3%. This means that at that time China achieved the target of supporting the high GDP growth with low energy consumption growth. However, it became impossible to support the high GDP growth with low energy consumption, and the reason for this was the closure of coalmines. Since the late 1980s, the energy consumption has increased rapidly, particularly in the industrial sector, and the increased energy was mostly supplied by coal, in particular, coal supplied by township coal companies (Lin, 1998). Although from 18% in 1980, the production share of small coalmines had increased by 1994 to 42%, the rate of coal consumption afterwards fell to lower levels because of the increasing use of oil. In 2000, because the productivity of small coalmines is very low and accidents frequently happen, in addition to the low growth rate of coal consumption, the central government decided to close up to 50% of coalmines (Wu and Li, 1995), while in the mid-1990s the central government had already limited the output of large state-owned coalmines in order to solve the financial problems of state-owned coal enterprises, and, as a result, 40 state-owned coalmines and 25,000 small non-state-owned coalmines were closed in 1998. Yet, in order to realize the development target of achieving by 2000 a GNP four times greater than that in 1980, at least 150 million tons of standard coal would have been required (Gu, 1992). Nevertheless, it is impossible to provide a larger share than twice that of fossil-derived energy. Since reform of the coalmining sector will inevitably reduce the coal supply, the government has turned its focus to the expanding of renewable energy for increasing the supply of energy.

The second problem is air pollution. According to the data supplied by China's atmospheric observation net, in 1989, the average concentration of SPM's (suspended particulate matter) was $432\mu g/m^3$: in northern cities, it was $526\mu g/m^3$, in southern cities it was $318\mu g/m^3$. The average urban concentration of SO_2 was $105\mu g/m^3$: in northern cities it was $93\mu g/m^3$, and in southern cities it was $119\mu g/m^3$. By 1992, however, the SPM had increased to 2 ten million tons, and SO_2 had increased to 1.68 ten million tons. In 1995, the area affected by acid rain was 2.8 million km^2, a growth of 60% when compared to 1985. In China, 90% of SO_2, 85% of CO_2, 87% of NO_X, 70% of fine particles are discharged by the direct combustion of coal (Byrne and Bo, 1996). As air pollution by the early 1990s had become a more and more serious hazard, the pressures of environmental degradation and growing awareness of the dangers forced the government to recognize that energy conservation had to become a priority of energy policy (Lin, 1998), and in August 1992, the Chinese government announced "emission standards for thermal power plants" in order to reduce SO_2 emissions. Although the implementation of the energy conservation policy has had an effect on the reduction of SO_2 emissions, and while the production of coal has been decreasing, the increase in steel production and the generation of electricity has meant that reliance on energy conservation for reducing air pollution has had only a limited effect (Jonathan and Fridley, 2000). Since an increase in power generation worsens air pollution, the Chinese government at that time also required an improvement in the structure of energy consumption so as to carry out energy conservation. An important feature of China's energy policy encourages two ways to improve energy consumption (Gu, 1992). One is to increase the percentage of clean energy while reducing the high proportion of coal consumption. The other is to reduce the direct consumption of coal, so as to increase conversion to secondary sources of energy: for example, to increase the consumption of clean energy and clean electricity. As previous studies have in fact pointed out, while the Chinese government is seeking to reduce the consumption of coal, it is also trying to enhance the production of electricity. Yet while coal has been turned to more efficient use, there is no doubt that the SO_2 and other air pollutants will increase if the electricity supplies increase. The world's energy consumption structure is shifting. Other countries have sought to rectify the serious situation caused by air pollution by expanding the use of renewable energy, and many incentives thus exist for the Chinese government to try to develop sources of renewable energy in China, too.

The third factor is the possible implementation of wind power. Sources of renewable energy include wind power, solar power, and biomass. When considering the balance of developing renewable energy, the Chinese government planned a variety of programs to develop the use of wind power, solar power, and biomass. The development of wind power has a long history and has evolved a more mature technology than other sources of renewable energy; most importantly, that it has the highest level of economic profit among these sources encouraged the government to attempt to implement wind power rather than other types of renewable energy. China is now the world's largest producer of small wind power equipment, while, at the same time, it is the most rich in wind resource, with the biggest wind power market (Zhou, 1996a).Consequently, wind power when compared to other renewable energy, has the best conditions for expansion, since not only the government but also investors pay attention to its benefits. In fact, the history of Chinese wind power promotion is very long, since already in the early 1950s small wind turbines were used as a power supply unit in regions far from the city. In recent years, China has for some time been operating a grid-connected wind power plant using imported equipment and technology. Indeed, the first grid-connected wind power plant was built as long ago as 1986, and in 1994, 14 wind farms with a total output of 30MW were built. Most of these wind farms were at the time located in rural areas, and they played a role in the power supply of rural communities (Zhou, 1996b). In 1997, large-scale wind power generation went into the early stages of commercialization. With the support of the World Bank, the relevant government departments who conducted a research project named "Study of the Financial Factors that Drive the Spread of Renewable Energy" found that wind power has the maximum power supply potential compared to other sources of renewable energy (Li and Zhu, 1999). While the market for the generation of energy through wind power has grown, to promote its commercialization penetration, the Chinese government and the World Bank carried out a project to expand the 190MW wind power generation facilities by 1999 (Han, 1999). Not only has China been carrying out research cooperation with international organizations, it has also been promoting a variety of research projects on wind power by itself. For example, in January 1995, the largest PV wind hybrid system in China was built on Xiaoguan Island in Shandong Province; this included five nationally made types of equipment, 5kW PV, a 110kAh battery, and was designed as a power system to be used mainly in rural areas (Li, 1997).As we have mentioned above, the promotion of wind power has a long history and has the potential to supply the greatest amount of power among sources of renewable energy: the Chinese government has therefore chosen to implement wind power as a major goal of national policy.

The background to efforts to promote wind power during the 2000s

As Table 4.1 shows, Chinese wind power installed capacity has been growing rapidly in recent years, especially since 2007 (Lin, 1998). The background to the efforts to promote wind power in the 2000s differs from the conditions in the1990s, the most obvious difference being that since 2000 official government policy has actively supported the development of wind power. Internationally, developed countries such as Germany and the United States have begun to accelerate the development of their renewable energy industries and have instituted a number of policies such as renewable portfolio standard (RPS) and feed-in-tariff (FIT) to support the development of sources of renewable energy. China has learned from the experience of these countries, and has instituted a great number of renewable energy development policies that are designed to cope with the realities of China's situation.

We can point here to three pillars of official policy: (1) a reduction in cost through the implementation of the competitive bidding system; (2) the dissemination of domestic equipment; and (3) the implementation of such renewable energy support policies as RPS and FIT, while the CDM project contributes to the rapid expansion of wind power.

Part of the background to this is that because of the need to establish the security of the power supply, the government aims to reduce the costs of wind power while attempting to spread its use on a large scale as soon as possible. As the economy grows rapidly, it becomes difficult for China to achieve a power supply balance. In the 1980s, the Chinese government responded to a serious power shortage by strengthening the expansion of power generation facilities, but between 1995 and 1999, the power supply again became unbalanced: in 1998, for example, the power supply in around 40% of the regions exceeded the demand, 20% of the regions suffered a surface power supply shortage, while only 40% of other regions were able to balance the supply and demand (Gu, 1992).Once China had joined WTO in 2001, however, because the demand since 2003 for energy and power increased rapidly to keep in step with increasing production as the economy was overheating. Since the construction of thermal power plants takes from 3–5 years, the power shortage that occurred before and since 2003 was caused by the failure of the nations' power generation to keep up with the power demand.

We cannot doubt that the imbalance in the power supply has seriously damaged economic growth, and the Chinese government, thinking of the difficulty of a coal supply that would meet the demands of electricity production and of the environmental pollution caused by thermal power plants, has consequently hurried to spread wind power as fast as possible. Since the price of foreign wind power equipment is 20% higher than domestically made units (Zhang, Chang, et al., 2009), the Chinese government believes that the spread of domestic facilities can lead to reduced costs, and so, on July 4 2005, the Chinese government issued "Notification about the Request of the Construction Management of Wind Farm," a directive that emphasizes the need for an increase in the domestic rate of equipment in order to expand the domestic equipment while reducing wind power costs. A reduction in costs along with the competitive bidding system mechanism that determines the system's interconnection price based on the contract price since 2003 offers incentives to the wider construction of wind farms, whose implementation since 2006 has entered a phase of rapid growth.

Since large-scale power plants in China are all state-owned power generation enterprises or central enterprises, direct regulation policies such as RPS are considered to be valid as a means to offer incentives to implement wind power. With the incentive to make profits, the power plant operators will choose the lowest cost for renewable power, with the exception of hydropower, which since 2007 has also been expanding rapidly.

Given such conditions as power plant locations, the investment environment and power interconnection since 2009 are becoming severe, and the annual increasing rate of wind power dropped from 100% to a rate of 52.79%in 2011. At this stage, the FIT, in which the benchmark prices are appointed in four different areas plays a role in pushing the growth of wind power.

The progress of China's wind power industry is largely attributed both to the effective implementation of a bundle of domestic public policies (such as the wind power concession programme, mandatory renewable power market share, power surcharge for renewables, and tax relief) and international support (in the forms of technology transfer, CDM, and public finance support) (Zhang, Chang, et al., 2009). At this point, it is also necessary to analyze the effect of the CDM project on wind power implementation, for which provided finance for Chinese wind that has been analyzed by previous studies(Gang and Morse, 2013; Tang and Popp, 2014; Zhou, 2010).It is concluded that the CDM, along with static investment and annual wind electricity production, is one of the most significant factors in promoting the development of wind power in China (Zhao et al., 2014). The financing impact of CDM certainly guarantees the profitability of Chinese wind power projects; however its effect in terms of the diffusion of technical information and technical capability is weak (Zhao et al., 2013).To analyze the effect of the CDM project, we have selected Huitengxile wind farm as an example. Table 4.2 shows the data, where if the carbon emission reduction credits (CERs) are sold at a price of 54 yuan/ton, then 54,000 tons CO_2 in the 10-year contract period can be reduced, and the revenue from

Table 4.2 The cost and profit of Huitengxile wind farm (39.6MW)

Cost		Profit	
Construction costs (yuan/kW)	10901	Grid connection price (yuan/kWh)	0.382
Interest (yuan/kWh)	0.041	Power generation (10^6kWh/yr)	142.97
Employee's wages (original/kWh)	0.068		
Operation maintenance costs (yuan/kWh)	0.156		
Other costs (yuan/kWh)	0.034		

Data Source: (Han et al., 2009)

CERs will be 270 million yuan (a revenue about 2.7 million yuan every year) (Han et al., 2009).

Table 4.2 shows that if the grid connection price is decided as 0.382 yuan/ kWh, the total cost is 0.45 yuan/kWh, and the annual deficit will be 10 million yuans. If the wind power investors can achieve 0.1 yuan/kWh from CDM projects, at the first stage 30,000h (about 10 years), the profit will be 45.7 million yuans, that is (0.382yuan/ kWh – 0.450yuan/kWh +0.1 yuan/kWh) 1429.7 million kWh, about 4.5 million yuans profit every year. These results prove beyond doubt that the CDM project is successfully promoting the dissemination of China's wind power. However, as the CDM projects application conditions become more and more severely, the wind power project cannot meet the conditions which the CDM projects required, so the chance of getting CDM credit turns to low. Furthermore, the CDM projects cannot solve technical problems of wind power, so the role of CDM in promoting the wind power has been limited.

To summarize the analysis above, the policies that in 2005 set the target of a 70% domestic equipment rate, the competitive bidding system that has been promoted since 2006, the mandatory share of renewable energy that forced the large-scale power plants to promote wind power that was issued in 2007, plus the Chinese version of FIT (benchmark prices divided into four kinds of wind resource areas) that was released in 2009, have all played an important role in expanding the use of wind power. We are left, however with the question that we posed at the beginning of this essay: since the profit from the competitive bidding system is very small, why has the competitive bidding system been implemented so smoothly? Let us analyze the incentives that push investors in the power industry to take part in the bidding, and try to answer this question.

When we consult the grid-connected price expressed in Table 4.3, we can see that the profits from wind power, which are determined by the competitive bidding system, are very low; for this, we can adduce three reasons.

Table 4.3 The bidding projects between 2003 and 2010

	Power generation capacity of the public tender by the State Reform Commission (MW) (percentage of the total installed capacity in brackets)	Result of the bid price (yuan/kWh)
September 2003	200 (36.5%)	0.4365–0.5013
September 2004	300 (39.3%)	0.3820–0.5190
August 2005	450 (35.5%)	0.4616–0.6000
August 2006	700 (26.2%)	0.4056–0.5006
September 2007	950 (15.8%)	0.4680–0.5510
September 2010	1000 (3.2%)	0.6235–0.7370

Source of data: (Jiang et al., 2011)

The first reason is that if we take into account the determination of the Chinese government and the movement of the international market, we can predict that the future of the wind power market is likely to be bright. Although the benefits from electric power sales at the contract price are small, the contract is valid for 25 years, and if the scale of wind power generation grows, then it looks likely that the costs will decrease. Moreover, this assumption is supported by the premise that the price of the interconnection of the wind power system will decline substantially. The price of connecting up the wind power grid must fall to a level that is able to compete with the interconnection price of the thermal power system. While the risks may be high, we can consider that the prospects for the development of wind power market are good, although this is not the greatest reason for believing that costs will fall.

The second reason for believing that costs will fall is that the promotion of wind farm can contribute the development of local economy. At the start of a wind power plant project, the foundation work, the land rent, the production of equipment, the operation of the wind farms and their management, all these are linked with the local economy. It is the local government, however, who will benefit from wind power projects, and if the local government does not offer special preferential policies for wind power investors, their incentive to invest will be small.

The third reason is the imperative need to secure renewable energy resources and the availability of wind. Yet while wind is a renewable energy resource and its supply is infinite, geography imposes limits, for since wind power plants cannot always be built in areas rich in wind resources, sites for the wind power plant will be restricted. When the scale of wind power grows stronger, the location will be tested more severely, and the building costs will increase. Because of the higher costs, the profit will be lower than the benefits derived from the bidding system. So, to profit from the enterprise, it will be a wise choice to ensure the location of wind plants as early as possible, and this is the enterprise's main incentive to participate in the bidding actively.

Conclusion

This chapter has offered a detailed analysis of the background to the promotion of wind power, while also evaluating the effect of CDM projects on wind power promotion. The analysis has shown that what lay behind the efforts to implement wind power in the 1990s was the fear of an energy supply shortage, the problem of air pollution, and the economic advantages of wind power to industry and local economies. Today, although the problems and advantages may not be much different, a new factor has come into play, and the most obvious difference between the 1990s and the 2000s is that since 2000, official policy has actively supported the development of wind power. The reduction in cost through the implementation of the competitive bidding system and the dissemination of domestic equipment, the implementation of such support policies as RPS and FIT, as well as the CDM project, have all contributed to the rapid expansion of wind power as a source of renewable energy. The analysis of the data proves beyond doubt that the CDM project has been active in promoting the dissemination of China's wind power, and the expansion of wind power in China not only contributes to a reduction of the world's greenhouse gases, but also constitutes an important element of the world's progress in wind power technology (Liao et al., 2010). At the same time, the Chinese government plays a more important role than do the governments of other countries, and it has formulated a large number of policies with regard to the expansion of wind power, while making sure that the policies are implemented thoroughly.

According to the report from REN21, China added an estimated 16.1 GW of new capacity in 2013, increasing total installed capacity by 21% to 91.4 GW. About 14.1 GW was integrated into the grid, with approximately 75.5 GW in commercial operation by year's end. Difficulties continued in transmitting power from turbines (particularly in remote northeast areas) to population demand centres, and about 16 TWh lost due to curtailment. However, new transmission lines and turbine deployment in areas with better grid access are reducing the number of idled turbines, and the rate of curtailment dropped from 17% in 2012 to 11% in 2013. Wind generated 140.1 billion kWh in China during 2013, up 40% over 2012 and exceeding nuclear generation for the second year running. By year's end, almost 25% of total capacity was in the Inner Mongolia Autonomous Region, followed by Hebei (10%), Gansu (9.1%), and Liaoning (7.3%) provinces, but wind continued its spread across China – 10 provinces had more than 3 GW of capacity (Renewable Energy Policy Network for the 21st Century, 2014).

The challenge of promoting wind power is not unique to China, for many developed and emerging countries are seeking to harness its potential, although the Chinese government's top-down centralized planning approach stipulates the most rapid implementation of wind power growth. The prospects for China's wind energy industry are still excellent, and the huge scope that exists in China for the application of all aspects of wind energy development offers the realistic prospect that wind energy will in future play a major role in helping China to meet its internal and international environmental obligations and its CO_2 reduction objectives. It will also open up new avenues for the perfecting of manufacturing and developmental skills in the construction of offshore wind parks, which will in turn enable China to become, and remain, a major player in the growing international markets for wind power expertise.

References

Byrne, J. and Bo, S. (1996), "The challenge of sustainability: balancing China's energy, economic and environmental goals," *Energy Policy* 24(5): 455–462.

China Wind Power Development Report 2012, GWEC (2012), *30 Years of Policies for Wind Energy.*

Chinese Wind Energy Association (CWEA) (2005–2010), *Statistics of China's wind power installed capacity.* Beijing: CWEA.

Cyranoski, D. (2009), "Renewable energy: Beijing's windy bet," *Nature* 457: 372–374.

Gang, H. and Morse, R. (2013), "Addressing carbon offsetters' paradox: lessons from Chinese wind CDM," *Energy Policy* 63: 1051–1055.

The Global Wind Energy Council (2001), *Global wind statistics 2011.* www.eoleres. com/media/944933/gwec_-_global_wind_statistics_2011[1][1].pdf (last accessed on November 1, 2013).

Gu, G. (1992), "China's dual-thrust energy strategy: economic development and environmental protection," *Energy Policy* 20(6): 500–506.

Han, J.Y., Mol, A.P.J., Lu, Y.L., and Zhang, L. (2009), "Onshore wind power development in China: challenges behind a successful story," *Energy Policy* 37(8): 2941–2951.

Han, Y. (1999), "Wind energy development in China: reality and market forces," *Renewable Energy* 16: 965–969.

He, Y. and Chen, X. (2009), "Wind turbine generator systems. The supply chain in China: status and problems," *Renewable Energy* 34(12): 2892–2897.

Horii, N. (2011), "The suggestions from the growth of wind power equipment company in China,"[The promotion of new energy in Fukuoka and trends of new energy policy in Asia],*Heisei 23 year Fukuoka – Institute of Developing Economies Collaborative Research Business Report,* Chapter 3 (in Japanese). www.pref.fukuoka. lg.jp/uploaded/life/103838_17780431_misc.pdf (last accessed on December 1, 2013).

James, P.D. and Clark, A.L. (1987), "China's energy resources: potential supply, problems, and implications," *Energy Policy* 15 (1): 73–90.

Jiang, L. et al (2011), "Wind Energy in China," *IEEE power & Energy Magazine* November/December, 36–46.

Jonathan, E.S. and Fridley, D.G. (2000), "What goes up: recent trends in China's energy consumption," *Energy Policy* 28: 671–687.

Kang, J., Yuan, J., Hu, Z., and Xu, Y. (2012), "Review of wind power development and relevant policies in China during the 11th Five-Year-Plan period," *Renewable and Sustainable Energy Reviews* 16: 1907–1915.

Li, J. (1997), "Renewable energy development in China: resource assessment, technology status, and greenhouse gas mitigation potential," *Applied Energy* 56 (3/4): 381–394.

Li, J. (2010), "Decarbonising power generation in China – Is the answer blowing in the wind?" *Renewable and Sustainable Energy Reviews* 14(4): 1154–1171.

Li, J. and Zhu, L. (1999), "Wind power commercialization development in China," *Renewable Energy* 16: 817–821.

Liao, C., Jochem, E., Zhang, Y., and Farid, N. (2010), "Wind power development and policies in China," *Renewable Energy* 35(9): 1879–1886.

Lin, G. (1998), "Energy development and environmental constraints in China," *Energy Policy* 26(2): 119–128.

Liu, W., Gan, L., and Zhang, X. (2002), "Cost-competitive incentives for wind energy development in China: institutional dynamics and policy changes," *Energy Policy* 30(9): 753–765.

Liu, Y. and Kokko, A. (2010), "Wind power in China: policy and development challenges," *Energy Policy* 38(10): 5520–5529.

Renewable Energy Policy Network for the 21st Century (2014), *Renewables Global Status Report 2014*. www.ren21.net/REN21Activities/GlobalStatusReport.aspx (last accessed on November 15, 2014)

The State Electricity Regulatory Commission (SERC) (2011), *Wind Power Regulation Annual Report 2011*, Beijing: SERC.

Tang, T. and Popp, D. (2014), The Learning Process and Technological Change in Wind Power: Evidence from China's CDM Wind Projects, *NBER Working Paper No. 19921*, February 2014.

Wang, Q. (2010), "Effective policies for renewable energy – the example of China's wind power-lessons for China's photovoltaic power," *Renewable and Sustainable Energy Reviews* 14(2): 702–712.

Wang, Q. and Chen, Y. (2010), "Barriers and opportunities of using the clean development mechanism to advance renewable energy development in China," *Renewable and Sustainable Energy Reviews* 14(7): 1989–1998.

Wu, K. and Li, B. (1995), "Energy development in China: National policies and regional strategies," *Energy Policy* 23(2): 167–178.

Xu, J., He, D., and Zhao, X. (2010), "Status and prospects of Chinese wind energy," *Energy* 35(11): 4439–4444.

Yang, M., Nguyen, F., De T'Serclaes, P., and Buchner, B. (2010), "Wind farm investment risks under uncertain CDM benefit in China," *Energy Policy* 38(3): 1436–1447.

Yu, J., Ji, F., Zhang, L., and Chen, Y. (2009), "An over-painted oriental arts: evaluation of the development of the Chinese renewable energy market using the wind power market as a model," *Energy Policy* 37(12): 5221–5225.

Zhang, P., Yang, Y., Shi, J., Zheng, Y., Wang, L., and Li, X. (2009), "Opportunities and challenges for renewable energy policy in China," *Renewable and Sustainable Energy Reviews* 13(2): 439–449.

Zhang X., Chang, S., Huo, M., and Wang, R. (2009), "China's wind industry: policy lessons for domestic government interventions and international support," *Climate Policy* 9(5): 553–564.

Zhao, Z., Li, Z., and Xia, B. (2014), "The impact of the CDM (clean development mechanism) on the cost price of wind power electricity: a China study," *Energy* 69: 179–185.

Zhao, Z., Sun, G., Zuo, J., and Zillante, G. (2013), "The impact of international forces on the Chinese wind power industry," *Renewable and Sustainable Energy Reviews* 24: 131–141.

Zhou, D. (2010), Application of CDM in China wind power generation, *2010 China International Conference on Electricity Distribution*.

Zhou, F. (1996a), Development of China renewable energy, *World Renewable Energy Congress (WREC) 1996*, 1132–1137.

Zhou, F. (1996b), Wind energy prospects in China, *World Renewable Energy Congress (WREC) 1996*, 785–788.

Part II
Trade and industrial structural change

5 Changes in trade and economic structure during the past 25 years

Have green growth, low carbon strategies made a significant impact in Northeast Asia?

Yasuhiro Ogura and Akihisa Mori

Introduction

Export-oriented growth has been an engine of economic growth in Northeast Asia since the late 1980s. International trade in the region has significantly increased in the decades since then (Table 5.1). Governments have often made selective interventions to foster specific industries through targeting and subsidizing credit that was clearly linked with specific export performance, making public investments in applied research, and sharing a wider range of information between the public and private sectors (World Bank, 1993). Countries also offered preferential measures to attract foreign direct investment. These measures accelerated export growth and increased per capita income. However, the current export-oriented growth has increased emission of untreated air and water pollutants and generation of solid wastes. In response, countries have gradually begun implementing stringent environmental regulations since the 1990s.

Stringent regulation, however, may impose too much cost on pollution-intensive industries and lead to the pollution haven effect. This effect occurs when a tightening of environmental regulations in one country deters exports (or stimulates imports) of dirty goods (Taylor, 2004) from other countries where environmental regulations are not as tight and industries are not required to reduce emissions (Mani and Wheeler, 1998). For example, the United States and Japan likely generated such an effect in Latin American and East Asia, respectively, during the period from 1960 to 1995 (Mani and Wheeler, 1998). East Asia, especially China, has increased inclusive carbon emissions and water consumption since 1985 to satisfy the import demands of the United States and Japan (Shimoda et al., 2009).

In response to increasing global concern about climate change and the emerging global climate regime, coupled with the 2008 global economic crisis, South Korea and China began to frame climate management as an economic opportunity. They regarded renewable energy as a strategic industry and made selective interventions to foster related industries by targeting and subsidizing credit through a green growth and low carbon strategy. Using this support, several

Table 5.1 Changes in trade of Japan, South Korea, and China during the past 25 years (in billions of US dollars)

Year		1992	1993	1994	1995	1996	1997	1998	1999	2000	2001	2002	2003	2004	2005	2006	2007	2008	2009	2010	2011	2012
Japan																						
Total	trade	572.7	601.6	670.3	779.0	760.1	759.9	668.8	727.6	859.0	752.7	754.3	855.4	1021.0	1110.8	1225.8	1336.6	1543.9	1132.7	1463.9	1678.6	1684.4
	export	339.7	360.9	395.6	442.9	410.9	421.1	388.1	417.6	479.3	403.4	416.7	472.0	565.8	594.9	646.7	714.3	781.4	580.7	769.8	823.2	798.6
	import	233.0	240.7	274.7	336.1	349.2	338.8	280.6	310.0	379.7	349.3	337.6	383.5	455.3	515.9	579.1	622.2	762.5	552.0	694.1	855.4	885.8
Environmental goods	trade	28.9	31.7	38.2	47.9	50.5	50.6	45.0	50.3	65.0	53.9	52.6	63.2	82.3	85.5	91.9	83.1	90.0	73.5	97.0	110.6	109.1
	export	22.6	24.9	30.0	37.1	37.2	36.5	32.4	36.9	48.6	38.7	38.0	45.9	61.1	61.8	63.1	58.1	63.8	52.9	71.5	80.8	78.3
	import	6.3	6.8	8.2	10.8	13.4	14.0	12.5	13.4	16.4	15.2	14.7	17.3	21.2	23.8	28.8	25.0	26.2	20.6	25.5	29.8	30.9
Dirty industries	trade	89.9	93.5	104.5	129.8	119.9	122.1	108.6	114.8	131.7	117.7	122.9	142.9	176.0	195.0	217.4	246.2	277.8	221.9	290.4	333.7	315.4
	export	52.0	54.9	61.2	74.6	69.5	71.5	65.9	69.8	78.4	69.0	74.8	86.4	107.3	119.5	132.4	149.4	167.1	137.5	179.6	194.6	185.3
	import	37.9	38.6	43.3	55.2	50.4	50.6	42.7	44.9	53.3	48.7	48.1	56.5	68.7	75.5	85.0	96.8	110.7	84.4	110.8	139.1	130.0
South Korea																						
Total	trade	158.4	166.0	198.4	260.2	280.0	280.8	225.6	263.4	332.7	291.5	314.6	372.6	478.3	545.7	634.8	728.3	857.3	686.6	891.6	1079.6	1067.4
	export	76.6	82.2	96.0	125.1	129.7	136.2	132.3	143.7	172.3	150.4	162.5	193.8	253.8	284.4	325.5	371.5	422.0	363.5	466.4	555.2	547.9
	import	81.8	83.8	102.3	135.1	150.3	144.6	93.3	119.8	160.5	141.1	152.1	178.8	224.5	261.2	309.4	356.8	435.3	323.1	425.2	524.4	519.6
Environmental goods	trade	8.7	8.9	12.2	17.5	18.4	17.1	11.1	14.4	16.3	14.2	16.5	20.3	30.6	40.8	53.2	53.6	63.4	60.6	81.5	82.1	85.9
	export	1.8	2.0	2.6	3.7	3.9	4.9	4.9	6.2	5.1	4.9	5.8	7.0	11.5	20.1	30.0	33.0	39.3	38.8	50.7	53.2	55.8
	import	6.9	6.9	9.6	13.8	14.6	12.2	6.2	8.2	11.2	9.3	10.7	13.3	19.0	20.8	23.2	20.6	24.1	21.8	30.8	29.0	30.1
Dirty industries	trade	32.0	34.4	40.8	55.7	54.0	55.6	46.8	51.8	61.9	55.9	61.6	74.6	102.2	120.7	140.3	168.2	200.1	154.4	202.5	245.6	236.1
	export	14.0	15.6	17.2	22.7	21.8	24.9	26.5	26.1	30.4	27.4	29.2	35.9	49.1	58.5	68.5	79.7	93.0	77.2	100.5	126.8	125.7
	import	18.0	18.8	23.5	32.9	32.2	30.7	20.3	25.7	31.4	28.6	32.4	38.7	53.1	62.2	71.8	88.5	107.2	77.3	102.0	118.8	110.4
China																						
Total	trade	165.5	195.7	236.6	280.9	289.9	325.2	324.0	360.6	474.3	509.7	620.8	851.0	1154.6	1421.9	1760.4	2176.2	2563.3	2207.2	2973.8	3641.8	3867.0
	export	84.9	91.7	121.0	148.8	151.0	182.8	183.8	194.9	249.2	266.1	325.6	438.2	593.3	762.0	968.9	1220.1	1430.7	1201.6	1577.8	1898.4	2048.8
	import	80.6	104.0	115.6	132.1	138.8	142.4	140.2	165.7	225.1	243.6	295.2	412.8	561.2	660.0	791.5	956.1	1132.6	1005.6	1396.0	1743.4	1818.2
Environmental goods	trade	7.1	9.9	12.9	15.1	16.3	16.6	16.8	18.4	22.6	26.6	35.6	56.5	88.4	108.4	132.1	160.0	195.5	172.6	236.8	270.8	275.2
	export	1.9	2.2	3.0	4.0	4.6	5.7	5.8	6.4	8.3	9.3	11.6	17.2	26.6	37.7	50.0	68.3	91.6	82.2	117.2	138.8	141.2
	import	5.2	7.6	9.9	11.1	11.7	10.9	11.1	12.0	14.3	17.4	24.0	39.4	61.8	70.7	82.1	91.8	103.9	90.4	119.6	132.0	133.9
Dirty industries	trade	33.6	41.5	46.6	61.5	62.4	69.4	70.2	78.9	100.9	104.8	124.5	164.9	224.6	275.9	335.6	429.7	503.1	411.5	551.8	689.7	694.4
	export	11.1	11.8	16.6	26.3	24.6	30.2	29.8	30.3	38.1	39.1	46.0	59.6	89.5	118.4	161.1	213.7	268.2	181.4	253.8	332.5	348.9
	import	22.5	29.8	30.0	35.2	37.8	39.2	40.4	48.6	62.7	65.7	78.5	105.3	135.1	157.6	174.6	216.0	234.9	230.1	297.9	357.3	345.5

Source: Author's compilation of data from UN Comtrade (2013).

wind turbine and solar photovoltaic cell manufacturers became world leading companies.

This chapter aims to explore how stringent environmental regulations and implementation of green growth, low carbon strategies in Northeast Asia have affected international trade, with a special focus on the impact on environmental and pollution-intensive industries since the 1990s. First we give definition for such "environmental" and "dirty" industries and provide an overview of our analytical methodology in Sections 2 and 3. Then, in Sections 4 and 5, this chapter explores the changes in production and trade for these industries in Japan, South Korea, and China.

Definitions of environmental and dirty industries

Environmental industry

Along with the progress in international negotiations regarding climate change, the recognition of environmental goods (i.e., products from the environmental industry) as important factors in mitigating climate change has led to a growing controversy about the scope of the 'environmental industry,' and policies such as more favorable tariff treatment for environmental goods in international organizations such as The Organisation for Economic Co-operation and Development (OECD) and Asia-Pacific Economic Cooperation (APEC) (Steenblik, 2005: 3). In international trade negotiations by such agencies, the existing classification of goods used to account for the tariff on each product is also applied to environmental goods. Countries trading in environmental goods have compiled lists of goods to define them as such, but definitions are still far from complete and controversy remains between member countries. The OECD prepared its first report regarding the environmental industry in 1992 and has discussed the issue continuously. OECD/Eurostat (1999) attempted to define the environmental industry and classify goods and services into the following three main categories: pollution management,[1] cleaner technologies and products,[2] and resource management (OECD/Eurostat, 1999).

APEC has also discussed the issue since 1995 and members have repeatedly nominated definitions of environmental goods (Steenblik, 2005). In September 2012, the 20th APEC economic leaders' meeting agreed on a list of 54 products that could be classified as environmental goods (APEC, 2012).

In this chapter, the two lists are referred to and defined as environmental goods (produced by environmental industry). As a result of the trade data collection methods for product codes included in the two lists, data are only available for 186 codes in UN Comtrade (2013) (see Appendix). In the following, trade data of environmental goods means the data of those 186 goods.

Dirty industries

Mani and Wheeler (1998) defined dirty industries as those that have incurred high levels of abatement expenditure per unit of output in the United States and other OECD economies, based on Hettige et al. (1994). For analytical purposes, however, they selected industries that rank high on actual emissions intensity (emissions per unit of output), namely, iron and steel, nonferrous metals, industrial chemicals, pulp and paper, and nonmetallic minerals. This chapter also uses the same five industries to determine what constitutes a dirty industry, given that they have the highest intensity of emissions, and analyzes these five pollution-intensive goods as the products from dirty industries.

Methodology

Environmental industry

Trade specialization coefficient (TSC) can be employed to see a country's trade specialization in the environmental industry. TSC is often used when measuring the competitiveness or trade structure of specific countries or industries (METI, 2013). TSC is defined as:

$$TSC = (X - M)/(X + M)$$

For a given industry, a TSC approaching 1 indicates a country's specialization in exports, and a TSC approaching −1 indicates a specialization in imports. Categories of environmental goods in OECD/Eurostat (1999) are used to define the environmental industry. The subcategory 'renewable energy plant' in the 'resource management' category is given special attention in this chapter to analyze the impact of low carbon strategies for green growth.[3]

Dirty industries

Mani and Wheeler (1998) employ the share of production in domestic manufacturing and import/export ratio to see if a country has become a pollution haven or generates a pollution haven effect. A country is classified as a pollution haven if it increases the share of production by dirty industries in domestic manufacturing while decreasing its import/export ratio. Companies in a country with much tighter discharge regulation may relocate their production sites to a country where regulation is lax. As a result, the pollution associated with the production of dirty industries may be transferred to countries or regions with lax regulation, which will increase production and export. Conversely, a country generates a pollution haven effect or becomes more dependent on pollution havens if it reduces its share of dirty industries in domestic manufacturing and its import/export ratio increases.

In examining the change in the structure of dirty industries in Japan, South Korea, and China, data for manufacturing production is obtained from United Nations Industrial Development Organization (UNIDO) (2013) and trade data is from UN Comtrade. Data collection is intended to cover as long a time series as possible and all the available data for Japan, South Korea, and China is used in the analysis of the years after the examination by

Mani and Wheeler (1998). However, there are some missing data by year or product in each country due to limitations in the database. Therefore, time period is non-uniform in the analysis.

Growth in the environmental industry

At a first glance, trade of environmental goods has grown over the past 25 years in Japan, South Korea, and China (Figure 5.1). In particular, the value of trade in China has risen sharply from the middle of 2000s and now is several times higher than that of Japan and South Korea. In case of Japan and South Korea, the degree of increase is rather gradual compared to that of China, although total value is actually increasing greatly.

Specialization in the export or import environmental goods

TSC shows no remarkable trend throughout the period because almost all the shifts are within the small range of 0.3 (i.e., between –0.1 and 0.2). The only exception in the three countries is the downward trend in Japan, although its fluctuation is not so large. However, when focusing on short-term changes, TSC in South Korea rose sharply in 1998, and there was also a sharp rise in TSC in China in mid-2000s.

The TSC of environmental goods shows an upward trend in South Korea and China. TSC in South Korea rose sharply in 1998 and in mid-2000s, after the period of Asian economic crisis and China's accession to World Trade Organization (WTO). In the case of China, TSC was on an upward trend in the mid-1990s and began rising again in 2005. While TSC in Japan shows a downward trend, its level is still higher than in South Korea and China (Figure 5.2).

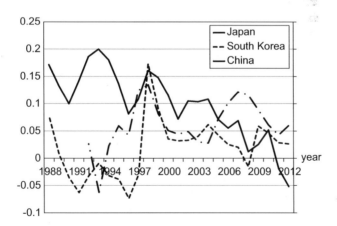

Figure 5.1 Shift in TSC in Japan, South Korea, and China during the past 25 years
Source: Author's compilation of data from UN Comtrade (2013).

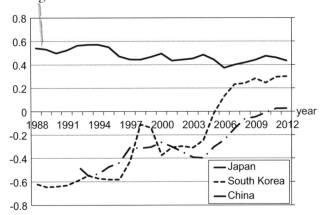

Figure 5.2 Shift in TSC of environmental goods in Japan, South Korea, and China during the past 25 years

Source: Author's compilation of data from UN Comtrade (2013).

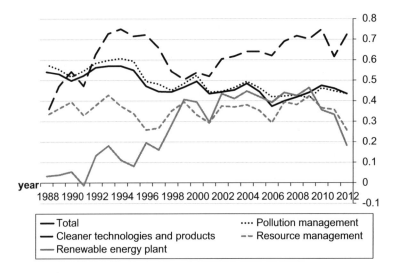

Figure 5.3 Shift in TSC of environmental goods in Japan during the past 25 years

Source: Author's compilation of data from UN Comtrade (2013).

In the case of Japan shown in Figure 5.3, TSC for the category 'resource management' rose in the late 1990s and remained around 0.4 throughout the 2000s. However, it has been falling since 2010. A similar trend can be observed for its subcategory 'renewable energy plant.' In the case of the 'cleaner technologies and products' category, TSC fell in the late 1990s and began to rise again beginning in 2002. The TSC for this category has remained at a high level compared to the other two countries.

In South Korea, The TSC of all categories rose in 1997 and 1998 immediately following the Asian economic crisis (Figure 5.4). In particular, the 'cleaner

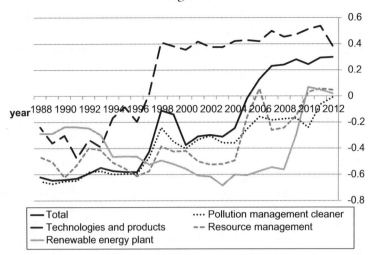

Figure 5.4 Shift in TSC of environmental goods in South Korea during the past 25 years
Source: Author's compilation of data from UN Comtrade (2013).

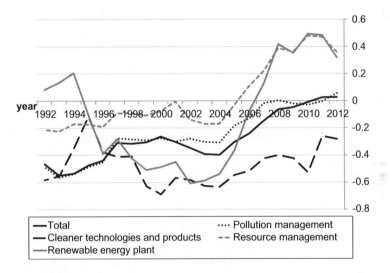

Figure 5.5 Shift in TSC of environmental goods in China during the past 25 years
Source: Author's compilation of data from UN Comtrade (2013).

technologies and products' category has increased its export specialization since 1997 and maintained a level around 0.4~0.5. TSC also had an upward trend in mid-2000s.[4] In particular, the TSC of the 'resource management' category and its subcategory 'renewable energy plant' both drastically shifted to an export specialization sharply after 2008. South Korea turned to net exporter in those categories in 2010.

The TSC of all categories in China shifted upward from 2005 to 2008, several years after China's accession to the WTO (Figure 5.5). In particular, the TSC of the 'resource management' category has risen sharply since the mid-2000s and China has shifted to an export specialization, which has exceeded that of Japan. The TSC of 'cleaner technologies and products' decreased in 2009 and 2010. However, it has increased again in 2011.

Summary

The shifts in the TSC of environmental goods in South Korea and China imply that the impact of the green growth and low carbon strategies on the trade structure of such goods is rather small, especially when compared with the impact of the Asian economic crisis and China's accession to the WTO. South Korea has become more specialized in the export of environmental goods in the period after those two events, while China also became more export-oriented since it joined the WTO.

However, radical shifts in the TSC of the 'renewable energy plant' subcategory in South Korea may show that green growth strategies may have actually had a significant impact on transforming the trade structure of such products and industries to being more export-oriented.

There seemed to be no radical shift in the TSC of Japan over the past 25 years. Despite this fact, Japan still has the highest level of TSC among the three countries examined in this chapter.

Change in trade patterns of dirty industries

Trade in dirty industries shows the same trend as that of the environmental industry. South Korea, China, and Japan have increased trade in dirty industries during the past 25 years, with China having the largest increase among them (Table 5.1).

Production and dirty industry share of the manufacturing sector

Production in dirty industries in Japan dropped around 2000, but rose again since then, becoming 30 percent higher than the 1988 level. The dirty industry share of all manufacturing rose since 2003, reaching 5 percent (Figure 5.6).

South Korea has steadily increased production in dirty industries, except for one interruption in 1998, reaching 4.3 times larger in 2012 than in 1988. On the other hand, the dirty industry share of all manufacturing has increased only slightly (Figure 5.7).

China has increased production in dirty industries throughout the period, and it eventually became about six times larger in 2012 compared with the 2003 level (Figure 5.8). The dirty industry share in all manufacturing also continued to rise gradually, reaching 3 percent in 2012.

While all three countries have increased both the production value and share of all types of dirty industries, their rates of increase differ slightly in terms of production value. The rate of increase in production value in Japan is smaller than that in the other two countries.

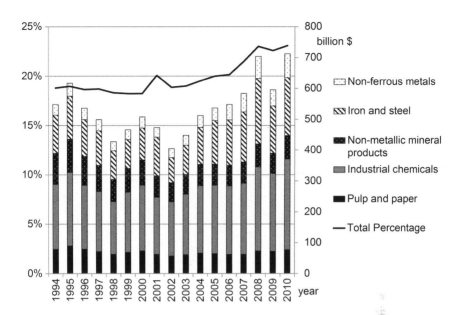

Figure 5.6 Shift in production value and share of all manufacturing for dirty industries in Japan

Source: Author's compilation of data from UNIDO (2013).

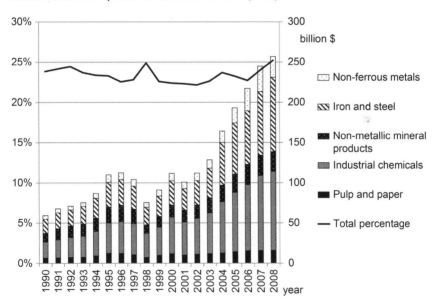

Figure 5.7 Shift in production value and share of all manufacturing for dirty industries in South Korea

Source: Author's compilation of data from UNIDO (2013).

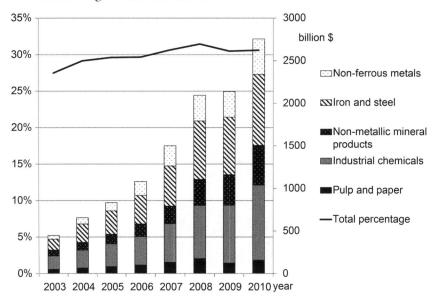

Figure 5.8 Shift in production value and share of all manufacturing for dirty industries in China

Source: Author's compilation of data from UNIDO (2013).

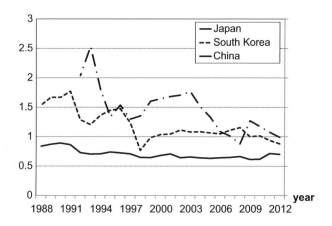

Figure 5.9 Shift in import–export ratio of dirty industries in Japan, South Korea, and China

Source: Author's compilation of data from UN Comtrade (2013).

Import–export ratio

As shown in Figure 5.9, the import/export ratio of dirty industries in Japan has stayed below 1 throughout the period. The ratio fell slightly over the period, but with a slight increase in 2011. Its import–export ratio for trade with the

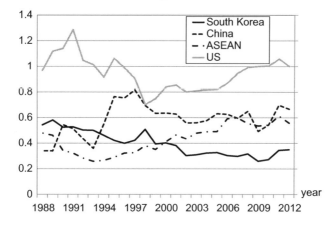

Figure 5.10 Shift in import–export ratio of Japan with specified trade partner
Source: Author's compilation of data from UN Comtrade (2013).

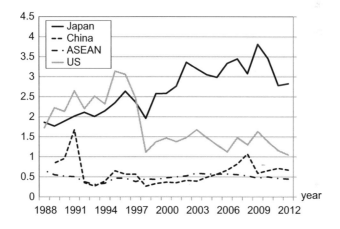

Figure 5.11 Shift in import–export ratio of South Korea with specified trade
partner
Source: Author's compilation of data from UN Comtrade (2013).

United States and ASEAN decreased in the 1990s, while the ratio has increased
since the late 1990s (Figure 5.10). The ratio for South Korea has been decreasing. The import–export ratio for China has decreased since the Asian economic
crisis, but began to increase in 2010.

In South Korea, the ratio dropped below 1 in 1998. It drifted just over 1
throughout the 2000s and again shifted just a bit below 1 in 2011. It is noted
that import/export ratio has increased for trade with Japan, China, and the
United States since the Asian economic crisis (Figure 5.11).

The import–export ratio in China dropped drastically in mid-1990s and mid-
2000s and fell below 1 in 2008. It kept shifting downward throughout the

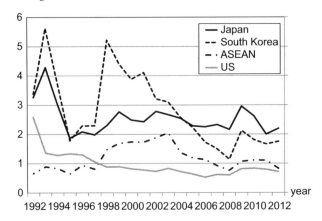

Figure 5.12 Shift in import–export ratio of China with specified trade partner
Source: Author's compilation of data from UN Comtrade (2013).

period, although it rose temporarily in 2009 when overall trade decreased, especially in export. China's import–export ratio with South Korea and ASEAN decreased after rising briefly following the Asian economic crisis period (Figure 5.12).

Summary

In Japan, South Korea, and China, the domestic production share of dirty industries has shown an upward trend over the period. The import/export ratio has trended downward in China and has also decreased slightly in Japan and South Korea. Overall, these three countries have become pollution havens, as pollution-generating production shifts to these countries from other countries.

However, this does not exclude the possibility that these countries also generate a pollution haven effect toward particular trade partners. For example, South Korea seemed to generate a pollution haven effect in the 2000s against China, Japan, and the ASEAN 6[5] countries. South Korea has increased its import/export ratio for trade with Japan and China, while only marginally increasing its share of dirty industries in the 2000s. Similarly, Japan continues to generate pollution haven effects against ASEAN countries, as its import–export ratio with ASEAN has risen gradually.

There does not appear to be a trend of dependence on the import of dirty industries in other countries after the green growth and low carbon strategies were implemented in South Korea and China. Instead, the shifts in the import/export ratio of these countries show that trade in dirty industries has become more specialized in export.

Discussion

This section discusses the results above with a focus on the shift in the value of exports or imports and the share of overall trade for environmental and dirty industries (Figures 5.13 and 5.14).

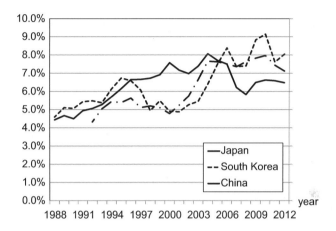

Figure 5.13 Share of overall trade of environmental goods in Japan, South Korea, and China

Source: Author's compilation of data from UN Comtrade (2013).

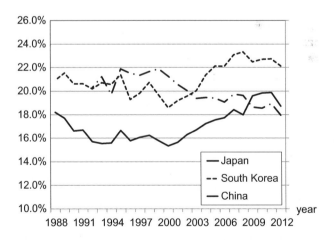

Figure 5.14 Share of overall trade in dirty industries in Japan, South Korea, and China

Source: Author's compilation of data from UN Comtrade (2013).

Japan

Japan has been a net exporter of both environmental and pollution-intensive goods during the past 25 years. The TSC of the environmental industry is still around 0.4, which is largest of the three countries. The import/export ratio in Japan has also been the lowest throughout the period.

However, the TSC of environmental goods is decreasing gradually, just like that of trade overall in Japan over the last 25 years. Such a trend seems to be unchanged after the government of Japan specified green innovation as growth field in its New Growth Strategy in 2009. The share of trade for environmental goods has been almost flat since 2009. The impact of the strategy on the trade of environmental goods seems to be marginal in Japan.

South Korea

South Korea became a net exporter in the 'cleaner technologies and products' category after the 1997 Asian economic crisis. Export from the environmental industry has significantly increased since China's accession to the WTO. After the 2008 global economic crisis, TSC drastically increased in 'resource management' category and the 'renewable energy plant' subcategory. Growth in the export of environmental goods seems to have accelerated during this same period, while import value has remained almost flat since 2010 (Table 5.2). The trade share of environmental goods has also shown an upward trend as a whole.

However, exports by dirty industries have also grown, although the extent is not as large as for the environmental industry. Now South Korea is a net exporter in these industries and net export value is growing. Growth of exports in dirty industries also seems to have accelerated in the last three years. The trade share of dirty industries has remained almost the same since 2009, which has had an upward trend during the 2000s.

These results imply that South Korea has focused on export promotion in both environmental and dirty industries. Green growth seemed to accelerate such a shift in trade structure by focusing on the export of certain specified goods.

China

Accession to the WTO has significant impacts on the trade structure of China. It accelerated the increase in TSC for almost all categories of environmental goods, especially resource management and renewable energy plant. The trade share of environmental goods has had an upward trend over the same period. In a similar way, the import/export ratio of dirty industries has decreased over the same period, while its share of overall trade has been on a decreasing trend. These results imply that China's accession to the WTO had a significant impact on China's trade structure and resulted in a shift to more export-oriented trade.

Table 5.2 Growth of exports and imports in Japan, South Korea, and China (value in 1992 = 100)

Year			1992	1993	1994	1995	1996	1997	1998	1999	2000	2001	2002	2003	2004	2005	2006	2007	2008	2009	2010	2011	2012
Japan	Total	export	100	106	116	130	121	124	114	123	141	119	123	139	167	175	190	210	230	171	227	242	235
		import	100	103	118	144	150	145	120	133	163	150	145	165	195	221	249	267	327	237	298	367	380
	Environmental goods	export	100	110	133	164	164	162	143	163	215	171	168	203	270	273	279	257	282	234	316	357	346
		import	100	108	130	170	211	222	198	212	260	241	232	274	336	376	456	395	414	325	403	472	488
	Dirty industries	export	100	105	118	143	134	137	127	134	151	133	144	166	206	230	254	287	321	264	345	374	356
		import	100	102	114	146	133	134	113	119	141	129	127	149	181	199	224	255	292	223	292	367	343
South Korea	Total	export	100	107	125	163	169	178	173	188	225	196	212	253	331	371	425	485	551	474	609	725	715
		import	100	102	125	165	184	177	114	146	196	173	186	219	275	320	378	436	532	395	520	641	636
	Environmental goods	export	100	114	147	207	218	277	280	351	288	278	329	395	653	1136	1700	1867	2226	2197	2867	3007	3155
		import	100	100	139	200	211	176	89	119	162	134	155	192	275	300	335	298	349	315	446	420	436
	Dirty industries	export	100	112	123	163	156	178	189	187	217	196	208	257	351	418	490	570	665	552	719	907	899
		import	100	104	131	183	179	171	113	143	175	159	180	215	295	346	399	492	595	429	567	660	614
China	Total	export	100	108	142	175	178	215	216	229	293	313	383	516	699	897	1141	1436	1684	1415	1858	2235	2412
		import	100	129	143	164	172	177	174	206	279	302	366	512	696	819	982	1186	1405	1248	1732	2163	2256
	Environmental goods	export	100	116	157	208	239	299	301	334	436	485	609	898	1392	1971	2616	3571	4792	4301	6132	7258	7387
		import	100	146	188	212	224	207	211	229	273	332	458	752	1179	1350	1568	1752	1983	1726	2283	2521	2557
	Dirty industries	export	100	106	150	238	222	273	270	274	345	353	416	539	810	1070	1457	1933	2426	1641	2296	3007	3155
		import	100	132	133	156	168	174	179	216	279	292	348	468	600	700	775	959	1043	1022	1323	1586	1534

Source: Author's compilation of data from UN Comtrade (2013).

Trade value has been increasing steadily, not only in exports but also in imports for both environmental and dirty industries. Such a trend is consistent throughout the period. Moreover, growth in both imports and exports seems to have accelerated since 2010 in those industries. Low carbon strategies may have impacts on promoting overall trade in both industries, while keeping with the broader trend of structural change to more export-oriented trade.

Conclusions

Major findings can be summarized as follows.

First, South Korea and China have shifted to export specializations following pivotal events: the Asian economic crisis and China's accession to the WTO. In particular, the shift to export specialization in the environmental industry seemed to be accelerated by China's accession to the WTO for both South Korea and China. Moreover, the trade share of environmental goods increased rapidly in the same period. Dirty industries in China also seem to have shifted to more export-oriented trade since then. Compared to such events, the impact of green industrial policy seems to be limited.

Second, the way in which green industrial policy influences trade varies by country. It caused a drastic shift in TSC in the 'resource management' category and its 'renewable energy plant' subcategory, and accelerated export growth of environmental goods in South Korea. In China, implementation of low carbon strategies accelerated trade growth while not generating a drastic shift in TSC or import–export ratio. This may suggest differences in the central focus of the policy.

Japan seems to have kept more export surplus than other two countries for both industries and is less dependent on dirty industry imports. However, the TSC of 'resource management' in Japan has fallen below that of China over the last three years. Policy influences on the trade of environmental and pollution-intensive goods in the last several years seems quite marginal in Japan.

However, challenges remain for this research. First, a causal relation between the change in trade patterns and trade volume and green industrial policy was not examined directly in this chapter. Trade itself is influenced by many factors. While there are suggestive results that have been observed, such as the shift in TSC of South Korea for specific environmental goods, that seem to be the result of the strategy government has adopted. However, it remains unclear exactly how much influence on trade are due to the policy decision, rather other factors such as the Asian economic crisis, China's WTO accession, and so on. There seems to be room for further research on this topic.

In terms of environmental goods, the Harmonized System classification does not perfectly fit with environmental goods in actuality. Therefore, both environmental goods and the other types of goods are counted in trade statistics with no classification in each code. Indeed, the list provided by APEC agrees with many of the 'ex-outs,' the annotation that is used for each produce (Zhang, 2011). Since we currently have no way to reorganize the data extracted from

UN Comtrade (2013) in accordance with such annotations, we have directly used the data based on the six-digit Harmonized System code. Consequently, our research includes data that may not directly relate to environmental goods. There is also room to study and improve the classification and treatment of trade data.

Notes

1 This category includes products related to air control, management of water and waste, environmental monitoring and assessment, etc. The product codes included are shown in the Appendix.
2 This category includes cleaner and more resource-efficient products. Product codes are cited in the Appendix.
3 Product codes included in these categories are shown in Appendix.
4 In the case of the 'resource management' category, there is lack of trade data after 2007 for some products. Therefore, this chapter holds off on examining the rise and fall of TSC in the mid-2000s in this category.
5 In this chapter, ASEAN 6 includes Indonesia, Malaysia, Philippines, Singapore, Thailand and Vietnam.

References

APEC (2012), 2012 Leaders' Declaration, Vladivostok Declaration – Integrate to Glow, Innovate to Prosper – ANNEX C: APEC List of Environmental Goods, www.apec.org/Meeting-Papers/Leaders-Declarations/2012/2012_aelm/2012_aelm_annexC.aspx (last accessed September 24, 2013).

Hettige, H., Martin, P., Singh, M., and Wheeler, D. (1994), IPPS: The industrial pollution projection system, *Policy Research Working Paper No.WPS1431*, The World Bank Policy Research Department Environment, Infrastructure and Agriculture Division.

Mani, M. and Wheeler, D. (1998), "In search of pollution havens? Dirty industry in the world economy, 1960 to 1995," *Journal of Environment & Development* 7 (3): 215–247.

Ministry of Economy, Trade and Industry, Japan (2013), Supporting industries and companies with potential to advance into foreign markets, *White Paper on International Economy and Trade 2013*, www.meti.go.jp/english/report/downloadfiles/2013WhitePaper/2–3.pdf (last accessed on August 1, 2014).

OECD/Eurostat (1999), *The Environmental Goods and Services Industry: Manual on Data Collection and Analysis*, Paris: OECD.

Shimoda, M., Watanabe, T., Yeh, Z., and Fujikawa, K. (2009), "Inter-linkage between industrial structure and environmental burden in East Asia," in Mori A. (ed.), *Economic Development and Environmental Policy in East Asia*, Kyoto: Minerva Shobo, 40–57 (in Japanese).

Steenblik, R. (2005), Environmental goods: A comparison of the APEC and OECD lists, *OECD Trade and Environment Working Paper, No. 2005–04*, OECD Joint Working Party on Trade and Environment.

Taylor, S.M. (2004), "Unbundling the pollution haven hypothesis," *Advances in Economic Analysis & Policy* 4 (2): 1–26.

UN Comtrade (2013), http://comtrade.un.org/db/ (last accessed on December 10, 2013)

UNIDO (2013), *INDSTAT4*, CD-ROM.

World Bank (1993), *The East Asian Miracle: Economic Growth and Public Policy*, Washington, DC: Oxford University Press.

Zhang, Z. (2011), "Trade in environmental goods, with focus on climate-friendly goods and technologies," *East-West Center Working Papers, Economic Series No.120*, Honolulu: EastWest Center.

Appendix

In this chapter, five products are identified as dirty industries: iron and steel, non-ferrous metals, industrial chemicals, pulp and paper, and non-metallic mineral products. Data by UNIDO (2013) and UN Comtrade (2013) are used for the analysis. Product codes and years that are applied in each database are listed below:

- UNIDO (ISIC Rev.3): 210 (for pulp and paper), 241 and 242 (for industrial chemicals), 2610 and 269 (for non-metallic mineral products), 2710 and 2731 (for iron and steel), 2720 and 2732 (for non-ferrous metals). Years: Japan 1994–2010, South Korea 1990–2008, China 2003–2010.
- UN Comtrade (HS): 47 and 48 (for pulp and paper), 28–40 (for industrial chemicals), 68–70 (for non-metallic mineral products), 72 and 73 (for iron and steel), 74–81 (for non-ferrous metals). Years Japan, South Korea 1988–2012, China 1992–2012.
- The definition of environmental goods in this chapter leans on the lists of OECD/Eurostat (1999) and APEC (2012). Data for 186 products code in those lists was found to be available.

Product codes are below:

220710, 230210, 252100, 252220, 280110, 281410, 281511, 281512, 281610, 281830, 282010, 282090, 282410, 283210, 283220, 283510, 283521, 283522, 283523, 283524, 283525, 283526, 283529, 284700, 285100, 290511, 320910, 320990, 380210, 391400, 392020, 392490, 392690, 441872, 460120, 560314, 580190, 591190, 681099, 690210, 690220, 690290, 690310, 690320, 690390, 690919, 700800, 701710, 701720, 701790, 701990, 730900, 731010, 731021, 731029, 732510, 780600, 840290, 840410, 840420, 840490, 840510, 840690, 840991, 840999, 841011, 841012, 841013, 841090, 841182, 841199, 841290, 841320, 841350, 841360, 841370, 841381, 841410, 841430, 841440, 841459, 841480, 841490, 841780, 841790, 841911, 841919, 841939, 841940, 841950, 841960, 841989, 841990, 842119, 842121, 842129, 842139, 842191, 842199, 842220, 842381, 842382, 842389, 842490, 842490, 842833, 843680, 846291, 847290, 847410, 847420, 847432, 847439, 847982, 847989, 847990, 848110, 848130, 848140, 848180,

850164, 850231, 850239, 850300, 850590, 851410, 851420, 851430, 851490, 851629, 853931, 854140, 854389, 854390, 870892, 890710, 890790, 901320, 901380, 901390, 901540, 901580, 901590, 902229, 902290, 902511, 902519, 902580, 902590, 902610, 902620, 902680, 902690, 902710, 902720, 902730, 902740, 902750, 902780, 902790, 902810, 902820, 902830, 902890, 903010, 903020, 903031, 903039, 903083, 903089, 903090, 903110, 903120, 903130, 903149, 903180, 903190, 903210, 903220, 903281, 903289, 903290, 903300, 960310, 960350, 960390

Years are the same as analysis of dirty industries.

Details of product description that are listed can be found on OECD/Eurostat (1999) and APEC (2012).

Category 'pollution management' of environmental goods by OECD/Eurostat (1999) are referred in this chapter.

Product codes classified in these are below:

'Pollution management': 230210, 252100, 252220, 280110, 281410, 281511, 281512, 281610, 281830, 282010, 282090, 282410, 283210, 283220, 283510, 283521, 283522, 283523, 283524, 283525, 283526, 283529, 380210, 392020, 392490, 392690, 560314, 580190, 591190, 681099, 690210, 690220, 690290, 690310, 690320, 690390, 690919, 701710, 701720, 701790, 701990, 730900, 731010, 731021, 731029, 732510, 780600, 840410, 840510, 840991, 840999, 841011, 841012, 841013, 841090, 841320, 841350, 841360, 841370, 841381, 841410, 841430, 841440, 841459, 841480, 841490, 841780, 841790, 841940, 841960, 841989, 842119, 842121, 842129, 842139, 842191, 842199, 842220, 842381, 842382, 842389, 842490, 842833, 846291, 847290, 847410, 847432, 847439, 847982, 847989, 847990, 848110, 848130, 848140, 848180, 850590, 851410, 851420, 851430, 851490, 851629, 854389, 870892, 890710, 890790, 901320, 901540, 901580, 901590, 902229, 902290, 902511, 902519, 902580, 902590, 902610, 902620, 902680, 902690, 902710, 902720, 902730, 902740, 902750, 902780, 902790, 902810, 902820, 902830, 902890, 903010, 903020, 903031, 903039, 903083, 903089, 903090, 903110, 903120, 903130, 903149, 903180, 903190, 903210, 903220, 903281, 903289, 903290, 903300, 960310, 960350, 960390

Category 'cleaner technologies and products' of environmental goods by OECD/Eurostat (1999) are referred in this chapter. So far, this category includes only three product codes: 284700, 320910, 320990

Category 'resource management' and its subcategory 'renewable energy plant' of environmental goods by OECD/Eurostat (1999) are referred in this chapter.

Product codes classified in these are below:

'Resource management': 280110, 854389, 285100, 391400, 841911, 841919, 854140, 841381, 850231, 220710, 290511, 841011, 841012, 841013, 841090, 700800, 701990, 840420, 840999, 841950, 841990, 853931, 902810, 902820, 903210, 460120, 84368

6 Taiwan's development of environmental industry and green growth

Lih-Chyi Wen and Chun-Hsu Lin[1]

Introduction

The idea of green economy or green growth has been globally initiated for a few years. For example, as the United Nations Environment Programme (UNEP) defined in 2011, 'green economy' is the one that results in 'improved human well-being and social equity, while significantly reducing environmental risks and ecological scarcities' (UNEP, 2011: 12). Also in 2011, the Organisation for Economic Co-operation and Development (OECD) used the term 'green growth' and defined it as

> fostering economic growth and development, while ensuring that natural assets continue to provide the resources and environmental services on which our well-being relies. To do this, it must catalyse investment and innovation which will underpin sustained growth and give rise to new economic opportunities. (OECD, 2011: 4)

Actually, both definitions are substantially close to the idea of sustainable development, in which economic, social development and environmental protection should be achieved simultaneously, taking into account of the needs of future generations.[2] Notably, both concepts of green economy and green growth do not replace sustainable development. UNEP explains that the idea of green economy recognizes that 'achieving sustainability rests almost entirely on getting the economy right' (UNEP, 2011: 17), while OECD argues that 'green growth is narrower in scope, entailing an operational policy agenda that can help achieve concrete, measurable progress at the interface of the economy and the environment' (OECD, 2011: 5). This chapter uses the term green growth in order to be consistent with other chapters of the book.

As green growth has become a global international but trend and rising concept among governments, new environmental regulations and policies, technological development, awareness of the public to the need of environmental protection and so on create demand for green technologies; that is a new green market for environmental goods and services. This market could be either domestic or international, but the supply of green technologies is definitely international under the liberalization of trade and investment.

Table 6.1 Taiwan's competitiveness on green technology, 2010–2014

Year	Ranking in the world	Ranking in Asia
2010	6	2
2011	11	4
2012	17	5
2013	18	6
2014	21	6

Sources: IMD (2010; 2011; 2012; 2013; 2014), *World Competitiveness Yearbooks.*

The economy of Taiwan has heavily relied on international trade for at least three decades. The report of the International Institute for Management Development (IMD) shows that Taiwan has been ranked 14th on the performance of international trade in the world (IMD, 2014: 242). The reason generally recognized is that the domestic market in Taiwan is relatively small and limited compared to European, American, and other markets in developed countries, so export is the only way for them to survive. The global trend of green growth opens a new global market and has boosted the technological development of environmental goods and services in Taiwan. Taiwan's LED and solar photovoltaic equipment productions are both ranked number two in the world in 2010. Also, Taiwan is considered one of the most competitive countries in Information and Communication Technology (ICT) industry in the global market. However, according to IMD, Taiwan's green technology competitiveness was dropped year by year, from the second in Asia and the sixth in the world in 2010 to the sixth in Asia and the twenty-first in the world in 2014 (See Table 6.1). It seems that Taiwan's advantage on ICT industry does not contribute to the competitiveness of Taiwan's green technology.

The purpose of this chapter is to examine the market performance of Taiwan's environment-related industries to see whether they have international competitiveness, and what kind of goods and services to what markets they are exporting. To this end, this chapter first analyzes Taiwan's policy and legislation on green growth. It then conducts a survey on Taiwanese companies for the aspects including company characteristics, their annual sales values, and their major exporting markets. In the survey questionnaire, the opinion questions were also included, such as what the major barriers they face in the global markets and what governmental assistances they need in order to enhance their green competitiveness.

Taiwan's policy and legislation on green growth

The term 'green growth' was initiated after the outbreak of financial crisis in 2009. Unlike South Korea or some other countries, however, Taiwanese government has not yet set up the policy or legislation specifically in terms of 'green growth'; rather, the government continues to revise the contents of Sustainable Development Policy Guidelines (hereinafter the Guidelines). Since the initiative of the idea of sustainable development in Bruntland Report in 1987 and in the Earth Summit in 1992, Taiwanese government has begun to follow the contexts of international agreements and made its visions and plans for sustainable development, even though Taiwan is not a member of the United Nations. The Guidelines was announced on 18 May 2000, and revised on 27 July 2009. In the Guidelines from 2009, Taiwan showed its sustainable development vision that 'Present and future generations will all be able to enjoy a "tranquil and diverse environmental ecology", "vital, open and prosperous economy," and "safe and harmonious welfare society."'[3] Accordingly, several documents were announced after the issuing of the Guidelines, including the 'Taiwan Declaration on Sustainable Development' in 2003, 'Taiwan Agenda 21 – National Sustainable Development Vision and Strategy Guidelines' in 2004, and 'Sustainable Development Action Plan' in 2009. Further, Basic Environmental Law was also announced in 2002 to be a fundamental law to achieve the balanced concern on social equity, economic development and environmental protection.

Although the contents of the Guidelines and the related documents are more declarative policies rather than legally binding obligations, some important policies were made accordingly. For example, National Sustainable Energy Policy Agenda was announced in June 2008. The Agenda declares Taiwan's energy vision is that

> sustainable energy development should take into account of energy security, economic development and environmental protection in order to meet the needs of development of the future generations. Sustainable energy policy should make efficient use of limited resources, develop environment-friendly and clean energy, and secure the stability of energy supply, so as to create a win-win-win vision on energy, environment and economy across generations.

The three targets were proposed as follows:

1. Increasing energy efficiency: annual energy efficiency should be increased by 2 percent or above in the coming eight years; energy intensity should be reduced by at least 20 percent off the 2005 level by 2015, and 50 percent off the 2005 level by 2025;
2. Developing clean energy: national emissions of carbon dioxide should be reduced to the 2008 level during 2016 to 2020, and to the 2000 level by 2025; the rate of low carbon energy in electricity-generating system should be increased from 40 percent to 55 percent or above by 2025; and
3. Securing the stability of energy supply: establishing an energy security supply system which meets the goals of 6 percent of economic growth rate and US$ 30,000 of income per capita in the coming four years.

However, these targets were soon revised in 2010. The Executive Yuan of the ROC (the Cabinet of Taiwan) announced the National Aggregate Action Plan on Energy Saving and Carbon Reduction in May 2010, recently renamed as 'National Aggregate Action Plan on Green Energy and Low Carbon' on 17 September, 2014. Inter alia, Taiwan government vowed to improve annual energy efficiency by more than 2 percent so as to decrease energy intensity at least 20 percent of the 2005 level by 2015, and at least 50 percent by 2025. It also conveyed the target to reducing its CO_2 emissions of the 2005 level by 2020 (i.e., 245 million tons) and of the level of 2000 by 2025 (i.e., 209 million tons).[4] In addition, the Executive Yuan announced Energy Development Guidelines under the authority of article 1.2 of Energy Management Act in October 2012 to be a framework for Taiwan's national energy development.

To this end, four main drafts of legislation have been submitted to the Parliament for consideration: Greenhouse Gas Reduction Act, Renewable Energy Development Statute, Energy Tax Statute, and the amendment of Energy Management Act. Unfortunately, due to the standstill on the political negotiation and business lobbying, only Renewable Energy Development Statute was passed in 2009 so far. Further, the draft of Basic Act on Sustainable Development is also pending in parliament. Due to the lack of new legislation, therefore, Taiwanese government can only use existing laws and decrees to enforce the tasks. For example, Statute for Upgrading Industries is the law which mainly relates to industrial development. Article 6.1(4) of this Statute provides that:

> To meet the requirement for industrial upgrading, a company may credit five to twenty percent of the amount of funds disbursed for any of the following purposes against the amount of profit-seeking enterprise income tax payable in each year within a period of five years from the then current year: . . . The funds invested in equipment or technology used for the *reduction of greenhouse gas emissions* or the enhancement of energy efficiency.

Another example is that due to the long-lasting pending of the legislation of Greenhouse Gas Reduction Act in parliament, Environmental Protection Administration (EPA) has announced greenhouse gases as new air pollutants under the authority of Air Pollution Abatement Act and its decree since 9 May 2012, so that EPA can regulate the greenhouse gas emissions on a legal basis. The uncertainty of legislation becomes the first obstacle to green industry.

Definition of the environmental goods and services sector

There is no clear definition on the environmental goods and services sector. Some international organizations have made efforts to define it, but disagreement still exists during the process of negotiation. For example, Para 31(iii) of the Doha Ministerial Declaration of the World Trade Organization (WTO) calls for 'the reduction or as appropriate elimination of tariff and non-tariff barriers to environmental goods and services.' The special sessions of the Committee on Trade and Environment (CTE) have discussed the definition for more than ten years but no final agreement has been reached yet. The definition has also been elaborated in Asia–Pacific Economic Cooperation (APEC) since the mid-1990s. Since the progress has been stalled for years, APEC changed its strategy from deciding the scope of environmental goods and services in advance to an early-harvest approach. In Annex C of APEC 2012 Leaders' Declaration, members of the APEC agreed to put 54 items on the list as the first step to reduce the tariff rates of environmental goods. As the APEC committed, it will reduce applied tariff rates to 5 percent or less by the end of 2015 taking into account economies' economic circumstances and without prejudice to their positions in the World Trade Organization (WTO).[5]

Contrary to the vague definition of environmental goods and services at the international levels, the European Union (EU) has created its own definition and classification on the environmental goods and services for the purpose of data collection. When the EU published its data collection handbook for the environmental goods and services sector in 2009 (European Commission, 2009: 29–30) it clearly adopted the definition of environment-related activities specified in the OECD/Eurostat environmental industry manual made in 1999. (OECD/Eurostat, 1999) As it states, the environmental goods and services sector consists of a heterogeneous set of producers of technologies, goods and services that can be divided into two categories: 'environmental protection' and 'resource management' as follows:

'Measure, control, restore, prevent, treat, minimise, research and sensitise environmental damages to air, water and soil as well as problems related to waste, noise, biodiversity and landscapes. This includes "cleaner" technologies, goods and services that prevent or minimise pollution' (environmental protection); and

'Measure, control, restore, prevent, minimise, research and sensitise resource depletion. This results mainly in resource-efficient technologies, goods and services that minimise the use of natural resources.' (resource management)

In Taiwan, the environmental goods and services are not defined by law; they are instead illustrated by a different approach. The Executive Yuan of ROC (Taiwan) adopted 'The Development Guidelines on Environmental Protection Services Industry and Action Plan' on 15 November, 2004. In the Guidelines, environmental protection industry was described as 'a synthetic technology-applying industry . . . and environmental products also have multi-functions in general which can be used not only in improving the environment but also in other sectors.' Actually, it does not help to clarify the definition well. EPA, the competent authority for environment and resources, defines environmental products by itself as:

Category 1: products which obtain environmental labels certified by the EPA, and products with foreign environmental labels mutually certified or recognized by ROC (Taiwan);

Category 2: products which do not fall into the items of environmental labels certified by the EPA, but are renewable, recyclable, low pollutive or energy saving recognized by the EPA; and

Category 3: products that, certified by the authority in charge, increase social benefits or reduce social costs and thus recognized by the EPA.[6]

International market performance of environment-related industries in Taiwan

Export countries of Taiwan's environmental protection equipment

In recent years, Taiwanese pollution control equipment has been increasingly exported to other countries. As shown in Table 6.2, the United States, China, and Japan are the biggest markets for Taiwan. Table 6.2 also shows to some extent that the market demand in these countries for pollution control equipment has improved.

Number of firms and output value

Industrial Development Bureau (IDB, 2010a and b) compiled the census data during the target years from the Environmental Protection Administration (EPA), the Directorate-General of Budget, Accounting and Statistics (DGBAS), Department of Statistics, Ministry of Economic Affairs (MOEA) and other official data sources in 2010. Data not provided in the survey was estimated in accordance with previous growth rates and updated by the study in 2013 (Sinotech Engineering Consultants, Ltd., 2013). Table 6.3 shows the number of firms of Taiwanese environment-related industries. The number of firms increased from 4,612 in 2005 to 6,891 in 2012. In terms of subsectors, the number of firms in environmental services, environmental resources and environmental equipment in 2012 are 5,044; 1,401; and 445. In this chapter, firms in renewable energy sector are not yet considered.

Table 6.4 shows the output values of environment-related industries from 2005 to 2012. The output value was 162 billion in 2005, and reached 235 billion in 2007. Because of the financial crisis in 2008 and 2009, the output value of environment-related industries fell sharply and then gradually picked up in 2011 and 2012 with the overall environmental industry output of NT$ 244 billion and NT$ 258 billion respectively.

In terms of percentage, environmental services sector accounted for 44.66 percent in all environment-related industries, followed by the environmental resources sector, 40.17 percent, and 15.18 percent of environmental equipment industry. Due to the rapid growth in 2007, environmental services industry accounted for 53.94 percent, but fell to 45.79 percent in the following year and remained at about 44 percent since then.

Based on the observation above, the output value of the environmental services industry is more vulnerable; when the economy grows, which increases

Table 6.2 Top 10 export countries of Taiwan's environmental protection equipment, 2006–2012 Unit: thousand US $

Year	Rank	1	2	3	4	5	6	7	8	9	10
2006	Destination	US	China	Japan	Singapore	UK	Hong Kong	Thailand	Malaysia	Germany	Denmark
	Total Export	67,003	61,448	15,752	11,961	9,242	9,030	8,824	8,085	6,004	5,697
2007	Destination	US	China	Japan	Singapore	UK	Thailand	Denmark	Vietnam	India	Germany
	Total Export	85,066	63,693	15,435	12,285	9,048	8,572	8,188	7,877	7,749	7,037
2008	Destination	US	China	Japan	Vietnam	Vietnam	Singapore	Hong Kong	Thailand	UK	Germany
	Total Export	3,076,338	102,545	68,277	16,359	11,099	10,876	10,560	9,704	9,500	9,288
2009	Destination	US	China	Japan	Vietnam	Singapore	Thailand	Turkey	Germany	UK	India
	Total Export	95,436	50,277	12,304	11,451	8,674	8,342	8,061	7,024	7,009	6,269
2010	Destination	US	China	Japan	Vietnam	Singapore	Malaysia	Thailand	Germany	Turkey	India
	Total Export	112,183	77,229	17,088	11,997	10,620	10,577	9,842	9,680	9,079	8,243
2011	Destination	US	China	Japan	Germany	Singapore	Vietnam	Turkey	Hong Kong	Malaysia	India
	Total Export	99,357	73,302	47,736	15,433	14,329	12,220	11,144	7,765	7,533	7,456
2012	Destination	US	China	Japan	Germany	Vietnam	Singapore	Thailand	N/A*	Hong Kong	Turkey
	Total Export	109,016	78,291	37,726	13,986	12,995	10,149	9,724	N/A	9,194	8,320

Source: Compiled from EPA and DGBAS by Sinotech Engineering Consultants, Ltd. (2013), 'Environmental Protection Industry and Water Saving Guidance Project', entrusted by Industrial Development Bureau, MOEA.

* Due to the error of the original data, it is presented as N/A.

Table 6.3 Number of firms in Taiwanese environment-related industries, 2005–2012

Class	2005	2006	2007	2008	2009	2010	2011	2012
1. Environmental testing services	67	184	82	84	88	92	97	103
2. Wastewater treatment	540	556	309	304	306	311	657	323
3. Waste disposal industry	1,608	2,649	2,134	2,364	2,462	2,550	2,969	2,662
4. Environmental engineering and technical consultancy services	160	213	96	94	97	103	110	117
5. Pest control operators	410	433	502	537	582	591	624	659
6. Recycling industry	702	543	849	880	877	794	1,155	844
7. Remediation services	238	241	134	132	133	135	157	140
8. Energy Technical Services (ESCO)	20	23	27	30	62	130	127	175
9. Environment-related verification services	11	11	11	11	11	11	12	13
10. Environmental management and technical services	14	14	6	6	6	7	7	7
Subtotal	**3,771**	**4,867**	**4,150**	**4,442**	**4,624**	**4,723**	**5,915**	**5,044**
Environmental services								
1. Environmental equipment	226	251	242	237	238	224	330	335
2. Environmentally materials	75	83	77	80	83	81	82	111
Subtotal	**301**	**334**	**319**	**317**	**321**	**305**	**412**	**445**
Environmental equipment								
1. Water supply	10	11	8	8	8	8	10	8
2. Recycled material manufacturing	530	686	915	1,126	1,100	1,252	1,319	1,393
Subtotal	**540**	**697**	**923**	**1,134**	**1,108**	**1,260**	**1,329**	**1,401**
Environmental resources								
Total Environment-related Industry	**4,612**	**5,898**	**5,392**	**5,892**	**6,053**	**6,288**	**7,656**	**6,891**

Note: 'Renewable energy industries' are not included in the census data.

Source: Compiled from EPA and DGBAS by Sinotech Engineering Consultants, Ltd. (2013), 'Environmental Protection Industry and Water Saving Guidance Project', entrusted by Industrial Development Bureau, MOEA.

Table 6.4 Output value of Taiwanese environment-related industries, 2005–2012
Unit: thousand NT $

Class	2005	2006	2007	2008	2009	2010	2011	2012 (e)
1. Environmental testing services	2,494,989	3,443,991	1,698,134	2,041,614	1,670,940	2,523,222	2,727,098	2,947,448
2. Wastewater treatment	2,082,939	3,506,996	3,742,510	3,993,840	4,262,048	4,548,267	4,853,708	5,179,661
3. Waste disposal industry	23,392,742	32,159,209	71,179,173	50,348,514	44,065,687	41,177,263	49,807,482	50,818,574
4. Environmental engineering and technical consultancy services	4,878,107	4,551,947	5,530,286	5,590,180	6,086,369	6,636,372	6,644,192	6,542,993
5. Pest control operators	1,216,521	1,342,918	1,185,863	1,509,043	1,391,950	1,554,312	1,715,805	1,894,077
6. Recycling industry	26,710,046	16,933,827	37,299,925	26,461,354	27,082,556	23,453,086	32,049,067	34,840,541
7. Remediation services	3,139,823	2,456,658	2,423,910	2,391,599	2,359,718	2,328,262	2,297,226	2,266,603
8. Energy Technical Services(ESCO)	372,700	537,300	1,198,400	2,252,200	2,065,100	3,591,700	6,650,000	7,920,000
9. Environment-related verification services	1,627,567	1,599,417	1,571,754	1,544,570	1,517,856	1,491,604	1,465,805	1,440,000
10. Environmental management and technical services	941,059	784,035	1,144,677	1,247,473	1,019,331	1,020,773	1,061,910	1,104,705
Subtotal Environmental services	66,856,493	67,316,298	126,974,632	97,380,387	91,521,555	88,324,861	109,272,294	114,954,602

(Continued)

Table 6.4 (Continued)

Class	2005	2006	2007	2008	2009	2010	2011	2012 (e)
1. Environmental equipment	11,684,160	7,500,075	12,430,597	14,415,603	11,354,509	12,830,122	13,796,230	14,835,086
2. Environmentally materials	13,867,432	17,397,800	20,368,129	18,808,199	19,490,140	26,536,926	19,433,905	20,984,731
Subtotal Environmental equipment	25,551,592	24,897,875	32,798,726	33,223,802	30,844,649	39,367,048	33,230,135	35,819,817
1. Water supply	32,788,093	33,284,025	33,620,000	33,841,542	32,600,000	33,841,000	35,754,783	36,287,529
2. Recycled material manufacturing	36,400,000	38,500,000	42,000,000	48,200,000	48,700,000	54,400,000	65, 800,000	65, 800,000
Subtotal Environmental resources	69,188,093	71,784,025	75,620,000	82,041,542	81,300,000	88,241,000	101, 554,783	107, 660,789
Total Environmental-related Industry	161,596,178	163,998,198	235,393,358	212,645,731	203,666,204	215,932,909	244,057,212	258,435,208

Note: This table shows only environment-related industries, 'renewable energy industries' are not included.

Source: Compiled from EPA and DGBAS by Sinotech Engineering Consultants, Ltd. (2013), 'Environmental Protection Industry and Water Saving Guidance Project', entrusted by Industrial Development Bureau, MOEA.

demands and outputs, the output value of the environmental services industry changes dramatically. Conversely, environmental resources industry is less vulnerable. Even with the financial tsunami in 2008 and 2009 making the domestic market demand decline, environmental resource industry still remained at 82 billion of output value in the year of 2008 and 81.3 billion or so in 2009 (see Table 6.4). Total output value of environment-related industry accounts for 2 percent of GDP in Taiwan, not including renewable energy industries.

Imports and exports of environment-related equipment

Table 6.5 shows the aggregated amount of Taiwanese environment-related equipment import and export from 2006 to 2012. From the overall trends, the total imports of environment-related equipment remained stable, ranged from NT\$ 9.7 to 13.4 billion. The exports show steady growth with total exports growing from NT\$ 7.7 billion in 2006 to 11.9 billion in 2012. Compared with imported environment-related equipment for the period between 2001 and 2005, the sum of imports and exports has shown relatively large magnitude of changes since 2006. The growth rate of imports was 21.49 percent while with 14.90 percent of growth in exports in 2007. But in 2012, the growth rate of import was −4.54 percent while with only 1.34 percent of growth in export. In 2008 and 2009, due to the global financial crisis, both import and export of environment-related equipment fell sharply.

Further, Table 6.5 compiles not only the amount of environment-related equipment import and export and the growth rate in Taiwan, as mentioned above, but also includes the percentage of imports and exports for which the environment-related industry account in the total imports and exports of Taiwan from 2006 to 2012. In recent years, environment-related equipment imported accounts for 0.16 percent of the total annual imports of Taiwan. And environment-related equipment exports accounts for about 0.12 percent on average. The percentage is still low, and to some extent shows that Taiwanese companies have not yet put too much input in this field.

Current status of the generation of electricity by renewable energy in Taiwan

Although the figures in Table 6.3 and 6.4 did not include renewable energy industry, current status of electricity generated by renewable energy in Taiwan can be seen in Table 6.6. The figures are divided into two parts: electricity generated from government-controlled Taiwan Power Company (TPC) and private companies. Due to the fact that the competent authority has announced the preferential feed-in-tariffs to which renewable energy equipment can apply under article 9 of the Renewable Energy Development Statute, the capacities of wind and solar power, especially generated by private companies, have increased faster than before (See Table 6.6.).

Table 6.5 An overview of Taiwanese environment-related equipment trade volume, 2006–2012
Unit: thousand NT$; %

	2006	2007	2008	2009	2010	2011	2012
Total imports of environment-related equipment (A)	9,736,430	11,828,710	10,636,476	8,467,571	13,329,112	14,349,677	13,698,191
Annual growth rate	–	21.49%	–10.08%	–20.39%	57.41%	7.66%	–4.54%
Total exports of environment-related equipment (B)	7,719,372	8,869,751	10,552,500	9,053,140	11,267,615	11,718,013	11,875,150
Annual growth rate	–	14.90%	18.97%	–14.21%	24.46%	4.00%	1.34%
Country's total imports (C)	6,604,336,706	7,211,790,352	7,551,085,183	5,757,179,343	7,943,487,728	8,280,368,637	8,021,457,258
Country's total exports (D)	7,279,319,454	8,087,933,801	8,010,375,849	6,708,883,860	8,656,831,128	9,041,591,432	8,899,963,477
The proportion of total imports (A/C)	0.15%	0.16%	0.14%	0.15%	0.17%	0.17%	0.17%
The proportion of total exports (B/D)	0.11%	0.11%	0.13%	0.13%	0.13%	0.13%	0.13%

Source: Compiled from the Republic of China Customs Statistics database by Sinotech Engineering Consultants, Ltd. (2013), 'Environmental Protection Industry and Water Saving Guidance Project', entrusted by Industrial Development Bureau, MOEA.

Table 6.6 Total capacities of renewable energy electric power generation in Taiwan, 2002–August 2014 Unit: 10,000 kW

Year	2002		2003		2004		2005		2006		2007		2008	
Items	TPC	private	TPC	private	TPC	private	TPC	private	TPC	private	TPC	private	TPC	private
Wind power	0.24	0	.024	0	.024	0	1.776	0	4.776	4.980	11.176	4.980	13.176	11.420
Solar power	0	0	0	0	0	0	0	0	0	0	0	0	0	0
Hydropower	n/a	n/a	n/a	n/a	n/a	n/a	n/a	n/a	n/a	n/a	n/a	n/a	164.88	28.91

Year	2009		2010		2011		2012		2013		2014	
Items	TPC	private	TPC	private	TPC	private	TPC	private	TPC	private	TPC	private
Wind power	17.976	16.710	24.916	22.230	28.678	23.150	28.676	27.290	28.676	32.300	28.676	34.370
Solar power	0	0	0.053	0	0.612	3.827	1.001	12.429	1.052	27.232	1.052	36.824
Hydropower	164.78	28.91	168.83	28.91	175.16	28.91	179.22	28.91	179.22	28.90	179.22	28.91

Source: Taiwan Power Company (TPC), available at www.taipower.com.tw/content/new_info/new_info-b31.aspx?LinkID=8 (last accessed on 29 October 2014).

A survey on environment-related enterprises in Taiwan

This study conducted a survey on environment-related enterprises in Taiwan to identify key issues about the industry. The targeted enterprises for survey are all of 5,927 enterprises under registration, excluding those with false addresses in the database (Foundation of Taiwan Industry Service, 2011).[7] Those targeted enterprises are mainly those manufacturers in the business with environment and energy-related industry, focusing more on the environmental protection industry and green energy industry. After further selection, questionnaires were sent to 1700 firms with 12.7 percent of reply rate. The questionnaires were more completed by finance and accounting (46.3 percent) and business owners or managers (33.2 percent). Those companies who completed the survey can be classified by their business characteristics in Table 6.7.

Table 6.7 The characteristics of environment-related firms

Sectors	Sub-sector	Number of firms surveyed	Subtotal
Environment-related equipment industry	Environment-related equipment manufacturing	42	48
	Environmentally materials	6	
Environment-related services	Recycling	14	126
	Environmental testing services	10	
	Wastewater treatment	15	
	Waste treatment	16	
	Environmental engineering and technical consultancy	50	
	Pest control	12	
	Remediation	2	
	Energy Technical Services (ESCO)	2	
	Environment-related verification services	2	
	Environmental management technology	3	
Green Energy Industry	Refrigeration and air conditioning	12	38
	Solar photovoltaic	9	
	Biofuel	3	
	Wind power	2	
	LED lighting photoelectric	6	
	Hydrogen and fuel cell	1	
	Energy information and communication	4	
	Electric cars	1	
	Total		212

Source: Foundation of Taiwan Industry Service (2011).

Overview on manufacturers' operation

Among the 212 enterprises, most of them (193/212) focus more on Taiwan's domestic market. Very few enterprises have exporting experiences: only 10 enterprises export to China, 2 to Japan, 1 to Korea, 3 to South Asia, 1 to North America and 6 to Europe. The others did not answer the question.

The net incomes of those enterprises surveyed are relatively low, only 4 percent of them earning 16 percent of net profit rate or above, 33 percent of them earning 13 percent to 15 percent of net profit rate, 10 percent of them earning 7 to 12 percent of net profit rate, 9 percent of them earning 4 to 6 percent of net profit rate, and 30 percent of them earning 3 percent of net profit rate or under.

In addition, most of the enterprises (76 percent) do not invest on environment-related research and development. Also most of the enterprises (75 percent) have no intention to invest on environment-related goods and services in the future.

Difficulties and needs in operation

In operation, the enterprises have encountered many issues or difficulties. 37 percent of the enterprises think intense competition in the domestic market is the primary difficulty which they are facing. Also, 24 percent of the surveyed enterprises need more assistance from government. 17 percent of the enterprises think regulations and supporting measures are not enough, while 15.5 percent of them are in the need of financial capital. The need for market and bidding information is ranked number one by enterprises (33 percent). Other types of information needed by enterprises include the subsidy measures for R&D (25.4 percent), low-interest loan (17 percent), and training opportunities (14.6 percent). 13.6 percent of those enterprises also need advanced technology from abroad, and 11.8 percent need the opportunities to expand their market globally. The result of this survey, to some extent, resonates the above argument that stagnated legislation is the first obstacle for Taiwanese green industry to expand the market.

Willingness to invest

By the enterprises surveyed, solar photovoltaic industry is the most preferred investment (10 of 212 enterprises), following by energy saving/green building technology (8 of 212). Also, energy saving services (ESCO), environmental consulting services and LED lighting manufacturing are generally preferred (7, 6, and 6 of 212 enterprises, respectively).

Considering the amount of investment, about 50 percent of the enterprises are willing to invest NT$15 million or less, while only 13 percent of the enterprises are willing to invest more than NT$15 million in the future.

Conclusion

The purpose of this chapter is to investigate the market performance of Taiwan's environmental related industries, and then to see whether the firms have international competitiveness in the global market under the trend of green growth. In addition, this study investigated in the major market barriers they face and governmental assistances they need.

As shown above, Taiwan has around 7,000 environmental related companies, including 450 pollution abatement equipment companies, 1,400 resource management companies, and 5,000 environmental service companies. The industry production values are not high, compared to most of Taiwanese industries. However, resource management companies, including water resource management and recycled material production, are growing fast with production value around NT$ 107 billion per year. Pollution abatement equipment production value is NT$ 35 billion per year, and the value of environmental service industry is NT$ 115 billion per year.

This chapter compiled the census data from Taiwan EPA and DGBAS survey during the targeted years. It found that Taiwan's environment-related businesses are small in terms of the market size and focusing more on the domestic market. Expanding the global market for them is not easy even though the competitiveness of green technology of Taiwan is not bad compared to most of the countries in the world. Also, the willingness to invest is low as well. The result of the survey explains to some extent why the ranking of Taiwan's competitiveness on green technology has dropped so quickly both in the world and Asia year by year (See Table 6.1.).

In terms of the assistance they need, government should accelerate the process of green legislation, such as adopting the three main energy acts and Basic Sustainable Development Act as soon as possible and new measures such as green certification, so as to promote their green supplying capacity and provide a legal basis for financial assistance. Further, the industries need not only the information of international green regulations and public procurements, but also financial measurements, such as loaning, and overseas demonstrating opportunities, and assistances to compete against international competitors.

Notes

1 The authors would like to thank our colleague Fu-Lin Cheng for his valuable inputs and discussion on the chapter.
2 For example, see paragraph 5 of the Johannesburg Declaration on Sustainable Development, A/CONF.199/20, adopted on 4 September 2002.
3 Sustainable Development Policy Guidelines, English version is available at http://nsdn.epa.gov.tw/en/index.htm (last accessed on 28 October 2014).
4 Executive Yuan of R.O.C. (Taiwan), *National Aggregate Action Plan on Green Energy and Low Carbon Reduction*, http://web3.moeaboe.gov.tw/ECW/reduceco21/content/Content.aspx?menu_id=2535 (last accessed on 28 October 2014). (In Chinese.)
5 See Annex C of APEC List of Environmental Goods www.apec.org/Meeting-Papers/Leaders-Declarations/2012/2012_aelm/2012_aelm_annexC.aspx (last accessed on 16 October 2014).
6 EPA, Green Living website. http://greenliving.epa.gov.tw/GreenLife/Digital Study/LearnPeopel-2.aspx (last accessed on 30 October 2014).

References

EPA, Green Living website. http://greenliving.epa.gov.tw/GreenLife/DigitalStudy/LearnPeopel-2.aspx (last accessed on 30 October 2014).

European Commission (2009), *The Environmental Goods and Services Sector – A Data Collection Handbook*, Luxembourg: Office for Official Publications of the European Communities.

Foundation of Taiwan Industry Service (2011), *A Survey Report of Current Status and Future Direction of Green Industry in Taipei*, entrusted by Taipei City Government, Taipei: Taipei City Government (in Chinese).

International Institute for Management Development (IMD) (2010), *World Competitiveness Yearbooks 2010*, Lausanne: The World Competitiveness Center.

IMD (2011), *World Competitiveness Yearbooks 2011*, Lausanne: The World Competitiveness Center.

IMD (2012), *World Competitiveness Yearbooks 2012*, Lausanne: The World Competitiveness Center.

IMD (2013), *World Competitiveness Yearbooks 2013*, Lausanne: The World Competitiveness Center.

IMD (2014), *World Competitiveness Yearbooks 2014*, Lausanne: The World Competitiveness Center.

Industrial Development Bureau (2010a), *An Overview and Survey of Taiwan's Environmental Protection and Environmentally Friendly Industry Development*, Ministry of Economic Affairs, Taiwan (in Chinese).

Industrial Development Bureau (2010b), *Green Industry Promotion Plan: 102–103 Environmental Protection Industry Analysis Report*, Ministry of Economic Affairs, Taiwan (in Chinese).

The Organisation for Economic Co-operation and Development (OECD) (2011), *Towards Green Growth – A Summary for Policy Makers*. www.oecd.org/greengrowth/keydocuments.htm (last accessed on 29 October 2014).

OECD/Eurostat (1999), *The Environmental Goods and Services industry: Manual for Data Collection and Analysis*, Paris: OECD Publication Service.

Sinotech Engineering Consultants, Ltd. (2013), *Environmental Protection Industry and Water Saving Guidance Project*, entrusted by Industrial Development Bureau, MOEA.

United Nations Environmental Programme (UNEP) (2011), Towards a Green Economy: Pathways to Sustainable Development and Poverty Eradication. www.unep.org/greeneconomy (last accessed on 29 October 2014).

7 Economic and environmental implications of economic integration in East Asia

Satoshi Kojima, Pongsun Bunditsakulchai, and Mustafa Moinuddin

Introduction

Trade and investment liberalisation is evolving rapidly in East Asia. The most prominent action has been taken by the Association of Southeast Asian Nations (ASEAN). ASEAN has played a central role to promote economic integration with other East Asian countries and has concluded free trade agreements (FTAs) or economic partnership agreements (EPAs) with China, South Korea and Japan, respectively. Furthermore, negotiations on Regional Comprehensive Economic Partnership (RCEP) were launched in May 2013 among the ASEAN+6 (ASEAN plus Japan, China, South Korea, India, Australia and New Zealand).

These processes are expected to boost economic growth. For example, Ando (2009) simulated the potential economic impacts of various regional FTAs and EPAs scenarios in East Asia, such as ASEAN+3 (ASEAN plus Japan, China and South Korea) FTA and ASEAN+6 FTA with different degrees of trade liberalisation, using a computable general equilibrium (CGE) model. The main conclusion is that FTA with a larger number of members with full trade liberalisation will generate greater economic benefits. Kitwiwattanachai et al. (2010) also applied a CGE model to analyse the economic benefits of different regional economic integration schemes and found that the East Asia multilateral FTA is more beneficial than the bilateral agreement such as ASEAN+ Japan FTA.

The importance of analysing the impacts of reducing or removing investment barriers has been pointed out by several trade liberalisation studies (Mérette et al., 2008). For example, Markusen (1997) investigated the relationship between trade and investment liberalisation with a stylised general equilibrium model and concludes that trade and investment liberalisation are not substitutes for each other and although they often have an opposite effect when implemented separately, they would complement each other when implemented together. Egger et al. (2007) also investigated the welfare implications of trade and investment liberalisation based on numerical simulations of stylised general equilibrium model. They obtained a similar insight to Markusen (1997) that investment liberalisation policy alone is not beneficial but trade and investment liberalisation together may improve welfare. However, very few studies have assessed the potential impacts of investment liberalisation in a quantitative manner.

Investment barriers consist of various elements including qualitative restrictions such as complicated administrative procedures and restrictions on foreign ownership and are associated with difficulty in quantification (Merette et al., 2008). The methodological challenge is also significant. A standard CGE framework assumes no mobility or perfect mobility of capital across region without explicit treatment of foreign direct investment (FDI).

Investigating the environmental implications of trade and investment liberalisation is no less important. The primary motivation of trade and investment liberalisation is to reduce costs, such as economic transaction costs due to trade barriers and obstacles to FDI. By reducing these costs, the integration process is expected to lead to improved economic efficiency and stronger economic growth. When negative externalities exist, however, economic actors have incentives to free ride such externalities to improve economic efficiency. Under such conditions there will be a tendency to overuse natural resources and to cause negative environmental impacts.

In this study, we investigate the economic and environmental implications of both trade and investment liberalisation with explicit treatment of FDI. For this purpose we developed a global CGE model with endogenous investment allocation across countries/regions with sector specific capital stock, and we applied this model to several scenarios of trade and investment liberalisation among ASEAN+6 countries to investigate the potential economic and environmental impacts of trade liberalisation and investment liberalisation. The following Section 2 discusses the modelling methodology of investment liberalisation in the CGE framework. Section 3 describes the model developed in this study. Section 4 explains the scenarios of trade and investment liberalisation and Section 5 reports on the simulation results. Section 5 also presents the results of sensitivity analysis. Section 6 summarises the main findings of this study and concludes the chapter.

Modelling investment liberalisation in CGE framework

Mérette et al. (2008) classified three approaches to address investment liberalisation in the CGE framework. The first approach assumes that service trade liberalisation implicitly includes the reduction of investment barriers and assesses the impacts of service trade liberalisation. The second approach tries to capture the impacts of investment liberalisation through increased capital mobility across regions by changing certain parameters and variables affecting inter-regional capital mobility. The third approach explicitly models FDI by assuming that the multinational firms in the same sector operating in the same region but headquartered in different countries produce different goods.

The first approach is apparently the least straightforward when analysing the impacts of investment liberalisation as this approach does not directly model either inter-regional investment allocation or dissemination of foreign production technologies, both of which are important functions of FDI. The second approach focuses on the former inter-regional investment allocation function, while the third approach can capture both. In this regard the third approach is the most relevant when looking to capture the potential implication of investment liberalisation. A drawback of the third approach is that it requires intensive data collection to disaggregate each sector based on the location of the headquarters, which makes it difficult to disaggregate sectors and regions in detail. A pioneering work in this approach by Petri (1997) employed three sectors (the primary, manufacturing and service sectors) with seven-country/region disaggregation, and many others with this approach employ the same three sector-disaggregation scheme (e.g. Brown and Stern, 2001; Dee and Hanslow, 2000; Lee and van der Mensbrugghe, 2001). Mérette et al. (2008) employed an 11-sector disaggregation scheme but covering only three regions (United States, Canada and the rest of the world). On the other hand, the second approach focusing on inter-regional investment allocation can easily employ a much more detailed disaggregation scheme thanks to the database of FDI flows and stocks provided by CEPII that employs the 57-sector 113-region disaggregation scheme of GTAP database Version 7.

Previous studies of the second and the third approaches generally modelled the inter-regional investment allocation function of FDI as inter-regional capital (not investment) allocation. This is a conventional specification for static CGE models in which investment does not directly affect the production decisions because the capital endowment is already given. Considering the dynamic nature of investment, however, it seems more appropriate to model FDI as inter-regional investment allocation in a dynamic setting. The same consideration can also be applied to inter-sectoral investment allocation. Conventional CGE models including dynamic models assume that the investment is added to the nationwide capital stock and the nationwide capital stock is endogenously allocated to each sector such that the rates of return to capital are identical across sectors. Instead we assume that investment is endogenously allocated to each sector and the sector-specific capital stock is increased by the investment. Annabi et al. (2004) employed this sector-specific capital approach in a single country recursive dynamic CGE model in which the ratio of sectoral investment to the sectoral capital stock is determined by the ratio between the rate of return to capital to the replacement cost of capital of the sector (analogous to Tobin's "q").

Measuring FDI barriers in a quantitative manner is another challenge. The barriers consist of various elements including those related to institutional or procedural issues. For example, Golub (2003) constructed the FDI barrier index based on the scoring of various types of FDI restrictions such as foreign equity limit, screening and approval, and nationality restriction on members of the board of directors. Petri (1997) estimated FDI barriers as tax equivalents imposed on FDI revenues based on trade barriers (tariff equivalents) for the primary and manufacturing sectors as well as estimates for the service sectors as reported in Brown et al. (1996).

In this study, we model FDI as inter-regional investment allocation to sector-specific capital and FDI barriers are specified as the "subjective" tax equivalents to FDI revenues that discourage FDI without actual tax payment. Foreign technology dissemination effects of FDI are not reflected in our model.

The model

Overview

We developed a global recursive dynamic CGE model with a relatively detailed sectoral and regional disaggregation scheme to capture the economic and environmental impacts of regional trade and investment liberalisation among ASEAN+6 countries. We employed a 19-region and 29-sector disaggregation scheme in which most ASEAN+6 countries (except for Cambodia, Lao PDR and Myanmar which are aggregated as "the rest of ASEAN") are treated as a region. The region outside ASEAN+6 is disaggregated into United States, EU, Russia, Brazil, other major oil and gas exporting countries (such as Venezuela, Nigeria and Iran) and the rest of the world. The sectoral disaggregation scheme is shown in Table 7.1.

Firms are assumed to maximise their profit given production technologies represented by Leontief function and constant elasticity of substitution (CES) function with 3-level nesting structure. At the bottom level, various primary

Table 7.1 Sectoral disaggregation scheme

Sector		Sector	
1	Agriculture	16	Other metals
2	Forestry	17	Metal products
3	Fishing	18	Motor vehicles and parts
4	Coal	19	Other transport equipment
5	Oil	20	Electronic equipment
6	Gas	21	Other machinery and equipment
7	Other minerals	22	Other manufactures
8	Food products	23	Electricity
9	Textiles and wearing apparel	24	Gas manufacture, distribution
10	Other light industries	25	Construction
11	Paper products, publishing	26	Transport services
12	Petroleum, coal products	27	Other financial service
13	Chemical, rubber, plastic products	28	Insurance
14	Other mineral products	29	Other services
15	Ferrous metals			

factors (skilled labour, unskilled labour, natural resources, land and capital goods) are combined as a value added composite, and various energy commodities are combined as an energy composite using the respective CES functions. At the second level, the value added composite and the energy composite are combined as an energy-value added composite using the CES function. At the top level, various intermediate inputs and the energy-value added composite are combined using the Leontief function. This specification allows substitutability between energy commodities and primary factors. Another unique feature of our model is that the capital stock in each sector is given at the beginning of the period, as a consequence of the investment decision in past periods, and the sector specific rate of return to capital is determined by the zero profit condition and the sector specific capital market clearance condition. Sectoral investment allocation is determined based on these sector specific rates of return to capital, and the capital stock in the next period is consequently determined.

The representative household maximises utility subject to the Cobb-Douglas utility function given the budget constraints. The household earns factor incomes including those from its capital stock in foreign regions (i.e., the return on FDI). The household savings are assumed to be a fixed ratio of the disposable income deflated by the average cost of consuming a fixed bundle of commodities in the base year data.

The government in each region collects various taxes and provides subsidies. The levels of government consumption and saving are assumed to be constant at the levels recorded in the base year data, and the direct transfer from the government to the household is endogenously determined to satisfy this condition.

Bilateral trade flows are determined by the demand side. The same type of commodities imported from various sources form an import composite commodity based on the CES function. Then, the Armington assumption is applied in which the import composite and domestically produced commodities of the same type are combined using the CES function. The bilateral exports are determined to satisfy the corresponding bilateral import demands. In this setting, there is no global market of commodities and the prices of traded commodities are specific to trade partners.

This model is equipped with a carbon emission module that calculates carbon emissions from the combustion of fossil fuels by each sector as well as by households.

Investment decisions including inter-regional investment allocation

We assume a two-stage investment decision mechanism in which the total savings are first allocated to destinations (either domestic investment or FDI outflows), and then the total investment in a region consisting of the domestic investment and all the FDI inflows are invested to produce a composite capital good that is allocated to each sector.

At the first stage of inter-regional investment allocation we assume that the total savings are distributed to each region according to the following distribution share:

$$\theta(s,r,t) = \frac{\theta_0(s,r) \times \tilde{r}(s,r,t)^\rho}{\sum_r [\theta_0(s,r) \times \tilde{r}(s,r,t)^\rho]} \tag{7.1}$$

where $\theta(s,r,t)$ is the share of FDI from source region s to destination r among the total savings in s, of which base year share is $\theta_0(s,r,t)$, $\tilde{r}(s,r,t)$ is the region-wide average expected rate of return to capital of region r for the investment source region s in time t, and ρ is the parameter representing the degree of influence that the expected rates of return have on the distribution decision.

The region-wide average expected rate of return is determined, reflecting the subjective FDI barriers, as follows:

$$\tilde{r}(s,r,t) = [1 - tfdi(s,r,t)] \times \frac{\sum_i [ror(i,r,t) \times K(i,r,t)]}{\sum_i K(i,r,t)} \tag{7.2}$$

where $tfdi(s,r,t)$ is the subjective FDI barrier (tax equivalent) on FDI from source region s to destination r, $ror(i,r,t)$ is the sector specific rate of return to capital of sector i in region r, and $K(i,r,t)$ is the sector specific capital stock of sector i in region r.

Note that the subjective FDI barrier discourages FDI through lower expected rate of return to capital but there is no actual money transaction for this barrier as mentioned above.

At the second stage of sectoral allocation of a newly produced capital good, the decision is expressed by the constant elasticity of transformation (CET) function. The decision variables are the sector-specific rates of return to capital that are determined by the zero profit condition and the market clearance of a given sector specific capital stock as explained above.

In reality, FDI consists of various forms including monetary investment such as ownership of equity share and physical investment such as the construction of plants using some goods produced in the source country. Our model assumes the monetary FDI that is used to produce capital goods in the destination country. Because of the perfect substitutability of money CET specification is not applicable to the FDI allocation decision in our model. Note that an alternative specification of FDI as inter-regional capital goods allocation is associated with difficulty in reflecting transportation of capital goods or in differentiating FDI transaction from other trade transactions.

Balance of payment and foreign exchange rate

It is common for multi-regional CGE models to employ a macroeconomic closure either with endogenous foreign exchange rates given the fixed balance of payment or with endogenous balance of payment given fixed foreign exchange rates. These two closure rules, fixing either exchange rates or balance of payment, seem to be too strong particularly for the models with endogenous FDI flows. Instead, we assume endogenous balance of payment with a simple exchange rate determination model. Empirical macroeconomic studies suggest that the determination of exchange rates is complicated. For example, Helliwell (1979) classified three main approaches to exchange rate determination modelling, that is, purchasing power parity models, interest rate parity models and structural balance-of-payments models. We assume that the exchange rate (to USD) of a region in the next time step is determined based on the ratio between the balance of payment to the real GDP of the region, as follows:

$$pexr(r, t+1) = pexr(r,t) \times a_r \left[1 + b_r \tan\left(\frac{bop(r,t)}{GDP(r,t)} \right) \right] \qquad (7.3)$$

where $pexr(r,t)$ is the exchange rate of region r in time t (local currency/USD), $bop(r,t)$ is the balance of payment of region r in time t (million USD), $GDP(r,t)$ is the real GDP of region r in time t (million USD), and a_r and b_r are coefficients (potentially region specific).

If the balance of payment is negative (i.e. net revenue from foreign transactions including FDI transactions is positive) the exchange rate to USD decreases, and vice versa. This specification is admittedly preliminary. The elaboration of this specification such as inclusion of purchasing power parity as a determinant or application of different functional forms is a subject for future research.

Data and calibration

The social accounting matrix (SAM) corresponding to the base year 2004 was constructed based on the GTAP database Version 7 (Badri and Walmsley, 2008). The CEPII macroeconomic projection data are used for recursive dynamic simulations (Fouré et al., 2012).

Data of bilateral FDI flows and owner-specific capital stock in each region are based on the CEPII FDI database for global CGE model (Gouel et al., 2012). The rates of tax equivalent to FDI barriers are derived from Petri (1997) taking the average rates across sectors based on the inward FDI capital stock of each sector (i.e. the primary, manufacturing and service sectors). The estimated rates are shown in Table 7.2.

To simulate CO_2 emissions the energy volume data provided as a part of GTAP database version 7 and the estimation of emission factors (Lee, 2008) are used.

Table 7.2 FDI inflow barriers in the base year

Region	FDI inflow barriers(tax equivalent)
Japan	0.378
China	0.517
South Korea, Singapore	0.344
USA, Canada, Australia, New Zealand	0.477
Indonesia, Malaysia, Philippines, Thailand	0.406
Other regions	0.357

Source: Authors' estimate based on Petri (1997).

For static calibration, capital depreciation rates are assumed to be 4 percent for developed countries and regions (Australia, New Zealand, Japan, Korea, Singapore, USA, EU and Russia) and 7 percent for the remaining countries and regions. The initial rates of return to capital are calibrated such that the quantity of nationwide capital stock represented in firms' factor payment for capital and that represented in payment for capital depreciation recorded in the SAM are identical given the prices of capital stock and newly produced capital as well as the depreciation rate. The elasticities of substitution are set at 1 for energy related to CES functions, at 1.5 for trade related CES functions, and at 0.5 for the sectoral investment CET function. The parameter in the FDI distribution model (ρ) is assumed to be 0.5, and a_r and b_r in the exchange rate determination model are assumed to be 0.2 and 0.5, respectively.

In addition to static calibration in the base year, annual growth rates of total factor productivity (TFP) are dynamically calibrated such that the GDP projection by CEPII can be achieved given projections of population, skilled and unskilled labour force with endogenously determined sectoral capital stock. This dynamic calibration is done for the business-as-usual (BAU) scenario in which FDI barriers estimated for the base year are assumed to remain. For the policy simulations, the calibrated TFP growth rates as well as projections of population and skilled and unskilled labour force are given and GDP is endogenously determined.

Trade and investment liberalisation scenarios

We assess the potential policy impacts of trade and investment liberalisation among ASEAN+6 as changes from the BAU trajectories. The trade and investment barriers in the BAU scenario are assumed to be fixed at the base year rates.

These barriers are gradually reduced or removed between 2010 and 2014 in the trade liberalisation scenario (TL), the investment liberalisation scenario (IL), and the trade and investment liberalisation scenario (TIL) as follows:

TL scenario

- Complete removal of trade barriers in terms of import tariffs and export subsidies of non-agricultural commodities among ASEAN+6 by 2014
- 50 percent reduction of trade barriers in terms of import tariffs and export subsidies of agricultural commodities among ASEAN+6 by 2014

IL scenario

- Complete removal of tax equivalent investment barriers among ASEAN+6 by 2014

TIL scenario

- Trade liberalisation is assumed to be the same as the TL scenario
- Investment liberalisation is assumed to be the same as the IL scenario

Reduction or removal of trade and investment barriers is gradually implemented between 2010 and 2014 with linear interpolation during this period.

Simulation results

We first assess the impacts of trade and investment liberalisation scenarios on trade flows and investment flows to see whether our model works as we expect. Then, the economic and environmental impacts of trade and investment liberalisation scenarios are assessed in terms of the following assessment indicators.

- Real GDP
- Equivalent variations (EV)
- Government revenue
- CO_2 emissions

Indicators in monetary units are expressed in USD. Policy impacts are expressed as percentage changes from the BAU if not indicated otherwise. Trade and investment liberalisation policies are applied from 2010 and we evaluate the policy impacts between 2009 and 2020.

Impacts on trade and FDI flows

First, we assess the policy impacts on trade and FDI flows that are directly affected by trade and investment liberalisation scenarios.

Figure 7.1 shows the trajectories of policy impacts on the total imports (in value) of ASEAN+6 (left) and of the world (right).

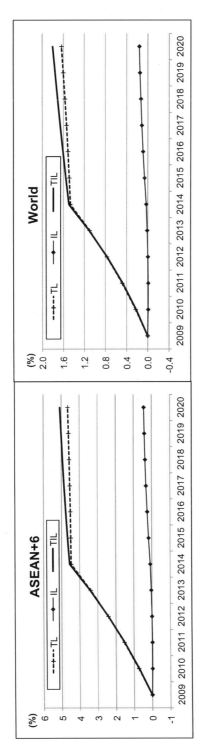

Figure 7.1 Policy impacts on import volume (in value)

The impacts of trade liberalisation (TL) on import volumes are consistent with our expectation. Gradual removal of trade barriers during 2010 and 2014 results in a gradual increase in positive impacts on import volumes of ASEAN+6 as a whole when implementing liberalisation, and after 2014 positive impacts of around 4.5 percent remain nearly constant. The positive impacts on import volumes of ASEAN+6 induce a similar pattern as those of the world but with lower rates of around 1.6 percent. Investment liberalisation (IL) also has slight positive impacts on import volumes. These observations are applicable to the export volume as shown in Figure 7.2.

Policy impacts on cumulative trade flows (during the evaluation period) of each country/region are shown in Table 7.3.

Trade liberalisation increases the volume of both imports and exports for all ASEAN+6 countries as we expected. For countries or regions outside ASEAN+6, trade liberalisation among ASEAN+6 has negative impacts on import volumes, which is expected as these countries/regions become relatively less attractive as trade partners compared to the ASEAN+6 members. The bilateral trade flows are determined by import demands in our model and the trade liberalisation impacts on export volumes of countries/regions outside ASEAN+6 are mixed. The impacts of investment liberalisation on trade volumes are also mixed.

Figures 7.3 and 7.4 show the trajectories of policy impacts on the total FDI inflows and outflows of ASEAN+6 (left) and of the world (right), respectively.

It is observed that trade liberalisation has a larger positive impact on FDI flows than investment liberalisation. This seemingly counterintuitive result can be explained by the fact that main determinants of FDI flows are both the size of funding source (total savings) and the ratio of FDI to total investment. We find that trade liberalisation has a larger positive impact on total savings than investment liberalisation and the consequent increase in FDI flows is mainly through the former driver. Investment liberalisation increases FDI flows mainly through the latter driver.

Policy impacts on cumulative FDI flows (during the evaluation period) of each country/region are shown in Table 7.4.

It is observed that some of the ASEAN+6 members reduce FDI flows under the IL scenario, which indicates the reduction in total savings of these countries.

Impacts on real GDP and welfare

Figure 7.5 shows the trajectories of policy impacts on the total real GDP of ASEAN+6 (left) and of the world (right).

For ASEAN+6 as a whole, trade liberalisation increases real GDP and investment liberalisation also marginally increases real GDP. During the gradual liberalisation period (2010–2014) the growth rates of these positive impacts gradually increase and after 2015 the rates become nearly constant. Interestingly, investment liberalisation (IL) has negative impacts on the gross world product (sum of all the national GDPs). It is noted that the inter-regional investment

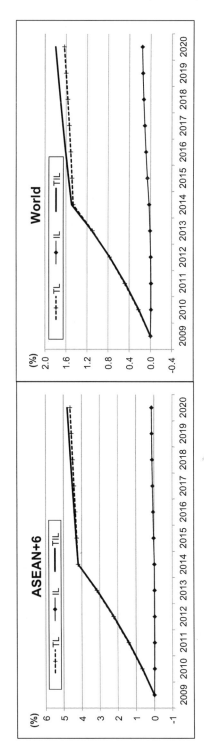

Figure 7.2 Policy impacts on export volume (in value)

Table 7.3 Policy impacts on trade volumes in value (cumulative for 2009–2020) (Unit: %)

Country/Region	Import volume			Export volume		
	TL	IL	TIL	TL	IL	TIL
Australia	4.509	0.398	4.939	5.291	0.047	5.349
New Zealand	1.584	0.711	2.320	4.069	0.051	4.140
China	2.570	0.094	2.659	2.675	0.060	2.745
Japan	3.224	0.077	3.321	3.748	0.092	3.844
South Korea	4.368	0.465	4.854	4.094	−0.019	4.078
Indonesia	3.238	0.234	3.483	5.615	0.156	5.786
Malaysia	4.995	−1.224	3.731	2.963	−0.007	2.951
Philippines	2.579	0.390	2.982	1.612	0.086	1.706
Singapore	2.100	1.411	3.583	2.776	−0.173	2.598
Thailand	5.409	0.604	6.039	4.318	0.075	4.406
Vietnam	13.359	0.065	13.287	4.263	0.089	4.364
Rest of ASEAN	19.860	−0.414	19.175	4.175	0.122	4.313
India	6.536	0.008	6.536	1.424	0.088	1.519
USA	−0.049	0.041	−0.005	−0.012	0.068	0.057
Brazil	−0.083	−0.021	−0.104	0.032	0.062	0.096
EU	−0.101	−0.042	−0.144	0.009	0.108	0.121
Russia	−0.100	−0.020	−0.120	0.171	0.048	0.219
Major oil and gas exporters	−0.169	−0.020	−0.189	0.290	0.074	0.367
Rest of the world	−0.037	0.018	−0.016	−0.073	0.069	−0.005
ASEAN+6 total	3.618	0.199	3.824	3.441	0.046	3.493
World total	1.197	0.070	1.270	1.197	0.070	1.270

allocation decision in our model is not based on optimisation (such as the CET allocation) and the removal of investment barriers does not necessarily improve economic efficiency globally.

Table 7.5 shows the policy impacts on the cumulative real GDP (during the evaluation period) of each country/region.

The impacts of trade and investment liberalisation on real GDP are mixed for the ASEAN+6 members but negative for all the countries/regions outside ASEAN+6.

The welfare impacts of trade and investment liberalisation in terms of equivalent variations (EV) exhibit quite different patterns from the impacts on real GDP, as shown in Figure 7.6.

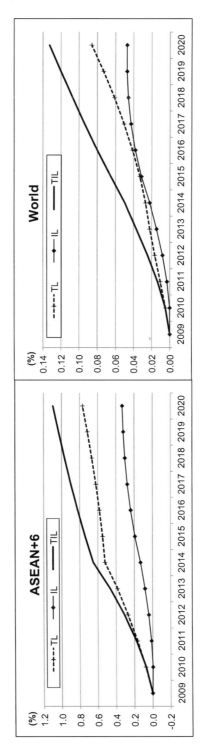

Figure 7.3 Policy impacts on FDI inflow

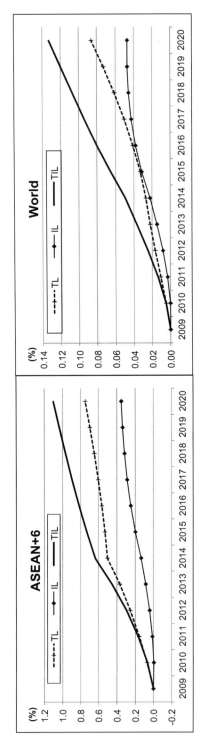

Figure 7.4 Policy impacts on FDI outflow

Table 7.4 Policy impacts on FDI flows (cumulative for 2009–2020)
(Unit: %)

Country/Region	FDI inflow			FDI outflow		
	TL	IL	TIL	TL	IL	TIL
Australia	−0.892	0.597	−0.270	−0.944	0.444	−0.479
New Zealand	−4.953	1.596	−3.342	−5.111	1.327	−3.777
China	0.416	0.087	0.492	0.418	0.078	0.487
Japan	−1.919	−0.189	−2.088	−1.980	−0.042	−2.011
South Korea	−0.192	1.572	1.415	-0.267	1.106	0.866
Indonesia	−3.133	0.311	−2.822	-3.231	0.268	−2.968
Malaysia	5.563	−3.091	2.382	5.363	−1.699	3.652
Philippines	3.821	1.342	5.183	3.949	1.323	5.294
Singapore	1.017	4.475	5.718	0.188	4.077	4.460
Thailand	3.048	1.894	4.965	3.049	1.738	4.814
Vietnam	27.130	−0.046	26.634	27.350	−0.026	26.902
Rest of ASEAN	24.284	−1.136	22.575	25.211	−0.846	23.915
India	4.670	−0.028	4.630	4.713	-0.038	4.663
USA	−0.091	0.012	−0.075	−0.065	−0.004	−0.066
Brazil	−0.176	−0.091	−0.268	−0.162	−0.090	−0.253
EU	−0.374	−0.186	−0.565	−0.372	−0.188	−0.566
Russia	−0.313	−0.073	−0.385	−0.321	−0.074	−0.395
Major oil and gas exporters	−0.620	−0.117	−0.740	−0.669	−0.127	−0.799
Rest of the world	−0.079	−0.050	−0.123	−0.051	−0.058	−0.103
ASEAN+6 total	0.501	0.191	0.691	0.485	0.201	0.687
World total	0.040	0.028	0.068	0.040	0.028	0.068

In terms of per capita EV, investment liberalisation has significant positive welfare impacts for ASEAN+6 as a whole and for the whole world. It is particularly interesting that the welfare impacts of investment liberalisation are positive in spite of negative impacts on real GDP. This result demonstrates a unique feature of our model with endogenous FDI that can accommodate household income derived from the production factors outside the country.

Table 7.6 shows the policy impacts in terms of the cumulative per capita EV (during the evaluation period) of each country/region.

The deviation of welfare impacts from the impacts on real GDP is clearer at country level. For example, Japan reduces its real GDP but enjoys significantly positive EV under all the three scenarios.

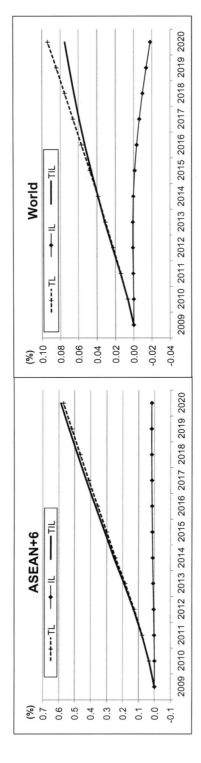

Figure 7.5 Policy impacts on real GDP

Table 7.5 Policy impacts on real GDP (cumulative for 2009–2020)
(Unit: %)

Country/Region	TL	IL	TIL
Australia	0.054	0.034	0.089
New Zealand	–0.481	0.156	–0.319
China	0.395	0.023	0.417
Japan	–0.127	–0.027	–0.154
South Korea	0.177	0.149	0.328
Indonesia	–0.369	0.091	–0.273
Malaysia	1.773	–1.112	0.611
Philippines	0.630	0.280	0.916
Singapore	–0.249	0.414	0.177
Thailand	0.773	0.388	1.174
Vietnam	6.182	–0.025	6.083
Rest of ASEAN	6.482	–0.269	6.131
India	1.414	–0.016	1.397
USA	–0.013	–0.002	–0.015
Brazil	–0.027	–0.010	–0.037
EU	–0.052	–0.015	–0.067
Russia	–0.057	–0.009	–0.067
Major oil and gas exporters	–0.137	–0.022	–0.159
Rest of the world	–0.041	–0.014	–0.054
ASEAN+6 total	0.570	0.018	0.587
World total	0.094	–0.018	0.075

It is noted that there is a trade-off between welfare during the evaluation period and welfare generation capacity after the evaluation period if the cumulative EV is positive but the household assets at the end of the evaluation period decrease. Our simulation results tell that increased welfare during the evaluation period is associated with increased welfare generation capacity after the evaluation period, at least for ASEAN+6 as a whole and for the world.

Impacts on government revenue

In our analysis the difference between government revenue and public spending is absorbed by the direct transfer from the government to the households, and the change in government revenue does not directly affect the welfare level. In

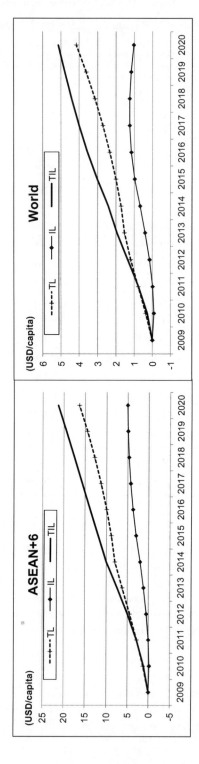

Figure 7.6 Welfare impacts in terms of per capita EV

Table 7.6 Welfare impacts in terms of per capita EV (cumulative for 2009–2020) (Unit: USD per capita)

Country/Region	TL	IL	TIL
Australia	1068.3	377.2	1445.4
New Zealand	292.8	582.1	873.2
China	–68.1	4.5	–64.5
Japan	947.8	175.8	1137.8
South Korea	2152.4	470.9	2616.3
Indonesia	–11.0	12.2	1.3
Malaysia	1346.8	884.2	2309.3
Philippines	41.8	10.6	51.9
Singapore	3922.0	1624.7	5537.1
Thailand	321.3	68.3	379.1
Vietnam	–17.0	0.7	–18.0
Rest of ASEAN	146.8	–2.5	142.8
India	70.4	–2.3	67.9
USA	–102.1	2.4	–97.6
Brazil	–27.9	–9.3	–37.3
EU	–214.7	–64.2	–280.3
Russia	–20.3	–11.8	–32.2
Major oil and gas exporters	11.9	–8.6	3.2
Rest of the world	–13.1	–2.2	–15.1
ASEAN+6 total	96.3	29.2	125.9
World total	23.5	7.9	31.6

the real world, however, policy impacts on government revenue are an important determinant of the policy implementability.

Table 7.7 shows the policy impacts on the cumulative government revenue (during the evaluation period) of each country/region.

The removal of import tariffs under the trade liberalisation scenarios (TL and TIL) results in negative impacts on government revenue. Investment liberalisation in which investment barriers are assumed to be tax equivalent without money transaction does not cause negative impacts but in fact has slight positive impacts on government revenue. Not only all the ASEAN+6 members but also many countries/regions outside ASEAN+6 reduce the government revenue due to trade liberalisation.

Table 7.7 Policy impacts on government revenue (cumulative for 2009–2020) (Unit: %)

Country/Region	TL	IL	TIL
Australia	−1.950	0.400	−1.555
New Zealand	−1.285	0.564	−0.735
China	−4.938	0.090	−4.855
Japan	−0.580	0.122	−0.447
South Korea	−2.801	0.514	−2.309
Indonesia	−9.078	0.209	−8.891
Malaysia	−15.389	0.508	−14.640
Philippines	−7.593	0.204	−7.427
Singapore	−4.493	2.284	−2.186
Thailand	−7.900	0.455	−7.527
Vietnam	−14.733	0.100	−14.710
Rest of ASEAN	−12.572	−0.145	−12.764
India	−4.178	0.008	−4.168
USA	−0.016	0.047	0.034
Brazil	−0.053	−0.011	−0.064
EU	−0.059	−0.012	−0.072
Russia	0.014	0.002	0.016
Major oil and gas exporters	−0.015	0.001	−0.013
Rest of the world	0.019	0.029	0.051
ASEAN+6 total	−2.750	0.192	−2.557
World total	−0.501	0.043	−0.456

Impacts on CO_2 emissions

Table 7.8 shows the policy impacts on the cumulative CO_2 emissions (during the evaluation period) of each country/region.

For example, trade liberalisation increases real GDP but reduces CO_2 emissions in Australia, and the opposite patter occurs in Japan and Singapore (refer again to Table 7.5).

The case of positive impacts on real GDP with a reduction in CO_2 emissions only applies to Australia under the TL scenario, but there are 10 cases of decoupling between welfare improvement and CO_2 emissions. It is particularly interesting that investment liberalisation achieves welfare gain along with a reduction in CO_2 emissions for the whole world, without any low carbon policies.

Table 7.8 Policy impacts on CO$_2$ emissions (cumulative for 2009–2020)
(Unit: %)

Country/Region	TL	IL	TIL
Australia	−0.047	0.055	0.008
New Zealand	−0.384	0.212	−0.169
China	0.266	0.020	0.283
Japan	2.480	−0.037	2.448
South Korea	2.915	0.281	3.192
Indonesia	−1.258	0.098	−1.159
Malaysia	1.592	−0.932	0.634
Philippines	1.079	0.140	1.220
Singapore	2.173	0.994	3.207
Thailand	1.408	0.284	1.684
Vietnam	8.713	−0.034	8.588
Rest of ASEAN	17.129	−0.395	16.520
India	7.334	−0.054	7.269
USA	−0.142	−0.006	−0.147
Brazil	−0.208	−0.026	−0.235
EU	−0.227	−0.042	−0.270
Russia	−0.113	−0.015	−0.128
Major oil and gas exporters	−0.249	−0.041	−0.291
Rest of the world	−0.424	−0.032	−0.454
ASEAN+6 total	1.473	0.015	1.483
World total	0.499	−0.008	0.489

Sensitivity analysis

Our model employs several parameters that are not well supported by empirical data. In particular, our specifications of exchange rate determination and inter-regional investment allocation are original and parameter values are set in an ad hoc manner. We conduct sensitivity analysis by changing the parameter values associated with these two mechanisms as follows.

- Case 1: 10 percent higher value of a_r in the exchange rate determination equation (7.3)
- Case 2: 10 percent higher value of b_r in the exchange rate determination equation (7.3)
- Case 3: 10 percent higher value of ρ in the investment share equation (7.1)

We see how these cases affect the cumulative real GDP, EV, CO_2 emissions, and trade volumes in value and FDI flows. First, it is found that the influence of Cases 1 and 2 are almost identical. Second, EV is sensitive to these parameter values. In terms of percentage change, Indonesian EV of the TIL scenario is the most sensitive to the parameters in the exchange rate determination equations. All the signs of EV under all three cases are not changed from the base case except for the Indonesian EV of the TL scenario under Cases 1 and 2. Other indicators are in general robust against these parameter values. In particular, real GDP, CO_2 emissions and export values are very robust against these parameter values. FDI flows are less robust against these parameter values.

Conclusion

In this chapter, we have developed a recursive dynamic global computable general equilibrium (CGE) model with sector-specific capital accumulation and endogenous foreign direct investment (FDI) allocation, and applied this model to the assessment of the impacts of trade and investment liberalisation among the ASEAN+6 countries. We assume the gradual reduction and removal of import tariffs/export taxes (recorded in the base year data) among the ASEAN+6 countries between 2010 and 2014 under the trade liberalisation (TL) scenario, and assume the gradual removal of investment barriers (expressed as ad valorem tax equivalent without actual money transaction) among the ASEAN+6 countries between 2010 and 2014 under the investment liberalisation (IL) scenario. We also assess the impacts of the combination of TL and IL scenarios (TIL scenario). We first see how these liberalisation scenarios affect trade and investment flows, and then we assessed the policy impacts from economic and environmental viewpoints.

We found that both the TL and IL scenarios increase the aggregate real GDP of ASEAN+6 as a whole but the magnitude of impacts by the former is much larger than that of the latter. The aggregate real GDP of the world also increases under the TL scenario but slightly decreases under the IL scenario. In this study FDI is modelled as the purchase of newly produced capital goods in other countries rather than the allocation of capital goods produced in the investing country to other countries, and consequently the investment allocation across countries/regions is specified in terms of money that is perfectly substitutable. This is why we employ an investment distribution function that is not based on optimisation (such as CET) and consequently the reduction in investment barriers among the ASEAN+6 countries does not necessarily improve global efficiency. This is an important difference between trade liberalisation and investment liberalisation in our model.

Policy impacts on welfare in terms of equivalent variations (EV) exhibit a different pattern from the impacts on real GDP. Both the TL scenario and the IL scenario improve welfare levels (presented by positive EV) not only for ASEAN+6 as a whole but also for the whole world. It means that the IL scenario improves the welfare for the whole world (positive EV) but decreases the global real GDP. Similarly, the IL scenario significantly improves welfare without significantly increasing real GDP for ASEAN+6 as a whole. FDI allows households to earn factor income not directly connected to the domestic production and the correlation between GDP and EV is much lower in our model than in the conventional CGE models without FDI.

Government revenues are reduced under the TL scenario as the tariff revenues are drastically reduced. In our analysis reduced government revenue is reflected in EV through the reduction in the transfer from government to households, affecting household income. In the real world, the impacts on government revenue are important as a criterion for policy feasibility.

By and large, the policy impacts on CO_2 emissions for ASEAN+6 as a whole and the world are similar to impacts on real GDP. Concerning the CO_2 emissions for ASEAN+6 as a whole, the TL scenario significantly increases emissions but the IL scenario only marginally increases them. Interestingly, global CO_2 emissions decrease under the IL scenario. This means that the IL scenario results in welfare gain along with a reduction in CO_2 emissions for the whole world. At the national level this kind of decoupling of welfare improvement and environmental impacts can be achieved by outsourcing production activities to other countries through FDI and trade, but at the global level this is not easily achieved.

These major findings demonstrate the importance of potential positive welfare impacts of investment liberalisation that would be obtained through different mechanisms from trade liberalisation. Investment liberalisation increases the overall return on the investment portfolios of households in the implementing countries. This mechanism is not necessarily associated with the improvement of production efficiency and household revenues can increase without significant increase in real GDP. This may facilitate the decoupling of welfare improvement from CO_2 emissions.

The synergy between trade liberalisation and investment liberalisation is not well observed in our study. Somewhat significant synergy is observed for household income for which the TIL impacts are larger than the sum of the TL and IL impacts by a few percent, but in general the TIL impacts and the sum of those corresponding to the TL and the IL scenarios are very similar. This observation is different from one of major conclusions of Markusen (1997) that the TIL impacts are quite different from impacts of either the TL or IL scenario alone. It must be noted that Markusen (1997) interpreted FDI as provision of skilled-labour intensive services to the host country, which is very different from our interpretation of provision of money investment to produce capital goods in the host country.

This study illustrates the usefulness of our model with endogenous FDI allocation for capturing the policy implications of trade and investment liberalisation. One serious drawback of our model is, however, the lack of a technology dissemination role of FDI. The flow of FDI from countries with advanced technology is expected to bring that advanced technology to the recipient countries, which will result in productivity improvement for the latter. Some studies (e.g. Petri, 1997; Mérette et al., 2008, among others) have differentiated the firms in one region based on the location of company headquarters in order to reflect the technology dissemination role of FDI. This approach will face technical difficulties when the number of sectors and regions increase. Alternatively we can introduce an assumption of different capital productivity based on the owner of the capital. This approach becomes more attractive if not only sector-specific capital but also owner-specific and sector-specific capital accumulation mechanisms can be introduced. This approach may be able to capture the foreign technology dissemination effects of FDI.

References

Ando, M. (2009), *Impacts of FTAs in East Asia: CGE Simulation Analysis*, Tokyo: The Research Institute of Economy, Trade and Industry (RIETI).

Annabi, N., Cockburn, J., and Decaluwe, B. (2004), *A Sequential Dynamic CGE Model for Poverty Analysis*, mimeo, CIRPEE-PEP, Québec City: Université Laval.

Badri, N.G. and Walmsley, T.L. (2008), *Global Trade, Assistance, and Production: The GTAP 7 Data Base*. West Lafayette, IN: Center for Global Trade Analysis.

Brown, D.K., Deardorff, A.V., and Stern, R.M. (1996), "The liberalization of services trade: potential impacts in the aftermath of the Uruguay Round," in W. Martin and Winters, L.A. (eds.), *The Uruguay Round and the Developing Countries*. Cambridge: Cambridge University Press.

Brown, D.K. and Stern R.M. (2001), "Measurement and modeling of the economic effects of trade and investment barriers in services." *Review of International Economics* 9 (2): 262–286.

Dee, P. and Hanslow K. (2000), *Multilateral Liberalisation of Services Trade*. Canberra: Productivity Commission.

Egger, P., Larch, M., and Pfaffermayr, M. (2007), "On the welfare effects of trade and investment liberalization," *European Economic Review* 51 (3): 669–694.

Fouré, J., Bénassy-Quéré, A., and Fontagné, L. (2012), *The Great Shift: Macroeconomic Projections for the World Economy at the 2050 Horizon*. Paris: CEPII.

Golub, S.S. (2003), *Measures of Restrictions on Inward Foreign Direct Investment for OECD Countries*. Paris: OECD.

Gouel, C., Guimbard, H., and Laborde, D. (2012), *A Foreign Direct Investment Database for Global CGE Models*. Paris: CEPII.

Helliwell, J.F. (1979), "Policy modeling of foreign exchange rates," *Journal of Policy Modeling* 1 (3): 425–444.

Kitwiwattanachai, A., Nelson, D., and Reed, G. (2010), "Quantitative impacts of alternative East Asia Free Trade Areas: A Computable General Equilibrium (CGE) assessment," *Journal of Policy Modeling* 32 (2): 286–301.

Lee, H. and van der Mensbrugghe, D. (2001). *A General Equilibrium Analysis of the Interplay between Foreign Direct Investment and Trade Adjustments*. Kobe University, Research Institute for Economics & Business Administration, Discussion Paper No. 119.

Lee, H.-L. (2008), *The Combustion-Based Emission Data for GTAP Version 7 Data Base*, West Lafayette, IN: Center for Global Trade Analysis.

Markusen, J.R. (1997), *Trade versus Investment Liberalization.* No. w6231. Cambridge, MA: National Bureau of Economic Research.

Mérette, M., Papadaki, E., Lan, Y., and Hernandez, J. (2008). "FDI Liberalisation between Canada and the USA: A CGE Investigation." *Atlantic Economic Journal* 36 (2): 195–209.

Petri, P.A. (1997). Foreign Direct Investment in a Computable General Equilibrium Framework. Making APEC work: Economic challenges and policy alternatives. March 13–14, 1997, Keio University, Tokyo.

8 International recycling by South Korea in the context of green growth

Soyoung Kim and Akihisa Mori

Introduction

The Seoul Initiative was adopted at the 5th Ministerial Conference on Environment and Development in Asia and the Pacific (MCED-5) in 2005 with the aim of addressing major policy issues pertaining to green growth and encouraged an international discussion on green growth. Maximizing social benefit while minimizing ecological impact is regarded as a basic principle of green growth (United Nation Economic and Social Commission for Asia and the Pacific [UNESCAP], 2008).

Faced with the global economic recession that was at its worst in late 2008, President Myung Bak Lee of South Korea laid out a "Low Carbon, Green Growth" strategy as a new means of domestic economic development and set the ambitious goal of 7% growth per annum (Cho, 2010). The Low Carbon, Green Growth strategy defines its goals as "growth achieved by saving and using energy and resources efficiently to reduce climate change and damage to the environment, securing new growth engines through research and development of green technology, creating new job opportunities, and achieving harmony between the economy and environment" (The Korean Prime Minister's Office, 2010, art. 2).

One of the important characteristics of South Korean green growth is that the aim is to ensure that resources are more used efficiently across the whole economy. Toward this end, resource productivity has been adopted as a key policy indicator for green growth (Green Growth South Korea, 2009). Resource productivity refers to the monetary yield per unit resource of domestic material consumption.

South Korea implemented the Extended Producer Responsibility (EPR) program as one of the main policy tools for green growth. This program is expected to increase the efficiency of resource use and eco-production. The EPR program focuses on two aspects: implementing a mandatory domestic recycling system, and reducing the amount of toxic material used in production (The Korean Ministry of Environment [KMOE], 2010). EPR is a policy concept recommended by Organisation for Economic Co-operation and Development in 2001 (OECD, 2001) and advocated as a tool for environmentally sound management of waste (OECD, 2007). OECD defines EPR as "an environmental policy approach in which a producer's responsibility for a product is extended to the post-consumer stage of a product's life cycle" (OECD, 2001: 9). EPR aims at internalizing the negative externalities accrued from the whole life cycle of a product as a means of improving overall social welfare (Walls, 2004). Most OECD countries are implementing EPR programs in key sectors (OECD and Japanese Ministry of Environment [JMOE], 2014).

The resource productivity of developed countries tends to increase with economic globalization. This is attributed to a gradual change in the structure of economic activity from resource-based and labor-intensive production to skill- and capital-intensive production (Alcorta, 2012). This structural change additionally increases the export of recyclable and hazardous waste from developed countries to developing countries (Taketoshi, 2009), which can result in increasing the resource productivity of developed countries simultaneously with increasing the negative externalities in developing countries. Rauscher (2001) asserted that, theoretically, international trade of hazardous waste is beneficial to the exporting countries, with the benefits increased by environmental laxity in the importing countries. When there is insufficient regulatory oversight in the waste disposal and processing industries, negative gains may be accrued to the importing countries, and this may cause welfare losses for the world as a whole. Therefore, to achieve global green growth, policies need to be implemented that will avoid the transfer of negative externalities from developed countries to developing countries.

In recent years, large amounts of waste of electrical and electronic equipment (WEEE) have been exported to developing countries. WEEE includes hazardous substances that can damage the environment and human health if not properly handled. International trade of WEEE can lead to welfare losses in developing countries where environmental governance is not sufficient to internalize the negative externalities. International trade of hazardous waste is regulated by the Basel Convention. However, there is no internationally unified regulatory framework for the international trade of used products. As a consequence, a great amount of WEEE was brought into non-OECD countries in the guise of used products intended for reuse (Nnorom et al., 2011).

As of 2009, in South Korea, WEEE regulated by the EPR program is collected at a rate of only 23–28% for televisions, washing machines, and refrigerator, and 7% for air conditioners (Kim et al., 2013). The flow of WEEE that is not collected under the EPR program has not been published. Accurate data on illegal exports of used electronics is not publicly available. However, according to the Japan China Commodities Inspection Company, only 28 cases of exports of used electronics from South Korea to China were found to be illegal in 2005 (Ahn, 2006). The reasons for those rejections were mixing of unsanitary or forbidden waste, falsification of export permits, and failing to undergo a preliminary inspection before shipment (Ahn, 2006). It is known that there were ship-backs of illegally exported used electronics disguised as products intended for reuse (KMOE, 2012a).

Against this background, this chapter first explores features of WEEE management in South Korea to focus on the institutions involved in the export of used electronics. The export rates of five types of goods are estimated and the export destinations of used cathode ray tube (CRT) computer monitors are identified. CRT monitors are chosen because they contain a very high concentration of toxic metals because of the lead included in the CRT glass (Oguchi et al., 2013). Field research in Nhat Tao market in Ho Chi Minh City, Vietnam, was used to create a cost–benefit incidence analysis in order to show how the benefits and costs of the export of CRT computer monitors are allocated under South Korea's international recycling program.

Features of EPR programs for WEEE management

Main features of WEEE management in South Korea, the EU and Japan are shown in Table 8.1. WEEE management in South Korea is the same as that in the European Union (EU) and Japan in that it focuses on mandated domestic recycling systems and the restriction of the use of certain hazardous substances (RoHS) in manufacturing covered by the EPR program. In South Korea, a mandatory recycling system for producers was implemented in January 2003 under the Act on the Promotion of Saving and Recycling of Resources. This law was superseded by the Act for Resource Circulation of Electrical and Electronic Equipment and Vehicles (ARCEEEV) in February 2008; ARCEEEV encompasses both recycling and RoHS. As of 2014, 26 types of electronics are regulated by the law.

South Korea has three unique features in comparison with the EU and Japan. First, South Korea exempts certain manufacturers and importers (producers) of regulated electronics from recycling duty on the basis of their production size (KMOE, 2014b, art. 14–15).

Second, a producer's duty in the EPR program is different from that of a producer in the EU or Japan. The South Korean recycling program assigns EPR producers both a minimum recovery target per unit and a quota for the recycling of targeted electronics. Recycling refers to the whole process of changing WEEE into recovered materials in facilities approved for that purpose (KMOE, 2012b). If the quota is not met, a fine that is set to greater than the cost of implementing proper recycling for the missing volume is imposed upon the EPR producers (KMOE, 2014a, art. 18). The recycling target of EPR producers is 6 kg per inhabitant per year, adjusted to reflect their share of total domestic shipment, by 2016 (KMOE, 2014c). In the EU, collection targets refer to the separately collected volume by producers, distributors, and collection facilities (including municipal facilities), but there is no penalty to producers for not achieving this failure. Japan does not impose a collection or recycling target on producers, but it requires producers of regulated electronics to achieve a minimum recovery target per unit.

Third, by determining the volume of recycling conducted by EPR producers, the South Korean government has qualified the export of used computer

Table 8.1 Institutions of WEEE management in South Korea, the EU, and Japan (as of 2014)

	South Korea	EU	Japan
Definition of Producer	Manufacturers and importers[1] Above standard[2]	Manufacturers and importers[1]	Manufacturers and importers[1]
Regulated items	Household appliances,[3] IT equipment,[4] etc. (26 types of EEE)	(102 types of EEE)	(8 types of EEE)
Collection (recycling) target (min.)	6 kg per inhabitant per year, in proportion to the shipment share of EPR producers in total domestic shipmentsby 2016	45% of average weight of EEE placed on the market in the prior three years, from 2016	–
Recovery rate (min.)	65–80%	50–80%	50–70% (laptop computer: 20%)
RoHS (max. level)	Lead (0.1%), Mercury (0.1%), Hexavalent chromium (0.1%), PBB (0.1%), PBDE (0.1%), and Cadmium (0.01%)		
Targeted item of RoHS	All of regulated items	All of regulated items	Regulated items and microwaves
RoHS penalty	Prohibition of sale and a fine below 30 million KRW	Prohibition of sale	Sale with a disconfirming mark
Export of used electronics	Approval of the export of used computer monitors for reuse as legitimate recycling	Monitoring duty / Cost of monitoring on producers / Burden of proof on exporters of used electronics	Specification of Harmonized System (HS) code for used household appliances and display/ Prior consultation

Notes:

[1] Any person or firm that, under its own brand name, manufactures and sells, or resells, or imports and sells the final electronics.

[2] More than 1 billion KRW of total sales in previous year, or more than 0.3 billion KRW of import amount in previous year.

[3] Air conditioners, clothes dryers, freezers, refrigerators, televisions, and washing machines.

[4] Computers (laptop and desktop) and computer displays (CRT and flat screen).

Source: EU (RoHS Recast, 2011; WEEE Recast, 2012), Japan (JISC0950, 2008; JOP, 2008; JOP, 2014), South Korea (KMOE, 2012b; KMOE, 2014a; KMOE, 2014b; KMOE, 2014c).

monitors for the purpose of reuse as legitimate recycling since 2004 (KMOE, 2003, 2012b). In fact, EPR producers requested this international recycling program for used computer monitors (Chung and Yoshida, 2008). EPR producers achieve the recycling target of computer monitors by paying exporters for documentary evidence of an export declaration issued by customs.[1] South Korea does not delineate a particular strategy to combat the illegal export of used electronics. The export of used electronics for direct reuse is exempted from related duty imposed on waste trade (KMOE, 2012a). The criteria for exemption from duty refer to "used electronics which function fully, have a contract ensuring the export for the purpose of direct reuse and have a document of evaluation on products' functionality from destination country" (KMOE, 2012a: 308). However, exporters of used electronics are not required to prove that the exporting products are actually eligible for exemption.[2]

In the EU a large proportion of WEEE is sent from retailers and municipalities to exporters after it is separately collected from consumers (European Electronics Recyclers Association, 2007), and this amount is still counted in the collection rate target. It is unclear how many of these exporters commit illegal practices. The EU set forth two main measures to deter illegal export of used electronics. One measure is to strengthen export inspections by requiring exporters to prove that the shipped items are reusable electronics intended for direct reuse, not WEEE, when requested by an inspection authority (WEEE Recast, 2012, art. 23, cl. 2). The cost of inspections and analyses for monitoring used EEE suspected to be WEEE can be charged to the producers or exporters (WEEE Recast, 2012, art. 23, cl. 3). The other measure is to set a high collection target to prevent the illegal export of used electronics by informal exporters (WEEE Recast, 2012, (15)).

In Japan, as a measure to curb illegal export of used electronics, Japan has regulated used home appliances and computer monitors since 2008 by using the Harmonized Commodity Description and Coding System (HS code) to categorize exports. Japan provides exporters with a prior consultation and presents a more detailed standard for the self-evaluation of legal exports of used electronics than is provided in South Korea and the EU. This standard is composed of five components: life span (below 15 years for air conditioner and television; below 10 years for freezer, refrigerator, washing machine, and clothes dryer) and appearance, function, packaging and loading, a contract proving sales for direct reuse, and empirical evidence of sales of direct reuse (JMOE, 2013).

Theoretical explanation of international recycling in South Korea

Figure 8.1 presents a simplified economic model of an EPR domestic recycling management scenario. In the diagram, P_R is the marginal revenue for recyclers and MC_R is the marginal cost of recycling. Thus, $P_R - MC_R$ is the marginal profit from recycling. MC_L is the marginal cost of landfill disposal. The value of $P_R - MC_R$ is read from left to right and the value of MC_L is read from right to left.

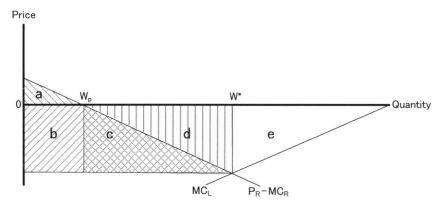

Figure 8.1 Domestic recycling of computer monitors
Source: Adapted from Pearce (2001) by author.

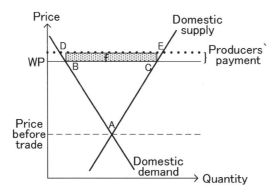

Figure 8.2 International trade of used computer monitors and producers' cost

In this instance, the recycling level in the market will normally be W_p, which is where recyclers' profits are maximized. We assume that the government imposes duties on producers to achieve the recycling level W^* that represents the optimal levels of recycling and landfill use. In this case, producers have to bear costs corresponding to b + c + d. In contrast, recyclers have gains of the area a + b + c, and society's cost of landfill is e.

Figure 8.2 shows the domestic market for used computer monitors in South Korea. The domestic equilibrium price before trade (A) is below the world price (WP), which means that South Korea is a net exporter. We assume that the line segment W_pW^* of Figure 8.1 and BC of Figure 8.2 are the same. Owing to the international recycling program, EPR Producers can fulfill the volume of recycling

Table 8.2 Additional costs (−) and benefits (+) in domestic and international recycling

	Producer	*Exporter*	*Recycler*	*Society*	*Sum*
International recycling	−f	f	0a	−e	a − e
Domestic recycling	−b − c − d	0	a + b + c	−e	a − d − e
Difference	−f + b + c + d	f	−b − c	0	d

duty corresponding to the line segment BC by providing exporters with a payment in exchange for export declarations for used computer monitors. In this case, the cost to the producers corresponds to the shaded area f. Theoretically, this can result in the increase of the supply to the length of the line segment DE because it has the same effect as increasing the product price by the amount of payment from producers to exporters (Chung and Yoshida, 2008).

Table 8.2 shows additional costs and benefits in domestic and international recycling of used computer monitors. Through international recycling, the producer's additional savings is the area −f + b + c + d. Recyclers suffer a loss of −b − c. For society, there is no change so long as the same residue for landfill disposal remains after recycling, and exporters can make additional profits corresponding to f. The additional net benefit of the international recycling is d as a whole.

Exports of used computer monitors in action

Data

International trade of used electronics and new electronics are not differentiated by HS codes, which are used globally for the classification of trade commodities, up to the level of six digits. Some countries, such as Japan, specify additional digits for the HS codes to classify used electronics. However, it is difficult for most countries to quantify the trade of used electronics from only trade statistics.

Because South Korea does not specify extended HS codes for used electronics, we examine the details of export declarations to estimate the total export volume of used electronics. In this chapter, we examine five types of electronic appliances: air conditioners, computer monitors, refrigerators, televisions, and washing machines. The HS codes for the selected electronics and details of the method for selecting data are provided in the Appendix.

Because the export volume of used electronics in this chapter is based on self-declarations by exporters, undeclared export shipments are not included in the export volume. In particular, comprehensive data on export freight of monetary value less than two million KRW are not available. The reason for this is that it is not necessary to declare such exports in South Korea; this exemption is based on South Korea Customs Service Notification (2014).

In order to observe the time-series data of exported used electronics not including fluctuations in the amount of discarded electronics generated in South Korea, we quantified the export rate on the basis of the volume of discarded electronics. The export rate is calculated by dividing the exported volume of the used electronics by the volume of discarded electronics generated in South Korea. For annual volumes of discarded electronics, we referred to Kim et al. (2013). Those data were estimated from sales data by using a delay model that considers the product lifespan distribution. The volume of computer monitors was updated to agree with the data according to the same method.[3]

The volume of discarded computer monitors is estimated from sales data (IDC Korea, 2010; KOSIS) and a product lifespan distribution. The shape parameter of the lifespan distribution of computer monitors is fixed at 2.4 in this chapter. This value is chosen because it represents the average shape of the 22 types of electronics (Oguchi et al., 2006). The average lifespan of computer monitors was assumed to be five to six years according to the Public Procurement Service (2011) and Baek (2006).

Export rate

The export rates of used electronics are shown in Figure 8.3. The export rates of used air conditioners and washing machines were estimated at below 1%, and refrigerators were below 3% during 2002–2009.

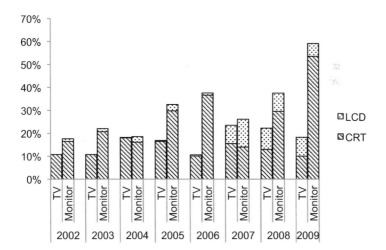

Figure 8.3 Export rates of used computer monitors and televisions from South Korea during 2002–2009 (weight basis)

Note: Air conditioners, refrigerators, and washing machines are not shown because their export sizes are negligible.

Source: Compiled by author from data in the Korea Customs Trade Development Institute (KCTDI) database.

Since 2002, the export rates of used computer monitors have increased, reaching 59% in 2009. During the entire period, most exported used monitors were CRT monitors. The export rates of used televisions were relatively low in comparison with the rates for used computer monitors, ranging between 11% and 24%. Since 2007, used flat screen televisions have accounted for around 40% of total exports of used televisions. It is noteworthy that the export rate of computer monitors declined in the years 2004 and 2007 despite EPR producers' subsidies to exporters of used computer monitors.

Export destination

The export destinations of CRT computer monitors are shown in Figure 8.4. CRT computer monitors were exported mostly to Asian countries during the entire period. The main destinations for used CRT monitors were Hong Kong (2003–2006) and Vietnam (2007–2009). Drastic decreases of export volume to Hong Kong can be observed in 2004 and 2007. The export rates of used computer monitors mirror those changes for those years (see Figure 8.3).

Hong Kong is famous as an entrepôt of China for recyclable resources and secondhand products (Kojima and Yoshida, 2007). As contamination by electronic waste in China intensified, the Environmental Protection Department (EPD) of Hong Kong conducted investigations and uncovered illegal electronic waste disguised as reusable electronics in 2003 (Kojima and Yoshida, 2007). In July of 2004, the EPD required the South Korean government to enact countermeasures against illegal export of used electronics (Byun, 2004). In April 2006, Hong Kong adopted a stringent policy, issuing the Advice on Import and Export of Used Electrical and Electronic Appliances having

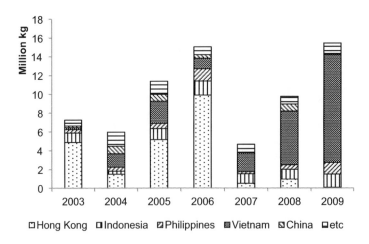

Figure 8.4 Export destinations of used CRT monitors during 2003–2009
Source: Compiled by author from data in the KCTDI database.

Hazardous Components or Constituents (EPD, 2006). Although exports to Hong Kong were decreased in response to these stringent regulations in 2004 and 2007, South Korea's total export volume of used CRT monitors has not declined since then. Instead, the main destination changed from Hong Kong to Vietnam. In 2009, 74% of export volume of used CRT monitors was headed for Vietnam.

Market conditions of Vietnam

Entrepôt for used electronics

Vietnam shares borders with China and some member countries of Association of Southeast Asian Nations (ASEAN). Vietnam has belonged to the ASEAN Free Trade Area (AFTA) since July 1995, and, as of 2008, Vietnam's import tariff is below 5% for 98% of the products in the Inclusion List when imported from an AFTA country but not when imported from a non-AFTA country (ASEAN, 2008). Additionally, in July 2005, Vietnam started abolishing tariffs with China (The Korean Ministry of Foreign Affairs and Trade, 2011), and Vietnam exempts goods imported temporarily for re-export from tariffs and value-added taxes (Japan External Trade Organization, 2014; HSK Vietnam Audit company). In these regards, Vietnam has economic and geographical conditions that make it likely to replace Hong Kong as an entrepôt for the trade of used electronics.

To protect the domestic market and the environment, Vietnam takes measures to avoid the illegal inflow of used electronics. In principle, Vietnam bans the import of used electronics (Government of Vietnam [GOV], 2006), especially used information technology appliances such as CRT computer monitors, desktop computers, mobile phones, and televisions (The Ministry of Post and Telecommunication of Vietnam, 2006). However, Vietnam allows the temporary import of used electronics intended for re-export (GOV, 2006). In 2012, Vietnam prohibited the import of refrigerators containing chlorofluorocarbon refrigerants, desktop computers, and televisions, even for the purpose of re-export (The Ministry of Industry and Trade of Vietnam [MOITV], 2012). Items not specified in MOITV (2012) can be legally imported for the purpose of re-export; hence, used computer monitors are still allowed to be imported into Vietnam so long as they are intended for re-export.

Hai Phong Harbor and Mong Cai City in northern Vietnam share a border with the city of Dongxing in China and act as hubs for the trade in used electronics (Shinkuma and Huong, 2009). Hai Phong harbor works as an export route to China, and is a known port for smuggling (Terazono and Yoshida, 2012). From Mong Cai city, a large amount of imported used electronics goes into Dongxing before being transported to Guangzhou (Shinkuma and Huong, 2009). Electronic waste from Guangzhou is supplied to Guiyu, which is in the same province (Lee, 2002). Plastic recovered in Guiyu is supplied to many global electronics companies (Watson, 2013).

Guiyu is widely known to experience severe environmental pollution as a consequence of substandard recycling of electronic waste (Leung et al., 2006). High levels of lead are present in the blood of children; high concentrations of persistent organic pollutants (POPs), such as flame-retardants, are present in various environmental media; and dioxin pollution is known to be severe (Huo et al., 2007; Li et al., 2007; Wong et al., 2007). These problems accrue from the hazardous constituent materials in the electronics in combination with improper recycling processes.

Another hub of trade in used electronics in the south central part of Vietnam is the Nhat Tao Market in Ho Chi Minh City. Used electronics are typically brought to Nhat Tao Market through Da Nang Port, Saigon Port, and the Sihanoukville Port in Cambodia (Hai et al., 2005; Kojima, 2005; Shinkuma and Huong, 2009).

Case study of Ho Chi Minh City

In Vietnam 17.3% of households have a computer and 90.3% have a television (General Statistics Office of Vietnam, 2012). This implies that demand for computer monitors is low, while that for new and replacement television purchases is high and stable.

New CRT televisions have not been sold in the market since 2014 because the Vietnamese government is pushing the transition from analog to digital broadcasting, with completion slated for 2020, and has banned production and import of televisions that cannot receive digital television signals (The Ministry of Information and Communication of Vietnam, 2013). However, CRT televisions are sold in the Nhat Tao market. CRTs removed from computer monitors are mostly used for rebuilding CRT televisions (Figure 8.5).[4] This is due in part to low demand for used CRT computer monitors and in part to high demand for CRT televisions. Rebuilding refers to not only refurbishment (which usually includes tests for functionality and defects before selling) but also changes and capability upgrades.[5] The price of a rebuilt 17-inch CRT television is around 35 USD, compared with around 300 USD for a brand new 32-inch flat screen television.[6]

Occupational health risks for recyclers and exposure of their children to high levels of toxins via breast milk are reported at Vietnamese electronic waste recycling sites (Tue et al., 2010). Occupational health risks are also high at the plastic recycling factories in the outskirts of Ho Chi Minh City. Such factories operate in a closed environment to conceal the smell of combustion of plastics and to avoid public attention (Figure 8.5).[7] A huge volume of waste is gathered in Ho Chi Minh city in response to active Chinese brokers who export many types of recovered materials from Cambodia and south central Vietnam to China (Yoshida, 2013).

According to retailers at the two markets, the CRT computer monitors exported from South Korea to Vietnam are mainly re-exported to Guangzhou, China or circulated domestically. In Guangzhou and Ho Chi Minh City, the rebuilding of used electronics is a thriving industry. Although the rebuilding

CRT monitors piled up in Nhat Tao market

Rebuilding a television with a CRT taken from a computer monitor

Rebuilt televisions displayed in Nhat Tao market for sale

Melting process in a plastic recovery factory on Ao Doi street

Figure 8.5 Recycling of CRT computer monitors in Ho Chi Minh City (Photos by Soyoung Kim)

process itself does not seem to cause severe environmental problems, parts that remain after rebuilding and used electronics unsuitable for rebuilding are supplied to substandard recyclers, who cause environmental pollution. Coupled with the above occupational health risks, it is highly likely that the negative externalities of CRT computer monitors are being transferred to Vietnam.

Cost–benefit analysis for used CRT computer monitor exports

South Korea admits the export of used computer monitors for the purpose of reuse as legitimate recycling. Additional benefits of export of used CRT computer monitors are estimated against domestic recycling in South Korea (Table 8.3). Our estimate shows that international recycling programs accrue a net benefit to South Korea.

In domestic recycling carried out under the EPR recycling program, producers provide reprocessing companies with a payment of 3,102 KRW per unit to cover collection and recycling costs (Association of Electronics Environment [AEE], 2012). International recycling enables producers to save 2,506 KRW per unit because the producers pay only 596 KRW per unit to the exporters (AEE, 2012).

Table 8.3 Additional cost/benefit per unit for international recycling against domestic recycling

		Producer	Exporter	Recycler	Government	(Vietnam)	Sum
Benefit	Recycling credits	3,102[a]	596[a]				
	Recycling			3,907[b]		(+)	
	Landfill savings				490[b, c]		
Cost	Loss of recycling credits	596[a]		3,102[a]			
	Recycling			3,426[b]		(+)	
	Loss of landfill saving				186[b, c]		
	Health risk					(+)	
Net benefit		2,506	596	−2,621	304	(−)	< 785

Sources: [a] AEE, 2012; [b] AEE, 2013; [c] Mok, 2005.

Exporters obtain an additional profit of 596 KRW per unit from EPR producers in return for reporting the export (AEE, 2012). On the other hand, international recycling deprives reprocessing companies of sales revenue of 3,426 KRW per unit and producers' payments of 3,102 KRW per unit, while saving 3,907 KRW per unit that is supposed to spend for recycling costs (AEE, 2012, 2013). The government additionally saves landfill disposal costs of 304 KRW per unit, where a unit corresponds to 9.5 kg of incombustible waste because the recycling rate of a CRT monitor is 38% (5.8 kg of 15.3 kg is recycled) (AEE, 2013). From interviews and observation at Nhat Tao market, we can guess that Vietnamese recyclers and consumers gain a bit at the cost of health and environmental risks.

In total, the net benefits from international recycling are estimated as at most 785 KRW per unit. In 2009, EPR producers exported 406,886 units of used CRT computer monitors as international recycling (Korea Environment Corporation, 2013). In total, 320 million KRW can be estimated as net additional benefits to South Korea from international recycling in 2009. The larger concern is the health and environmental cost in Vietnam, which overshadows the smaller net benefit generated from the international recycling program.

Discussion

In South Korea, used electronics that satisfy certain criteria are exempted from related duties imposed on waste export at the time of export. In addition, exporters of used electronics are not required to prove that the exporting products are eligible for exemption. Our estimate shows that 74% of the export volume of used CRT computer monitors was exported to Vietnam marked as being for reuse in 2009. This implies that South Korea does not strictly implement a monitoring system for export of used electronics because Vietnam permits only temporary import for re-export, not for reuse. EPR producers must ensure that exporters submit an export declaration, issued by customs, for the used computer monitors. However, they do not have to ensure proper reuse and/ or re-export at the export destination.[8] Exporters of used electronics do not face any sanctions for noncompliance unless they are uncovered at the time of export inspection.

The EU and Japan require exporters of used electronics to act more responsibly than is required in South Korea. The EU requires member states to strictly monitor for illegal exports of used electronics and clarifies that the relevant costs for inspection of used electronics suspected to be WEEE will be imposed on producers. The Japanese government presents a detailed standard for the used electronics and specifies the HS code for selected used electronics as a way of making the flow transparent. Compliance of exporters still depends on the strictness of government inspections.

This implies that comparably less stringent countermeasures against illegal and fraudulent export of used electronics have been established in South Korea than in the EU and Japan. These less stringent measures incentivize exporters of South Korea to export WEEE under the disguise of reuse and encourages importers having a contract with exporters of South Korea to shirk their responsibility to prove a sale for direct reuse.

In the future, RoHS-type legislation in South Korea, the EU, and Japan may reduce the transfer of negative externalities via international trade of used electronics. However, the impact of such legislation can be quite limited because South Korea sets a target of only 26 types of electronics for the RoHS framework.

Conclusion

One purpose of green growth is to achieve economic growth that maximizes social welfare while minimizing ecological impact (UNESCAP, 2008). South Korea aims to achieve this purpose through international recycling. This chapter demonstrates theoretically and empirically that EPR producers, exporters, and the government of South Korea obtain economic gains from international recycling and that this will increase South Korea's resource productivity. However, these gains come at the expense of health and environmental risks to importing countries, such as Vietnam.

The identified gains, however, accrue in part from South Korea's insufficient system for monitoring against illegal or fraudulent export of used electronics. Materials to prove that the exporting object is functionally reusable and directly reused in destinations are not monitored, and this causes severe asymmetry of information regarding the condition of exported objects. To maximize the economic and environmental benefits both domestically and globally, and to minimize negative externalities in the importing countries, South Korea should establish a more stringent monitoring system and enforce it more strictly.

Notes

1 Interview with the head of the Public Relations Department of the Association of Electronics Environment (AEE), 7 February 2014.
2 Interview with the Export Control Officer of Incheon Customs, 23 September 2014.
3 See Kim et al. (2013) for a complete description of the estimation procedure.
4 Interview at Nhat Tao Market, 28 March 2014.
5 Interview at Nhat Tao Market, 28 March 2014.
6 Interview at Nguyen Thi Minh Khai, 27 March 2014.
7 Interview at plastic recycling factory on Ao Doi street, 28 March 2014
8 Interview with the head of the Public Relations Department of AEE, 7 February 2014.

References

Ahn, H. J. (2006), *Proceeding for Parliamentary Inspection of the Government Offices* during 13–27 October, Seoul, The South Korean National Assembly (in Korean).

Alcorta, A. L. (2012), "Climbing the stairway of development," *Policy Brief* (May), UNIDO.

Association of Electronics Environment of South Korea (AEE) (2012), Price of recycling credits for 2011 and 2012, Seoul, print (in Korean).

AEE (2013), Recycling cost analysis of waste of electrical and electronic equipment, Seoul, print (in Korean).

Association of Southeast Asian Nations (ASEAN) (2008), Consolidated CEPT Package, 2008 – Vietnam. Retrieved from www.asean.org/communities/asean-economic-community/category/other-documents-24 (last accessed on 23 January, 2015).

Baek, B. S. (2006), *Lifespan by Item for Compensation of Consumers' Damage*, Seoul: Korea Consumer Agency (in Korean).

Byun, H. S. (2004, 4 July), "China demands for 'preventing illegal export of e-waste' to the Korean government," *Hankook Ilbo Newspaper* (in Korean).

Cho, M. R. (2010), International conference of interconnections of global problems in East Asia – Is the green economy secure in South Korea?: Dissecting Korea's green growth strategy, held in Namdaemunro, Seoul by Hanshin University and Nautilus Institute on October 18–21, 2010.

Chung, S. W. and Yoshida, F. (2008), "A study of the WEEE (waste of electrical and electronic equipment) recycling and export in South Korea." *Journal of the Japan Society of Waste Management Experts* 19 (4): 235–243 (in Japanese).

Environmental Protection Department of Hong Kong (EPD) (2006), Advice on import and export of used electrical and electronic appliances having hazardous components and constituents. Retrieved from www.epd.gov.hk/epd/english/environmentinhk/waste/guide_ref/files/advice_on_e-waste.pdf (last accessed on January 23, 2015).

European Electronics Recyclers Association (EERA) (2007), *Towards Sustainable WEEE Recycling – Proposals for the Revision of the Relevant Provision of the WEEE Directive*, Arnhem: EERA.

General Statistics Office of Vietnam (2012), Percentage of households having main durable goods by urban, rural region and sex of household head. Retrieved from www.gso.gov.vn/default_en.aspx?tabid=491 (last accessed on January 23, 2015).

Government of Vietnam (GOV) (2006), Decree 12/2006/ND-CP. Making detailed provisions for implementation of the commercial law with respect to international purchases and sales of goods; and agency for sale and purchase, processing and transit of goods involving foreign parties.

Green Growth South Korea (GGK) (2009), *National Strategy for Green Growth*, Seoul: GGK (in Korean).

Hai, H.T., Mai, C.X., and Huong, H.T. (2005), Current status of electronic waste and its treatment technology in Hanoi, in *Proceeding of the Second NIES Workshop on E-waste* held on November 23, 2005, 105–111.

HSK Vietnam Audit Company. Outline of value added tax in Vietnam (in Japanese). Retrieved from www.hskv.com.vn/ja/component/attachments/download/40 (last accessed on January 23, 2015).

Huo, X., Xu, X., Zheng, L., Qiu, B., Qi, Z., Zhang, B., Han, D., and Piao, Z. (2007), "Elevated blood lead levels of children in Guiyu, an electronic waste recycling town in China," *Environmental Health Perspectives* 115 (7): 1113–1117.

IDC Korea (2010), *Analysis of PC monitor market and prospect*, Seoul: IDC Korea (in Korean).

Japan External Trade Organization (JETRO) (2014), Basic information on export and import policies of Vietnam (in Japanese). Retrieved from www.jetro.go.jp/world/asia/vn/trade_03/#block3 (last access on January 23, 2015).

The Japanese Government (JOP) (2008), Act on the promotion of effective utilization of resources, enforcement ordinance. Retrieved from http://goo.gl/vDF85v (last accessed on January 23, 2015).

JOP (2014), Home appliance recycling law, enforcement ordinance (in Japanese). Retrieved from http://law.e-gov.go.jp/htmldata/H10/H10SE378.html (last accessed on January 23, 2015).

Japanese Industrial Standards Committee (JISC) 0950 (2008), The marking for presence of the specific chemical substances for electrical and electronic equipment (in Japanese). Retrieved from http://home.jeita.or.jp/eps/jmoss_en.htm (last accessed on January 23, 2015).

Japanese Ministry of Environment (JMOE) (2013), Criteria for exporting secondhand electronics (in Japanese). Retrieved from www.env.go.jp/press/files/jp/23042.pdf (last accessed on January 23, 2015).

Kim, S.Y., Oguchi, M., Yoshida, A., and Terazono, A. (2013), "Estimating the amount of WEEE generated in South Korea by using the population balance model," *Waste Management* 33 (2): 474–483.

Korea Customs and Trade Development Institute (KCTDI), Export database. Retrieved from http://trass.kctdi.or.kr/service/statistic/StatisticsViewServlet?mainServiceURL=P02M01D010 (last accessed on March 18, 2014).

Korea Environment Corporation (KECO) (2013), Recycling achievement by export under the EPR program, Incheon, Print.

Korean Ministry of Environment (KMOE) (2003), Notification on a contractor of recycling (No.2003–212) (in Korean).

KMOE (2010), *Eco-Assurance System Guidance*, Gwacheon, KMOE (in Korean). Retrieved from www.keco.or.kr/kr/business/resource/communityid/115/view.do?idx=185 (last accessed on January 23, 2015).

KMOE (2012a), *Handbook on the Export and Import of Waste*, Gwacheon: KMOE (in Korean).

KMOE (2012b), Regulation on guidelines of recycling and collection duty of WEEE (No. 450) (in Korean).

KMOE (2014a), Act for resource circulation of electrical and electronic equipment and vehicles (ARCEEEV) (in Korean).

KMOE (2014b), Enforcement ordinance of ARCEEEV (in Korean).

KMOE (2014c), Collection target 6kg of WEEE per capita [Press release], January 29 2014 (in Korean). Retrieved from www.kdi.re.kr/infor/ep_view.jsp?num=131084 (last accessed on January 23, 2015).

Korean Ministry of Foreign Affairs and Trade (KMOFAT) (2011), *Commercial Environment Asia/Oceania* Vol. 2. Seoul, KMOFAT (in Korean).

Kojima, M. (2005), "Transboundary movements of recyclable resources in South East Asia," in Kojima, M. (ed.), *International Trade of Recyclable Resources* (Spot survey Nr. 9), Tokyo: IDE-JETRO, 85–94.

Kojima M. and Yoshida, A. (2007), "Hong Kong as an intermediary provider of recovered sources and used products," in Kojima, M. (ed.), *Trade of Secondhand Resources in Asia*, Tokyo: IDE-JETRO, 70–83 (in Japanese).

Korean Statistical Information Service (KOSIS), Production data on mining and manufacturing industries (Data ID: DT_1F01012). Retrieved from http://kosis.kr/statHtml/statHtml.do?orgId=101&tblId=DT_1F01012&conn_path=I3 (last accessed on January 23, 2015).

The Korean Prime Minister's Office (2010), Framework act on low carbon, green growth. Retrieved from www.moleg.go.kr/english/korLawEng?pstSeq=54792 (last accessed on January 23, 2015).

Lee, S. (2002, May 12), "Ghosts in the MACHINES," *South China Morning Post Magazine*. Retrieved from http://ban.org/library/ghosts_in.html (last accessed on January 23, 2015).

Leung, A., Cai, Z.W., and Wong, M.H. (2006), "Environmental contamination from electronic waste recycling at Guiyu, Southeast China." *Japan Society of Material Cycles and Waste Management* 8: 21–33.

Li, H., Yu, L., Sheng, G., Fu, J., and Peng, P.A. (2007), "Severe PCDD/F and PBDD/F pollution in air around an electronic waste dismantling area in China," *Environmental Science and Technology* 41: 5641–5646.

Ministry of Information and Communication of Vietnam (MOICV) (2013), Circular 07/2013/TT-BTTT, Regulating the points of time to integrate the ground digital televisions produced and imported for use in Vietnam.

Ministry of Industry and Trade of Vietnam (MOITV) (2012), Decision 5737/QD-BCT, 2012. On the temporary list of goods temporarily imported for re-export, transmitted, and in bonded warehouses.

Ministry of Post and Telecommunication of Vietnam (MOPTV) (2006), Decision 20/2006/QD-BBBCVT. Promulgating the list of used information technology appliances banned from import.

Mok, J.H. (2005), *Improvement Plan of Waste Charge Program*, Incheon: KECO (in Korean).

Nnorom, I., Osibanjo, O., and Ogwuegbu, M. (2011), "Global disposal strategies for waste cathode ray tubes," *Resource, Conservation and Recycling* 55: 275–290.

Organisation for Economic Co-operation and Development (OECD) (2001), *Extended Producer Responsibility – A Guidance Manual for Government*, Paris: OECD.

OECD (2007), *Guidance Manual for the Implementation of OECD Recommendation C(2004)100 on Environmentally Sound Management of Waste*, Paris: OECD.

OECD and JMOE (2014), Issues Paper. Global Forum on Environment: Promoting sustainable materials management through extended producer responsibility (EPR), June 17–19, 2014.

Oguchi, M., Kameya, T., Tasaki, T., Tamai, N., and Tanigawa, N. (2006), "Estimation of lifetime distribution and waste numbers of 23 types of electrical and electronic equipment," *Journal of Japan Society of Waste Management Experts* 17: 50–60 (in Japanese).

Oguchi, M., Sakanakura, H., and Terazono, A. (2013), "Toxic metals in WEEE: Characterization and substance flow analysis in waste treatment processes," *Science of Total Environment* 463–464, 1124–1132.

Pearce, D. (2001, August), What is a rational waste management policy, from section 1 of 'Development and application of policies for promoting sustainable waste management' draft report, International Forum of the Collaboration Projects, Economic and Social Research Institute, Cabinet Office, Government of Japan.

Public Procurement Service (2011), Durable years of equipment (No. 2011–18) (in Korean).

Rauscher, M. (2001), "International trade in hazardous waste," in Schulze, G.G. and Ursprung, H.W. (eds.), *International Environmental Economics: A Survey of the Issues,* Oxford: Oxford University Press, 148–165.

RoHS Recast (2011), Directive 2011/65/EU of the European Parliament and of the Council of 8 June 2011 on the restriction of the use of certain hazardous substances in electrical and electronic equipment.

Shinkuma, T. and Huong, N. (2009), "The flow of E-waste material in the Asian region and a reconsideration of international trade policies on E-waste," *Environmental Impact Assessment* 29: 25–31.

South Korea Customs Service Notification (2014), Notification about the paperwork of the export entry (No. 2014–65) (in Korean).

Taketoshi, K. (2009), "Environmental interdependence in East Asia," in Mori, A. (ed.), *Economic Development and Environmental Policy of East Asia,* Tokyo: Minerva Shobo, 58–79 (in Japanese).

Terazono, A. and Yoshida, A. (2012), "Current international flows of electronic waste, future tasks, and possible solutions," in Hieronymi, K., Kahhat, R., and Williams, E. (ed.), *E-waste Management,* Oxfordshire: Routledge, 137–163.

Tue, N.M., Sudaryanto, A., Minh, T.B., Isobe, T., Takahashi, S., Viet, P.H., and Tanabe, S. (2010), "Accumulation of polychlorinated biphenyls and brominated flame retardants in breast milk from women living in Vietnamese e-waste recycling sites," *Science of the Total Environment* 408: 2155–2162.

United Nations Economic and Social Commission for Asia and the Pacific (UNES-CAP) (2008), Greening Growth in Asia and the Pacific, Bangkok: UNESCAP.

Walls, M. (2004), "EPR policy goals and policy choices: What does economics tell us," in OECD (ed.), *Economic Aspects of Extended Producer Responsibility,* Paris, OECD, 21–49.

Watson, I. (2013, March 31), China: The electronic wastebasket of the world. CNN Asia. Retrieved from http://edition.cnn.com/2013/05/30/world/asia/china-electronic-waste-e-waste/ (last accessed on January 23, 2015).

WEEE Recast (2012), Directive 2012/19/EU of the European Parliament and of the Council of 4 July 2012 on waste electrical and electronic equipment (recast).

Wong, M.H., Wu S.C., Deng, W.J., Yu, X.Z., Luo, Q., Leung, A.O., Wong, C.S., and Wong, A.S. (2007), "Export of toxic chemicals – a review of the case of uncontrolled electronic waste recycling," *Environmental Pollution* 149 (2): 131–140.

Yoshida, A. (2013), "Recyclable waste trade of mainland China," in Kojima, M. and Michida, E. (ed.), *International Trade in Recyclable and Hazardous Waste in Asia.* Northampton: Edward Elgar, 44–50.

Appendix

Export declarations for South Korea consists of a 56-item list which must be filled out when exporting. The shipped products must be identified as either brand new or used. The "condition of goods" item must be specified as either "N" (new) or "O" (used). As the second component, "name of goods", used goods are specified as "USED" along with the commercial name of the exported product, and new goods lack the "USED" prefix. In this paper, we used the sum of the total amount of shipped goods specified as "O" in the condition of goods and, from among the shipped goods specified as "N", those having the word "USED" in the name of the goods. The reason for adding the latter criterion is to capture shipments that were mistakenly declared as used electronics for only one component.

Table 8A.1 The HS Code list of the five selected electronics from 2002–2009

Year	Air conditioner	Computer monitor	Refrigerator	TV	Washing machine
2002–2006	841510	8471602021	84181010	85281290	84501
	84158	8471602023	84182	85281390	845020
2007–2009	841510	8528410000	84181010	852872	84501
	84158	85285110	84182	852873	845020

9 The policy impact of product-related environmental regulations in Asia

Etsuyo Michida*

Introduction

Environmental and health regulations that impose requirements on products, product-related environmental regulations (PRERs), have been introduced in many countries, and both the number and variety of PRERs has increased in recent years (see Table 9.1). The European Union (EU) has been leading the introduction of PRERs in the past decades. The examples are the EU RoHS Directive (Directive of the European Parliament and of the Council on restriction of the use of certain hazardous substances in electrical and electronic equipment), which was implemented in 2006 and restricts the amount of hazardous substances[1] that is permitted in electronic and electrical (E&E) equipment and the EU REACH Regulation (Regulation of the European Parliament and of the Council concerning Registration, Evaluation, Authorization and Restriction of Chemicals), which was implemented in 2007, and regulate chemical substances and chemicals contained in products that cause serious concern for consumer health and the environment.[2] Regulating countries are not limited to Europe. More recently, many Asian developing countries as well as Middle East countries such as United Arab Emirates have implemented various PRERs.

PRERs are aimed at protecting consumer's health, safety, and the environment by requiring products sold in regulated markets to meet certain requirements. An important characteristic of PRERs is that regulations on products apply equally to those domestically produced and imported products that fall within the scope of the regulations. Therefore, PRERs affect both domestic and foreign firms through trade in a similar way. For example, RoHS and REACH have imposed requirements on foreign firms that produce final goods as well as components exported to EU markets. For exporting firms, failure to adapt to a PRER leads to a loss of market access to EU and impede firms' competitiveness. However, many small and medium firms (SMEs) may not be aware of destination markets of their own products which are mere parts of some final products as marketing of final products is conducted by other firms. Nevertheless, these component suppliers need to adapt to PRERs if they are remotely affected by PRERs. Adaptation to PRERs in midstream firms of supply chains is now an important challenge for manufacturing.

Table 9.1 Examples of PRERs

Country	Year enacted	Regulation	Description
EU	1994	Packaging and Packaging Waste Directive	Requirement for packaging to minimize packaging volume and weight and to use design to permit reuse or recovery
	2000	ELV (End-of-Life Vehicle)	Recycle rate of ELV to be 95% by 2015
	2005	WEEE (Waste Electrical and Electronic Equipment)	Recycle rate of WEEE to 70–80%
	2006	RoHS (Restriction of the Use of Certain Hazardous Substances)	Restriction of lead, mercury, cadmium, hexavalent chromium, PBB, and PBDDE in E&E products
		Battery Directive	Setting maximum quantities for certain chemicals and metals in certain batteries
	2007	REACH (Registration, Evaluation, Authorisation and Restriction of Chemicals)	Chemical regulations that regulate chemicals in articles
	2009	Toys Safety Directive	Restriction of chemicals, toxic substances and allergenic fragrances that are harmful for children under 14 years old
	2009	Regulations on Automobile Exhaust Gas	Emission regulation
	2009	Rules on Exhaust for Greenhouse Gasses from Automobiles	Regulation on CO_2 emission from new automobiles
	2009	ErP (Energy related Products)	Products that do not have an eco-friendly design through procurement, production, packaging, transport, consumption, and disposal are not permitted to be put on markets.

U.S.	1978	CAFÉ (Energy Policy and Conservation Act of 1975 & Motor Vehicle Information and Cost Saving Act)	Requires automobiles that are sold in U.S. market to meet average fuel efficiency standards.
China	2007	China RoHS (Electronic and Information Product Pollution Prevention Act)	Relating to the regulation of 6 substances in the Chinese market
UAE	2013	Prohibition of Unregistered Biodegradable Plastic Products Circulation	Decision obliging manufacturers and suppliers of plastic products to register 15 new biodegradable plastic products, the plastic products need to conform with UAD standard No.2009:5009

Source: Author.

A PRER introduced in one country could affect economic and environmental policies in other countries as some governments introduce policies to support domestic firms' efforts to comply with PRERs introduced in an export market. Moreover, introduction of a PRER in one part of the world signals to both producers and consumers that environmental and health related problems might need to be addressed in their own regulations; thus, similar PRERs tend to be introduced in multiple countries. The enactment of a PRER will induce extensive reaction, both in and out of the enacting jurisdiction. PRERs such as the REACH Regulations of the EU are relevant not only to chemical industry but also to other industries because chemicals are used extensively in products such as garment, wood products, and E&E products.

PRERs introduced in important export markets can impact policy in other countries and provide a new mechanism for affecting other countries' policies through trade. In fact, implementation of EU PRERs triggers Asian governments to enact policies in response. Developed countries such as the United States and EU members have been the primary regulators for a long time, but in recent years China, South Korea, Vietnam, and other Asian countries have introduced PRERs similar to EU RoHS and EU REACH. PRERs have been introduced around the globe and multiple regulations have impacted on manufacturing firms producing export goods. Some governments introduce PRERs to tackle their own environmental, health, and safety problems, such as waste and safe products; others do so to improve access to export markets, with a similar PRER introduced across industries and borders. Introducing PRERs is not used solely to mitigate environmental and health related risks in each country, but it can also change industry competitiveness. Asia is not exceptional in having production networks extensively impacted, but it is one of the most important areas in which firms could have been affected by PRERs and thus need to take adaptation measures. Increased trade volume in the Asian region along with globalization implies that the impact of PRERs is increasingly important.

This chapter discusses EU PRERs, specifically the EU RoHS directive and REACH regulation, which have impacted Asian firms and Asian policies. Section 1 shows how REACH and RoHS impact Asian firms, and Section 2 describes the effect on Asian adaptation policy. Section 3 shows how REACH and RoHS affects PRER development in Asian countries. And finally, conclusion discusses the future challenges.

Impact of PRERs on Asian firms

Environmental regulations such as air and water pollution control regulations have been examined extensively in the literature of environmental economics since the 1970s (see Jaffe et al., 1995) but research on PRERs has received limited attention until recently. As number, variation, and coverage of the PRERs has increased in recent decades, more research has been recently conducted (e.g., Angerer et al., 2008; Tong, et al., 2012). PRERs and pollution control regulations differ in objectives, actors, geographical coverage, and mechanism of effect. Regulations on air pollution and water effluent from factories are aimed at protecting workers, residents, and the environment at production sites. PRERs, in contrast, are aimed at protecting consumer health and safety at consumption sites and the environment at end-of-life disposal sites, such as e-waste provisions in the EU RoHS. The actors who must adapt to pollution control regulations are producers and factories within the regulators' jurisdictions. Individual factories are required to take necessary measures for pollution control, and the choice of measures made by the factory management does not require help from input suppliers. On the other hand, PRERs impose requirements on both producers of a final good and of the input parts and components. Firms that produce final goods are often required to obtain information from their suppliers about the compliance of the parts and components of the final goods because compliance with PRERs requires compliance at each step. Suppliers asked by customers to comply with a PRER must ask the same of their own suppliers: each supplier along a supply chain must manage its suppliers as well. Therefore, in contrast to pollution control measures, which can be unilaterally addressed by a single factory, PRERs require supply chain or life cycle management by firms exporting to regulated markets. The extent and complexity of PRERs' impact has been made clear through an examination of the supply chain management required to meet regulations, such as RoHS directives and REACH regulations, on chemicals contained in products. Chemicals are used to improve the standard of living in a variety of ways. When chemicals contained in a final product are regulated, it becomes necessary to redesign, monitor, and test the materials, parts, and components composing the final product to prove that they meet the stipulated chemical thresholds. Further complicating compliance, although many PRERs regulate products in specific industries, the impact of PRERs that regulate chemicals spreads to various industries. REACH affects industries beyond the chemical industry: textile, garment, wood products, plastic, rubber, machinery, electric and electronic industries, and many others are affected. Adaptation is complex for industries whose products are composed of various materials. For example, a chair may contain wood, plastic, metal, cloth, and synthetic materials such as polyester; it may even contain some electric parts if it is equipped with extra features, such as an automatic reclining system. To export such a chair, all related suppliers across various industries must comply with the PRERs for the final product to be placed in the EU market. This means that the chemical information must be transmitted through a supply chain that includes multiple industries.

Due to globalization of production, the parts and components necessary to manufacture a final product are often produced by different firms located in different countries. Many suppliers who will need to comply with product regulations will be located beyond the regulator's jurisdiction. Because parts and components suppliers are located across jurisdictional borders, supply chain management takes cooperative effort from multiple firms, industries and countries. Suppliers may be located in various countries, including in developing countries. In Asia, the impact of PRERs seems significant. De facto globalization has enabled manufacturing firms to procure product parts from different countries, selecting on the basis of comparative advantage, and such activities have led to the formation of extensive supply chain networks in the region. However, an Asian manufacturer's long and complex supply chain might adversely affect its compliance with PRERs because each supplier at all production stages needs to comply with the PRERs for the final product to have market access. For a firm at the top of the production pyramid, obtaining the complex supply chain information from thousands of suppliers spread around different countries can be a formidable challenge. Moreover, some suppliers are direct exporters and thus fully aware of their market destination, but other suppliers are indirect exporters and may know neither how their products will be used nor to which markets the products are destined. For firms, both domestic and foreign, with suppliers in developing countries, it may be necessary to audit suppliers to verify compliance. A firm cannot simply take measures to restrict the amount of regulated chemicals entering its products; it must also disseminate chemical information to its customers. Michida and Nabeshima (2012) show case studies of Vietnamese firms. Larger multinational firms tend to adapt to regulations appropriately but smaller domestic firms do not have capacity to do so, consequently some firms that have not adapted to regulations lose opportunities to supply larger customers. Some large multinational firms have started to select only those suppliers that are able to comply with relevant PRERs and provide credible information on environmental performance.[3]

Those firms that lack the capacity to comply with PRERs by collecting information and adopting compliance technologies will lose market access. PRERs can thus act as technical barriers to trade (TBTs). If firms are unable to supply to multinational firms selling products in regulated markets, this is an entry barrier for the firms. The supply chain management required to comply with PRERs can create entry barriers for lower capacity firms wishing to participate in export markets; participation in multinational firms' supply chains is an important mechanism for allowing firms to gain access to regulated markets. In terms of both TBTs and entry barriers, PRERs have a large impact on firms, especially on SMEs and on firms in developing countries that have less capacity to comply. Therefore, the capacity to comply with PRERs is an additional component of being part of global production networks and continuing to export to regulated markets. However, for a majority of SMEs in developing countries, collecting the necessary information and complying with the regulations requires additional capabilities and imposes a cost burden; this create a new hurdle for exporting.

Michida et al. (2014) present the results of a survey of firms on how Asian firms are impacted by chemical-related PRERs, including EU RoHS and REACH. The survey was conducted in Penang, Malaysia in 2012 on a sample ($n = 370$) of manufacturing industry firms. From their results, 60.9% of Malaysian firms have taken measures to comply with regulations on chemicals in products: 78.3% of foreign owned firms and 55.8% local firms answered had taken measures. Among the firms, 9.2% faced customer rejection due to chemicals in products; this was higher for foreign owned firms than for local firms. These results show that a significant number of firms find it necessary to comply with regulations on chemicals in products, even outside of the EU. When asked if they had changed destination markets due to PRERs, 1.8% of firms answered that they had. This result implies that some firms have lost export market access due to PRERs. Similarly, Michida et al. (2014) present the results of survey on Vietnamese manufacturing firms of a sample ($n = 1,054$) which was conducted in 2011. They show that 43.1% of firms have faced needs to manage chemicals in products and 9.8% of firms have experienced product rejection by their customers due to contained chemicals above the permitted levels. These results show chemical PRERs have impacted on Asian developing countries extensively.

Impact of EU PRERs on Asian policy

PRERs introduced in important export markets can impact policy making in other countries and provide a new mechanism to affect other countries' policies through trade. In fact, implementation of the EU PRERs has triggered Asian governments to enact policy measures in response. PRERs imposed on important export markets, such as the EU, have raised concern among exporting countries. Exported products that do not satisfy regulatory requirements cannot be placed in regulated markets, and firms might thus lose market access. Otsuki et al. (2001) examine regulations on food safety in the EU and empirically measure the magnitude of impact on exports from African countries to EU markets. Honda (2012) has shown the impact of EU RoHS directives on trade from outside the EU. Both studies suggest that regulations significantly impact trade. Sankar (2007) addresses concerns about the impact of regulation on the Indian leather industry and examines the market structure of the industry. The worry that PRERs could have a negative impact on export is widespread among governments of exporting countries, both developed and developing. These concerns have been raised and shared in the WTO TBT Committee. From 1995 to June 2011, the most frequently raised trade concerns center on EU REACH regulations: 34 member countries expressed concern about the EU REACH regulations, and 13 member countries[4] expressed concern about EU RoHS directives.

Concern about the impact of PRERs is especially keen in East and Southeast Asia, which has been the center of the world manufacturing for decades and in which many suppliers of parts and components to global assemblers are located. Although developing Asian countries have increased manufacturing capability, the capacity of firms to comply with technical regulations seems limited. This is primarily because PRERs have been mainly implemented in EU countries, and the underlying concepts are relatively new to many Asian countries. Modern technical regulations such as RoHS and REACH-SVHC require the control of chemical substances in products, but the specifics are not always clearly understood by either supplying or buying firms. Each actor imposes its own interpretation of RoHS and REACH-SVHC requirements in writing its procurement specifications (Nudjarin et al., 2013). Faced with this situation, Asian governments have basically reacted to the EU RoHS and EU REACH in one of two manners. Here, we discuss one type of reaction; the other will be discussed in the next section.

Some Asian governments provide policy support to affected firms so that firms can continue exporting by smoothly adapting production to PRERs. Thailand is notable for this approach. As soon as the EU regulatory body disclosed the contents of the RoHS directives as part of a public comment period, the Thai government took substantial action and established an EU WEEE & RoHS impact assessment subcommittee comprising representatives from manufacturers, an industrial association, the Chamber of Commerce, relevant government agencies, and research institutes. This was begun during the EU drafting of the RoHS directives, as early as 2001 (Nudjarin et al., 2013). The Thai government acted in proactive and preparatory ways to build a platform to assist firms in building capacity to meet the various PRERs requirements. In Singapore, the SPRING Singapore, a statutory board of the Ministry of Trade and Industry, took action by providing technical information on the PRERs. SPRING Singapore provides support for firms by distributing a booklet on RoHS that provided information on RoHS for SMEs in 2007 and incorporated a list of RoHS compliant suppliers in 2009. It also publishes a booklet on REACH called "Complying with REACH: A Guide for SMEs"; this began in 2007, which is the year of that REACH was implemented in the EU and was revised in 2009.

Vietnam delayed response to PRERs until much later. The Vietnamese government established Chemicals Agency (*Vinachemia*) in 2009 and a RoHS/REACH information center was opened to assist firms with UNIDO support in 2011. In contrast to these countries, the governments of Cambodia, Laos, and Myanmar have lagged behind in assisting firms with PRER compliance.

Smooth adaptation of regulations implemented in export markets is key to maintaining market access. Many development stages can be found among Asian countries. The extent and timing of government support to firms in providing regulatory and technical information varies, and this might contribute to widening the development gap between countries in terms of local firm capacities and competitiveness for global production and in terms of investment environment for multinational firms.

PRERs spreading across Asian countries

Vogel (2012) and Vogel and Swinnen (2012) presents an in-depth and interesting comparison of regulatory introduction between the United States and the EU, revealing that environmental and safety regulations are introduced as a result of interactions among various factors such as consumer concerns, institutional influence, politics, and the actions of other countries. In Asia, the introduction of PRERs seems to be driven by concerns about industrial competitiveness. PRERs trigger Asian and other countries to introduce similar regulations and standards. Japan, Korea, China, and Vietnam have introduced RoHS-like regulations or standards (Table 9.2). This is the second types of reaction by Asian governments to EU RoHS implementation. In some countries, regulations are mandatory, as the EU RoHS is. In other countries, non-binding standards are introduced. J-Moss, a Japanese RoHS, is a set of regulatory requirements. However, in contrast to the EU RoHS, products are not required to be free of the restricted substances so long as they are labeled according to the levels of the substances contained in products. An orange label must be placed on every product whose regulated substances exceed the limit; a green label can be placed on product containing no more of regulated substances than the limit. The Thai version of RoHS was introduced in 2009, also as a non-binding and voluntary standard. The Chinese version of RoHS, implemented in 2007, imposes labeling requirements similar to those of J-Moss, although the targeted products differ from those targeted in the EU RoHS. California's regulations are also similar to EU RoHS, but the range of targeted products is narrower.

Nudjarin et al. (2013) describes three motives for the development of a Thai RoHS: coordinating product specifications to avoid the burden of multiple standards; increasing the initial volume of local-RoHS compliant supplies; and providing industry with the technical infrastructure to guide acceptable practices and verify product compliance. The development of Thai RoHS was driven by industry demands. An additional motive is preventing products that do not meet EU regulations from flowing into the country. Import of such products

Table 9.2 RoHS-like regulations and standards in various countries

Year of implementation	Country/Region	Name	Memo
2006/July	EU	RoHS Directive	Revised by 2011/65/EU
	Japan	JIS C0950 (J-Moss)	
2007/January	California, U.S.	California RoHS Law	The law required the government to adopt regulations prohibiting sale of electronic devices that are prohibited by EU RoHS.
2007/March	China	Administrative Measure on the Control of Pollution Caused by Electronic Information Products	
2008/January	South Korea	Act for Resource Recycling of Electrical and Electronic Equipment and Vehicles	
2008/January	Norway	Prohibition on Certain Hazardous Substances in Consumer Products	Regulate 18 substances for consumer products
2009/February	Thailand	Thai Industrial Standard TIS 2368–255	
2009/June	Turkey	Turkey RoHS	Turkey WEEE and RoHS implemented in 2012
2010/January	California, U.S.	The California Lighting Efficiency and Toxics Reduction Act or AB 1109	
2012/January	India	E-waste (Management and Handling) Rules, 2011	RoHS part is implemented in 2014.
2012/December	Vietnam	Circular No.30/2011/TT-BCT	

Source: Author.

may raise concern among consumers and also increase the risk that the country's exported products might use noncompliant import goods as intermediate goods.

Vogel (1995: 5–8) called the situation "the California Effect," which refers to the critical role of powerful and wealthy green political jurisdictions in promoting a regulatory "race to the top" among trading partners. The California effect especially well describes the national patterns of regulation on health, safety, and the environment. Not all countries race to the top in regulations, and there are a number of Asian countries that have not followed. Urpelainen (2010) describes the situation as a "partial race to the top" in his theoretical model, and this correctly shows the Asian situation.

In the Asian region, countries have different comparative advantages and play complementary roles in production. Depending on the comparative advantage, firms extend production networks, such as by procuring materials in a resource-rich country and producing parts from these materials by transporting them to other countries for labor-intensive processes and then sending the outputs to another neighboring country for assembly before final export. The Asian region acts a production hub for such production chains through the complementation of countries. However, the above-mentioned reaction of Asian governments to the EU RoHS may impede the competitiveness of the Asian region as a production hub.

The problem with the current situation is that the approach and scope of products covered varies among regulations introduced in different countries, which impedes smooth trade in the region. Whenever parts, components, and final goods are exported to different countries, it is necessary to meet or address different labeling and manufacturing requirements. While harmonization of PRERs at the global level seems difficult, how each country should respond in an efficient and effective way needs to be considered.

Conclusion

This chapter discussed the impact of chemical-related PRERs on Asian firms and policies. Asian firms have been affected by these regulations, and many of the firms have taken measures to adapt to the EU regulations. Traditional environmental regulations, such as pollution control regulations, affect firms in only the regulated location. In contrast, the mechanism of PRERs can require firms that operate in non-regulated countries to meet prescribed environmental and health standards. PRERs can be considered as a newer approach with the potential to change environmental governance. Developing countries are often weak in enforcement of environmental regulations, and if PRERs work, they might be effective measures for influence environmental governance in developing countries. However, the EU RoHS and REACH aim at protecting consumer health and the environment at the sites of consumption and disposal, and the regulations do not necessarily improve the environment in developing countries. These regulations do not impose any standards on traditional pollution at production sites. Therefore, the regulations may contribute to production of cleaner products, but it is too much to expect that the regulations will help maintain clean production sites.

An important issue is the multiplicity of similar regulations across Asia as well as in other parts of the world. When looking at the progress of globalization, production activities are rarely completed in a single country. Rather, parts and components are produced in different countries, depending on comparative advantage, before being assembled into a final product. Asian countries have individually tried to enhance their firms' competitiveness in the EU market by assisting in firms' adaptation to EU regulations. However, such actions by individual countries are not the best solution because the compliance of final products requires compliance by other firms in the supply chains, and these firms may be located in other countries. Contrary to their original intentions, requirements set by different countries could introduce unnecessary complexity for firms seeking to produce export products. This complexity will be quite disadvantageous for SMEs, which lack the capacity to learn the complex requirements of export markets. More coordinated policy efforts among countries are necessary. Governments now need to take into consideration the global production network of firms beyond their jurisdictions to set optimal policies.

The purpose of PRERs is to provide environmentally friendly and safe products to consumers, not to create trade barriers. Because of the diversity of Asian countries in terms of their stages of development, the capacities of governments and firms, and their needs, policy coordination within the region is essential, but this is not an easy task. The question of how to pursue coordination efforts in a way that efficiently and equitably helps firms needs to be examined in the international arena.

If the world agrees on a common target in threshold levels of chemicals contained in products, having multiple versions of similar regulations is obviously inefficient; different versions create different requirements. However, while achieving such global consensus and harmonizing regulations will be difficult, the current competition among countries pushes exporting countries to enact their own regulations. This is a big challenge in the area of regulation of trade and technical barriers to trade.

Notes

* The first version of this chapter is presented as Michida (2014).
1 The prohibited substances are lead, mercury, cadmium, PBB (polybrominated biphenyl), and PBDE (polybrominated diphenyl ether).
2 The chemicals contained in products regulated by EU REACH are called SVHCs (Substances of Very High Concern).
3 For example, Japanese electric and electronic assembler SONY has made its criteria for selecting suppliers. www.sony.net/SonyInfo/procurementinfo/activities/index.html (last accessed October 30, 2013).
4 WTO Committee on Technical Barriers to Trade document G/TBT/GEN/74/Rev.9, issued on October 17, 2011.

References

Angerer, G., Nordbeck, R., and Sartorius, C. (2008), "Impacts on industry of Europe's emerging chemicals policy REACH," *Journal of Environmental Management* 86: 636–647.

Honda, K. (2012), The Effect of EU Environmental Regulation on International Trade: Restriction of Hazardous Substances as a Trade Barrier, *IDE Discussion Paper* No. 341.

Jaffe, A. B., Peterson, S. R., and Portney, P. R. (1995), "Environmental regulation and the competitiveness of U.S. manufacturing: what does the evidence tell us?" *Journal of Economic Literature* 33: 132–163.

Michida, E. (2014), The Policy Impact of Product-Related Environmental Regulations in Asia, *IDE Discussion Paper* No. 451.

Michida, E. and Nabeshima, K. (2012), Roles of Supply Chains in Adopting Product Related Environmental Regulations; Case of Vietnam, *IDE Discussion Paper* No. 343.

Michida, E., Nabeshima, K., and Ueki, Y. (2014), Impact of Product-Related Environmental Regulations in Asia: Descriptive Statistics from a Survey of Firms in Vietnam, *IDE Discussion Paper* No. 466.

Michida, E., Ueki, Y., and Nabeshima, K. (2014), Impact on Asian Firms of Product-Related Environmental Regulations through Global Supply Chains: A Study of Firms in Malaysia, *IDE Discussion Paper* No. 453.

Nudjarin, R., Michida, E., and Nabeshima, K. (2013), Impact of Product-related Environmental Regulations/Voluntary Requirements on Thai Firms, *IDE Discussion Paper* No. 383.

Sankar, U. (2007), *Trade and Environment: A Study of India's Leather Exports*, New Delhi: Oxford University Press.

Tsunehiro, O., Wilson, J., and Sewadeh, M. (2001). "Saving two in a billion: quantifying the trade effect of European food safety standards on African exports," *Food Policy* 26: 495–514.

Tong, X., Shi, J., and Zhou, Yu (2012), "Greening of supply chain in developing countries: Diffusion of lead (Pb)-free soldering in ICT manufacturers in China," *Ecological Economics* 83: 174–182.

Urpelainen, J. (2010), "Regulation under economic globalization," *International Studies Quarterly* 54: 1099–1121.

Vogel, D. (1995), *Trading Up: Consumer and Environmental Regulation in a Global Economy*, Cambridge, MA: Harvard University Press.

Vogel, D. (2012), *Politics of Precaution: Regulating Health, Safety, and Environmental Risks in Europe and the United States*, Princeton, NJ: Princeton University Press.

Vogel, D. and Swinnen, J.F.M. (ed.) (2012), *Transatlantic Regulatory Cooperation: The Shifting Roles of the EU, the US and California*, Northampton, MA: Edward Elgar Publishing.

Part III
Perspectives

10 Renewable energy sources in energy abundant economy

Russian experience

Nikita Suslov

Energy sector of Russia: high output and inefficient use

Although Russia's fuel and energy industrial complex(FEIC)[1] is a substantial legacy of its national patrimony, with more than 40,000 operating enterprises, it actually represents a rather small share of all the production units involved in the country's economy, accounting for only 0.8 percent of the whole. Nevertheless, the share of the energy complex in the total output amounts to almost 20 percent, whereas in industrial production – about 45 percent in basic prices, that is, exclusive of rental elements – the FEIC provides no less than 43 percent of all budget revenues, and about 70 percent of the total currency earnings from foreign trade.

Despite the relatively small number of FEIC enterprises, they accumulate about a quarter of the country's fixed assets, and with reference to industrial production, nearly two-thirds, though, as a matter of fact, the official sources of statistical data provided by Rosstat RF[2] do not include information on the volumes of fixed assets in different spheres of the economy as measured in constant prices, which are exactly the investments in the form of fixed assets directed to the power and energy sector annually. This information provides evidence relevant to the estimates mentioned above, which, in addition to other lacunae, leave out of account the capital concentrated in pipeline systems. As for the latter, the abovementioned estimates of both investments and FEC assets need to be increased. According to the forecast prepared by the Ministry for Economic Development for the socio-economic development of the Russian Federation for the period up to 2030, the share of FEIC investments in 2011 was 32 percent. Perhaps, the difference between this figure and our estimates based on Rosstat data – 24.9 percent (Statistical Compilation, 2012: 642–643) – can be explained by taking into account investments in pipeline transportation.

What is the volume of FEC fixed capital in absolute terms? According to our estimates based on the analysis of economic growth model built on cross-country data for 2010, the ratio of fixed assets as measured in constant prices to the country's GDP was about 5.5:1. Thus, with the GDP amounting to RUB 45.2

Table 10.1 Russian energy sector in the world economy in 2011

	Volume	World position	Share in the world	Net exports
Oil, million ton	517	2	12.9	246
Gas, billion cubic meter	677	1	20	196
Coal, million ton	334	6	4.3	99
Energy from HPS, billion kWh	170	4	6.2	
Energy from NPS, billion kWh	168	5	4.8	
Petroleum products, million ton	240	3	6.3	111
Electric energy, billion kWh	1036	4	4.8	17
Energy production, million toe	1315	3	10.0	592
Energy consumption, million toe	731	3	5.6	
Renewables (RE), million toe	17.7		1.34	
RE without HPS, million toe	3.5		0.25	
GDP, $ bill. PPP	2363	6	3.0	
Population, million	142.9	9	2.06	

Sources: FSSS RF: www.gks.ru; IEA, Statistics: http://wds.iea.org/wds/ReportFolders/ReportFolders.aspx?CS_referer=&CS_ChosenLang=en; and IMF, World Economic Outlook Database, April 2014: www.imf.org/external/pubs/ft/weo/2014/01/weodata.

billion, Russia's fixed assets in 2010, including the cost of household property assessed at current prices, accounted for about RUB 300 billion; a quarter of this related to the FEC sector was RUB 75 billion, which is notably greater than the annual GDP.

Russia's FEIC is known to be one of the largest in the world, and it produces one-fifth of the world's total natural gas reserves, 13 percent of its oil, more than 6 percent of its hydropower and oil products, and 5 percent of the total electric and nuclear energy. At the same time, 46 percent of the total output is exported (Table 10.1). Although Russia's GDP amounts to only 3.0 percent of the world economy, its total FEC output accounts for 10 percent of the world energy production, while consumption is 5.6 percent. Russia can therefore be considered one of the world's greatest energy powers.

Among the many useful services that the energy sector renders to both the economy and society, such as the provision of comfortable living conditions for the population, power supplies for industrial production, support of the country's scientific and technical progress, satisfying the demand for services to assist other branches of the economy, etc., there is one service that we especially wish to single out – rent creation. Rent from the oil and gas industry was the basis for the existence of the Soviet Union, whose disintegration followed a two-fold drop in oil prices in 1985, rather than in 1980. In many respects, rental income explains the rapid growth of the Russian economy during the first eight years of the

Table 10.2 Energy consumption in Russia and other world economies in 2010, USA=100 percent

	Per capita			Per GDP	
	GDP PPP	Energy use	Electricity use	Energy use	Electricity use
Canada	83	103	125	124	125
Czech Republic	54	59	58	109	58
Finland	72	95	107	133	107
Germany	76	57	55	75	55
Greece	52	35	37	67	37
Israel	64	42	54	66	54
Japan	69	55	62	79	62
Netherlands	83	70	50	84	50
Russia	33	69	51	208	51
Sweden	80	76	112	96	112

Sources: Calculated from WB data: and IEA data; IEA, Statistics: http://wds.iea.org/wds/ReportFolders/ReportFolders.aspx?CS_referer=&CS_ChosenLang=en; and WB data, WB Data: http://data.worldbank.org/indicator/SP.POP.TOTL (2014).

21st century, and rent is certain to remain an important element for the country's economy over the long-term period. Calculated on the basis of production accounting of such resources in world prices for 2010, the volume of the rent created by hydrocarbon production was US$ 400 billion (Ickes and Gaddy, 2011), which at the current exchange rate was equal to more than a quarter of the GDP. Unfortunately, a considerable part of this sum was not spent effectively: only about US$ 120 billion passed through the budgetary sphere, and the bulk either went into indirect (hidden) subsidies for the inefficient economic sector or was taken "into shadow" (Suslov, 2012). Thus, the major task today is to increase rental incomes that can become a source for investments. Such a task is associated with significant growth in the relative prices of oil, gas, and consequently, other utilities, which cannot be "planned" in the short term. In this regard, the government should make attempts, at least, to minimize offshore trading schemes.

Before we discuss Russia's utilization of renewable resources, let us turn our thoughts to another related problem: the energy efficiency of the Russian economy. As a whole, Russia does not lag behind the developed countries in per capita consumption of energy, consuming about 70 percent of the US energy rate (see Table 10.2). Frankly speaking, when we consider that Russia's climate is more severe than that of most other countries, its energy consumption is likely to increase in the future and reach the levels associated with Canada and Finland. In particular, this will relate to the separate types of energy resource that provide technological progress – electric power, motor fuel and what are known as 'renewables' (RES). However, the lag here is not as significant since it falls within the efficiency of energy consumption. Russia's energy consumption per GDP PPP unit is twice as high as that of the United States, one and a half times higher than that of such northern countries as Canada and Finland and three times higher than that of the developed European countries and Japan. The research conducted by Bashmakov and Suslov (Bashmakov et al.,2008;Suslov, 2005; Suslov, 2007) show that severe climatic conditions only partly contribute to such a big difference in GDP energy consumption. The obsolete technological structure of the Russian economy, the energy losses caused by the depreciation of production facilities and failures in organizational management, as well as a lack of incentives to investment and energy saving, greatly contribute to this problem. Such a high rate of energy intensity calls into question Russia's economic development not only in terms of achieving sustainable growth but also the possibility of economic growth per se.

Renewable energy: though desirable, for now is disappointing

From this perspective, it seems clear that the development of alternative energy sources can become a very noticeable factor in reducing the energy cost per unit of output, given the present low level of energy consumption. Russia, with a population amounting to 2 percent of the world's people, produces and consumes only about 1.3 percent of global renewable energy production. If we set aside large-scale hydropower, the traditional source of our country's electricity generation and one that is especially widespread in Siberia and in the Far East, Russia's share in both the production and consumption of renewable energy (without the hydroelectric power plants) falls to an insignificant value – one quarter percent.

Besides such a poor performance, other figures testify to the fact that these days the role of renewable energy in Russia is quite insignificant. Even if we take into account large-scale hydropower, the production of energy resources from renewable sources of energy is twice as low as the world average, and in comparison with OECD this figure is three times lower. At the same time, Russia's production of alternative energy appears to be many times less than that of such countries as Finland, Norway, Denmark, Canada and the United States, not to mention Iceland, which consumes its own energy mostly produced from renewable sources (Table 10.3). At first sight, Russia's use of renewable sources corresponds approximately to the level of the United Kingdom and Japan – 0.12 tons of oil equivalent (toe) per capita against 0.1 and 0.15, respectively. However, it is necessary to point out that in Russia, the unit use of all energy resources is significantly higher than it is in the rest of the world. Moreover, according to 2011 IEA data, the energy consumed to energy produced ratio in Japan was about only 0.11 (in Russia – 1.8). As a result, of Japan's total energy use, for example, the share of renewable energy consumption is twice as high as in Russia, and in energy its total production reaches 37.8 percent, as against 1.3 percent in our country (Table 10.3).

Table 10.3 Renewable energy (RE) in the world and selected world economies, tone of oil equivalent, 2011

	Per capita energy output	*Per capita energy use*	*Per capita RE output*	*RE share in energy output, %*	*RE output to energy use ratio, %*
Australia	13.63	5.65	0.29	2.10	5.06
Canada	12.02	7.40	1.33	11.04	17.93
Denmark	3.80	3.25	0.55	14.43	16.84
Finland	3.25	6.61	1.73	53.14	26.13
Germany	1.52	3.83	0.38	25.19	10.04
Iceland	15.45	18.42	15.45	100.00	83.83
Ireland	0.38	2.83	0.16	40.82	5.52
Japan	0.41	3.65	0.15	37.80	4.23
Netherlands	3.82	4.60	0.19	4.88	4.06
Norway	41.64	6.00	2.55	6.12	42.50
Spain	0.68	2.69	0.29	43.31	10.96
United Kingdom	2.07	3.00	0.10	4.85	3.34
United States	5.70	7.00	0.43	7.61	6.20
World	1.91	1.89	0.25	12.89	12.98
OECD Total	3.13	4.31	0.35	11.09	8.05
Russia	9.20	5.12	0.12	1.35	2.43

Source: Calculated from IEA data: IEA, Statistics: http://wds.iea.org/wds/ReportFolders/ ReportFolders.aspx?CS_referer=&CS_ChosenLang=en; and WB data, WB, Data: http://data. worldbank.org/indicator/SP.POP.TOTL (2014).

In contrast to Japan and other world economies, all Russia's sources in the overall structure of renewable energy resources, apart from hydro, geothermal and solid biomass, are rather insignificant. Table 10.4 shows that Japan takes the leading position in the use of geothermal and solar energy; it also uses such sources as wind power and municipal waste. Wind power is more widespread in OECD countries, especially in Europe. Amongst OECD members, the production of biological motor fuel is rather well developed, while Europe specializes in the production of biofuel, and the American continent uses ethanol. And whereas many countries throughout world have started to recycle municipal waste, Russia has only to a very limited extent taken up this practice.

The only achievement of our country today is its leading position in the world's production of pellets (more than 2 million tons a year). Unfortunately, the pellets are mainly exported to European countries; their effective use in Russia is restrained by administrative and economic barriers. It seems relevant to add that nowadays Russia is successfully developing tidal power plants on the basis of original domestic technologies. A number of Russian companies have been paying much attention to the development of large-scale production technologies of photoelectric converters, a business that is again also mainly export oriented.

Russia's almost dead-end situation with regard to the production and use of green energy is a cause for especial concern given the breakthrough involved in green energy's balances abroad. By the end of 2008, the capacity of electric power generating plants using nontraditional RES (without large hydroelectric power stations) reached 280 GW, and in 2010 it exceeded the capacity of all nuclear power plants by 340 GW. By the end of 2009, the total capacity of 150 thousand wind power plants reached the level of about 159 GW. In 2009, when wind power plants with a total capacity of 39 GW came into operation, their capacity as compared to that at the end of 2008 (120 GW) grew by 32 percent. In 2009, WPPs generated 324 TWh of electric energy, and by 2011, this had grown to 416.8 TWh.

By the end of 2009, the world's total capacity of photoelectric converters had reached 21.3 GW, and over the year 2009, it increased by 7 GW, with the growth of sales in the world market being more than 50 percent. In 2009, the total annual output was 23.9 TWh, and in 2011 it reached 58.7 TWh. The total capacity of biomass power plants in 2009 was 60 GW, and the annual electric power output exceeded 300 TWh. The total capacity of geothermal power plants exceeded 10.7 GW, with the output of electric power amounting to 62 TWh annually. The total thermal capacity of solar heating systems in 2008 reached 145 GW (i.e. more than 180 million m2 of solar collectors); more than 60 million houses in the world now use a solar hot water supply, with annual growth rates being more than 15 percent.

The production output of biofuels (ethanol and biodiesel) in 2008 exceeded 79 billion liters per year (about 5 percent of the world's annual consumption of gasoline, bioethanol – 67, biodiesel – was 12 billion liters a year, which, when compared with 2004, marked a six times increase in the production of biodiesel, while the production of bioethanol doubled). In 2011, the world production and consumption of biofuel exceeded 50 billion liters, which is more than 1 percent of the world market of liquid fuels.

At present, 30 countries operate more than 2 million thermal pumps with a total thermal energy output of more than 30 GW, utilizing natural and waste heat and providing warm and cold supplies for buildings. Yet in Russia today the number of installed heating pumps does not exceed several hundred units.

At the same time, further development of alternative energy generation in Russia would be desirable because it would not only allow us to reduce the energy intensity of production but would also, as a result, release the resources for increasing economic growth. The fact is that two-thirds of the Russian territories, with a population of about 20 million people, are not covered by the networks of centralized power supply. As a rule, these are the regions with the highest prices and tariffs for fuel and energy (10–20 rubles per kW and more). The greater part of Russia's regions are known to be energy deficient and in

Table 10.4 Structure of renewable energy produced by sources (%) in 2011

	Russia	*Japan*	*OECD Europe*	*OECD Total*	*World*
Hydro	80.42	36.63	23.41	27.94	17.64
Geothermal	2.53	12.70	6.58	7.64	3.87
Solar photovoltaics	0.00	2.27	2.09	1.16	0.31
Solar thermal	0.00	2.10	1.51	1.49	1.08
Tide, wave and ocean	0.00	0.00	0.02	0.01	0.00
Wind	0.00	2.01	8.47	6.61	2.19
Renewable municipal waste	0.00	3.19	4.95	3.24	0.87
Solid biomass	17.05	40.54	41.29	38.27	68.91
Landfill gas	0.00	0.00	1.57	2.08	0.53
Sludge gas	0.00	0.00	0.69	0.34	0.09
Other biogases	0.00	0.56	3.34	1.53	0.90
Biogasoline	0.00	0.00	0.92	6.63	2.06
Biodiesel	0.00	0.00	4.29	2.61	1.02
Other liquid biofuels	0.00	0.00	0.86	0.42	0.50
Total of Renewable Energy	**100.00**	**100.00**	**100.00**	**100.00**	99.96

Source: Calculated from IEA data: IEA, Statistics: (2014) http://wds.iea.org/wds/ReportFolders/ReportFolders.aspx?CS_referer=&CS_ChosenLang=en.

need of both fuel and energy delivery. For them, as well as for energy importing countries, regional energy security is still a very urgent problem; and while it is one of the world's largest gas producers, Russia has gasified only about 50 percent of its urban and about 35 percent of its rural settlements. Otherwise, the Russian regions mainly consume coal and oil products, which are the main sources of local environmental pollution.

The continuous growth of tariffs, energy and fuel prices and the growing costs of a centralized power supply have accelerated the development of autonomous power engineering in the country: over the last 10 years, diesel and petrol generators with unit capacity of 100 kW have exceeded the total output of large power plants. Consumers of energy seek to provide themselves with their own sources of electric power and heat, which, as a rule, results in a reduction in the efficiency of fuel consumption as compared to the combined electricity and heat generation at heat and power plants, as well as a reduction in the efficiency of the country's energy as a whole. Here, the sources of renewable energy can really compete with the plants that use fossil fuel. An off-grid energy supply based on RES has proved its economic efficiency in many countries, since it allows the economies to avoid the high expenses associated with the laying of power lines. In Russia, it would be effective to use hybrid wind-diesel systems, biomass boilers, and small hydroelectric power stations that have the capacity to compete with traditional fossil fuel technologies.

Potential of RES utilization exists but is still not used

Besides these resources, Russia is also endowed with considerable potential for the economic application of renewable energy. Practically all regions of the country possess at least one or another source of renewable energy, and the majority of these resources constitute several types of RES, such as small rivers, the waste of agricultural and timber industry complexes, peat stocks, considerable wind and solar sources, low-potential heat of the earth, etc. In some cases their operation seems to be more commercially attractive when compared with the use of fossil fuel since deliveries of the latter are expensive and unreliable.

What, however, can we consider to be the proven experience of Russia in the use of RES in the national economy? According to O.S. Popel, the Chairman of the Scientific Council of the Russian Academy of Sciences on nonconventional renewable energy sources and the head of the laboratory for RES and power supply of the Joint Institute of high temperatures of the Russian Academy of Sciences, Russia has become one of the world leading wooden-pellet-producing economies (2 million ton per annum), yet the products are mainly exported to Europe (Popel, 2011). At the same time, we can note certain positive results in constructing tidal energy devices based on original national designs. In addition, a number of companies specialize in the large-scale development, production and export of photoelectric converters.

If we consider the potential application of RES by volume, we can find various and often discrepant data: for example, according to I.S. Kozhukhovskij, the General Director of Energy Forecasting Agency "APBE", the technical potential of alternative sources of energy accounts for about 4600 billion t of the equivalent amount of coal (3320 billion toe), whereas the economic potential, that is, the economically justified volume of their usage, is 300 million, here (210 billion toe) or about 30 percent of Russia's annual consumption (Kozhukhovskij, 2012). According to "RusHydro", which is a Holding Company that maintains the majority of large and medium Russian hydroelectric power stations (Pavlov, 2012), the general technical potential for the generation of electric power alone appears to be slightly lower than the figures specified above: it exceeds 45 trillion kWh, which amounts to about 4000 billion toe. "RusHydro" estimates the economic potential also as a smaller volume than "APBE", only at the level of 1566 billion kWh, which corresponds to about 135 million toe. Apart from this, it allocates "industrial potential", which means, apparently, assessing the possibilities for the use of renewable energy by industrial enterprises. Other available data provided by "RusHydro" includes a detailed structure of potential energy production for separate types of renewable energy source (Table 10.5).

Table 10.5 Potential of energy production using renewable energy sources in Russia

	Potential, billion kWh		
	Technical	Economic	Industrial
Small HPS (<25 MW)	372	205	6–10
Wind PS	6517	326	70–90
Geothermal PS	34905	335	40–60
Biomass PS	412	203	90–130
Tidal PS	253	61.6	16–45
Solar HPS	2714	435	5–10
Total	45173	1566	227–342

Source: Calculated from data of JSC "RusHydro", 2010 – Pavlov, M., "Renewable energy and sustainable economic development. Opportunities for Russia". *ESKO* (Electronic journal of energy service company "Ecological Systems"), No. 6, June 2012.http://esco.co.ua/journal/2012_6/art277.htm.

Here, the technical potential for the full deployment of RES can cover the nation's total energy production: this is possible in Russia by using modern advanced and projected technical means. The economic potential here is the contribution of the technical potential estimated as economically feasible. Finally, the industrial potential is the level of electric power generation that can be employed by industrial enterprises. Table 10.5 shows that the structure of technical potential is represented mostly by geothermal energy and wind sources; however, their economic potential does not significantly exceed the economic potential of the use of other types of RES, and even concedes priority to the economic potential of solar energy. In general, biomass, which rates low in technical potential, has the greatest weight in industrial potential. Despite the high technical potential of solar energy, the forecast of its use in the short run is far from optimistic. Industry can use about 227–342 billion kWh, which is equal to 40–60 percent of industry's general power consumption. Thus, biomass and wind sources seem to be industry's most probable sources of renewable energy.

In 2011, the G. M. Krzhizhanovsky Energy Institute developed the Program for the modernization of Russia's electric power industry for the period until 2020. The authors were able to offer an assessment of RES production by types, which can certainly be added to the IEA estimates and the data discussed above. Unlike the latter, the data shown in Table 10.6 include only electricity generation; that is, without heat and exported biomass. Another difference is that it takes into account only small hydropower plants with the power capacity of less than 25 MW. Thus, in 2010 the use of all renewable energy sources made it possible to generate only about 5889.4 billion kWh, which amounted to only 0.6 percent of its total output.[3]

Table 10.6 Summarized data on electricity production from renewable energy sources (RES) in Russia, 2010

Types of RES	Generation capacity, MW	Power generation, mill. KWh	Share in economic potential, %
Wind ES	13.2	14.2	0.04
Small HPS (<25 MW)	700	2800	1.37
Geothermal PS	81.2	474	0.14
Solar PS	0	0	0.00
Tidal PS	1.1	1.2	0.00
Biomass PS	520	2600	1.28
Total	**1315.5**	**5889.4**	**0.46**
Share of RES in total electricity production, %	0.57	0.58	

Sources: Calculated from data of Table 5 and data from "Elaboration of Program of Modernization of Power Sector of Russia for the period up to 2020", JSC G. M. Krzhizhanovsky Energy Institute, Moscow, 2011, p. 115.

A comparison of these data with the indicators of the potential use of RES given above testifies to the insignificant use of the latter. Actually, Russia does not use solar energy for electricity production, although in some areas solar collectors are used for heating dwellings. When wind and tidal power plants are used, their use is quite insignificant, and only small hydropower and biomass use their economic potential for more than 1 percent.

Reasons why Russia lags behind in developing RES: Economic non-competitiveness, institutional failure, and lack of infrastructure

Why does Russia, unlike most other countries, use RES so insignificantly? Generally speaking, there are several serious reasons for this:

- the non-competitiveness of RES projects in the existing market environment in comparison with the projects based on the use of fossil types of organic fuel;
- a number of institutional barriers associated with the lack of regulations necessary to stimulate the use of RES in electric power and the absence of both federal and regional programs to support large-scale use of RES;
- lack of infrastructure required for the successful development of an electric power industry based on RES, as well as an insufficient level and quality of scientific background for its development; the lack of an appropriate database of potential renewable energy sources as well as an authentic

database on projects already realized; the absence of normative, technical and methodical documentation and the software necessary for the design, construction and operation of power plants using RES; insufficient staffing and a lack of mechanisms to draw on public resources for the development of electric power industry though the use of RES.

According to data based on the materials provided by the International Energy Agency, EFC "APEEC" and JSC "RusHydro" (National Human Development Report, 2010: 115, Figure 10.1), the cost of electric power drawn from RES is on average much higher in Russia than in other countries this difference is especially notable in the case of solar, geothermal and wind energy. Of such sources, Russia can take advantages of small hydropower only, with the production cost of one kilowatt-hour at traditional power plants here being lower than abroad, which can be explained by cheaper fuel, a high share of cogeneration and favorable conditions for large scale hydro generation. The competitive

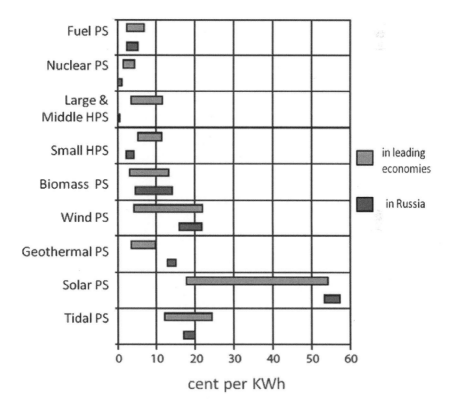

Figure 10.1 Electricity production cost in leading world economies and in Russia, 2007

Source: National Human Development Report in the Russian Federation 2009. Energy Sector and Sustainable Development, UNDP, Russia, Moscow, 2010: 115.

Prepared using data from IEA, EFC "APEEC" and JSC "RusHydro."

Table 10.7 Energy capacity utilization at power plants (%)

Fuel PS in Russia	52,9
Large Hydro PS	40
Small Hydro PS	~ 45
Wind PS	~ 25–40
Solar PS	~ 20

Source: Kozhukhovkij, I. S., Place of Renewable Energy Sources in Total Energy Balance of Russia. Agency for Forecasting Electric Energy Balance, Moscow, 2012, www.electrowind.ru/images/vozobn-istochn-v-energetike-rossii.pdf.

economic conditions for the development of RES in Russia are thus much less favorable than in other leading countries of the world.

The institutional environment in the Russian electric energy sector is the result mainly of two federal laws:

- The Law "On Energy Saving and Raising Energy Efficiency" of November 23, 2013
- The Federal Law "On Electric Energy Sector (revised)" of March 26, 2003 N 35-FL

These laws support the use of RES by providing:

- the opportunity to set feed-in tariffs or markups for RE;
- state guarantees and budget compensations for access to the grid;
- the chance for the network companies to purchase all renewable energy produced (e.g., by using green certificates).

Yet in practice, however, the specified possibilities for RES development are not taken up. The main reason for this is an extremely lengthy and expensive certification procedure. In particular, in Belgorod, it took a leading company developing RES[4]– a well-established company with strong lobbing power – a year to obtain a certificate to build a pilot solar power station. As a rule, local grids are reluctant to connect to RES plants due to their unstable character and the low quality of the energy produced (Table 10.7).

Government promises to support RES and what is expected

An important feature of Russian society is that most companies and organizations tend to perceive the government's advisory recommendations as directives. From this perspective, one cannot but admit that the formation of expectations and forecasts for RES development has been greatly influenced by the Federal Decree of January 8, 2009 No. 1-p "The main directions for the state policy to improve energy efficiency from renewable energy sources for the period up to 2020". This document set down that "state policy in the sphere of energy efficiency from renewable energy sources is an integral part of the energy policy of the Russian Federation and determines the purposes, directions and activities of the state bodies and public authorities for the development of energy industry from renewable energy sources", and assigned to the Ministry for Energy of the Russian Federation the responsibility of coordinating the activity of the Federal executive authorities in implementing the stated policy.

The main purpose of this directive is to increase the energy efficiency of the national economy by introducing high technologies and innovative equipment. The document also establishes target indicators of RES development as a share of electricity production from RES in the total generation of electric energy: for 2010 – 1.5 percent, 2015 – 2.5 percent and 2020 – 4.5 percent. The last figure shows that the capacity of electricity generation will amount to approximately 14700 MW, while electric energy production will reach 50 billion kWh.

Private-state partnership is expected to finance the implementation of state policy, and the government means to support the enterprises producing energy from renewable energy (except for hydroelectric power stations of more than 25 MW) by

- establishing and regularly adjusting the size and validity periods for markups to the energy equilibrium wholesale electricity/power price to determine the electricity price;
- obligating the wholesale electric energy buyers/consumers to purchase the specified volume of electric energy from RES;
- improving legal regimes for the use of natural resources in the construction and operation of electricity generating plants/facilities based on RES.

In addition, the government has promised "to use the mechanisms for providing additional support of the renewable energy sector in compliance with the budget legislation of the Russian Federation".

The Federal Decree of January 8, 2009 No. 1-p. has also established the following measures to increase the network and infrastructural support for the development of electric energy production to be derived from RES:

- improvement of scientific and engineering (i.e. technological services) support in production, realization and consumption of renewable energy;
- the use of potential capacity of domestic industry for the specified purposes;
- creation and development of the information environment and the expert and consulting engineering network as well as information support for the development of RES;
- development of normative, technical and methodical documentation for the design, construction and operation of power plants generating energy from RES;
- stimulation of electric energy consumers to increase the use of renewable energy.

Around the same time, the Russian government initiated the design of two more state programs aimed at facilitating RES development – the State Program of the Russian Federation "Energy efficiency and energy development", adopted in 2013(Ministry of the Energy of RF, 2013), and "The program to modernize the electricity sector of Russia for the period until 2020", although this has not yet been accepted. While the two programs contain similar subprograms of RES development and, judging by the contents, they generally correspond to the Federal Decree of January 8, 2009 No. 1-p., both of them focus mainly on the existing realities in the sphere of renewable energy production, that is, weak competitiveness, high institutional barriers and insufficient infrastructure; consequently, their target parameters are less optimistic. As a further consequence, the modernization program provides for the installation of only 3062 MW from all sources, with 4400 MW of installed capacity from RES to be reached by 2020. The "Energy efficiency and energy development" program goes even further and provides for the installation of about 9000 MW of power capacity over the period until 2020, which will make it possible to increase the generation of electric energy from RES up to 2.5 percent of its total output.

One further document that deals with RES development – "General scheme of allocation of electric power facilities for the period up to 2030" – has been published by the Energy Forecasting Agency "APBE" and was approved at the government meeting of the Russian Federation on June 3, 2010. However, the measures specified in it do not seem to be sufficient to achieve the targets and their associated indicators set forth in the Federal Decree adopted on January 8, 2009 No. 1-p. The more recent document offers two scenarios of the dynamics of RES input capacities – basic and maximum.

Table 10.8 shows that according to the basic or the minimum scenario only 6.1 million kW of generation capacity will be installed, whereas in the maximum scenario, it will be 14.3 million kW. Although these figures are less optimistic in terms of prospective use of RES, it seems relevant nonetheless to mention that since the government measures to support the development of RES still remain unclear, these forecasts are made on the basis of regional suggestions.

The minimum scenario suggests that there will be a 5.6 times increase in the use of RE as installed power generation capacity, while the maximum scenario presupposes a 12-fold increase. But even in this case, the share of RES in Russia's total power generation capacity will not exceed 4.0–5.0 percent. Wind power plants are expected to make the highest contribution to RES capacity increment, while biomass and small hydropower plants will take the second and the third positions. At the same time, since the share of biomass and small hydroenergy power plants in the total RE will decrease to the advantage of wind energy, the development of wind energy is highly likely to be the main direction that RES will take in our country.

The prospects for the development of wind energy in Russia have attracted the special attention of the experts, and consequently non-government organizations and independent experts are today developing a special program – "The

Table 10.8 The structure of RES installed power generation capacities according to "General layout of electric power facilities for the period up to 2030" (%)

	2010	By 2030	
		Basic	*Maximum*
Total RES capacities installed in thousand kW	1315.5	7400	15600
Wind ES	1.0	26.6	48.9
Small HPS (< 25 MW)	53.2	27.4	20.5
Geothermal PS	6.2	4.1	2.9
Solar PS	0.0	0.0	0.0
Tidal PS	0.1	0.2	0.1
Biomass PS	39.5	41.7	27.6
In Total	100.0	100.0	100.0

Sources: Joint data from "Elaboration of Program of Modernization of Power Sector of Russia for the period up to 2020", JSC G. M. Krzhizhanovskij Energy Institute, Moscow, 2011, p. 115 and Kozhukhovkij, I.S., Place of Renewable Energy Sources in Total Energy Balance of Russia. Agency for Forecasting Electric Energy Balance, Moscow, 2012, www.electrowind.ru/images/vozobn-istochn-v-energetike-rossii.pdf.

general scheme of allocation of wind power facilities in Russia for the period up to 2030" (Nikolaev, 2013). The writers of this document estimate that the technical potential of wind power until 2020 and 2030 will be 7 and 30 GW of the generating power with an annual output of 17.5 and 85 billion kWh, respectively, which considerably exceeds the figures estimated in the more general and already accepted program, "General scheme of allocation of electric power facilities for the period up to 2030". Taking into account the world experience, the authorities have selected the most energetic and cost-effective wind farms with the power capacity of 30–50 MW based on modern wind turbines of 2–3 MW as the first stations for the industrial development of electric power in Russia. This forecast relies on the supposition that wind farms are located mainly in the areas where production cost of electric energy generated at wind farms is lower than the cost of electric power generated at thermal power plants (using gas and coal) under construction, with the use efficiency coefficients of installed capacity of wind farms exceeding 30 percent (Nikolaev et al., 2008).

Some model analysis

Undoubtedly, the possibility and efficiency of RES largely depends on the micro-economic environment, that is, the situation in a certain district defined by the existence and quality of the type of the renewable energy source, the energy needs of the district, as well as the availability and the cost of traditional fuel and energy resources. At the same time, it seems relevant to take into account the average costs of RES involvement in economic turnover and energy balance. These conditions are formed at macroeconomic or zone levels and influence the competitiveness of RES proceeding from the practical availability of technologies to supply local energy needs, as well as the technical characteristics of all possible energy sources, including both traditional and renewable sources.

To assess the consequences and efficiency of the distribution of various production technologies and energy consumption, IEIE SB RAS[5] uses an economic inter-region and inter-sector forecast model that includes the energy sector of the economy with energy products in physical units – OMMM-Energy (optimization multi-sector multi-district model that includes energy with energy products in physical units) developed on the basis of the well-known model proposed by A.G. Granberg (Granberg, 1973).

OMMM-Energyisan optimization multi-sector multi-region model (MRIO model) that includes energy with energy products in physical units, and concerns both inter-sector and inter-region relations of national energy sector. It is a composition of two sub-models for the time periods 2008–2020 and 2021–2030, and views the dynamics of investment as a non-linear function adapted with the help of linearization techniques (Suslov, 2014).

The model covers 45 products, 8 of them energy products: rough oil, gas, coal, dark petroleum products, light petroleum products, products of coal processing, electricity, and heat. It also incorporates six large regions of Russia: the European region, the Ural region, the Tyumen region, Western Siberia, Eastern Siberia, and the Far Eastern region.

The model includes non-energy sectors that are important for a given energy sector analysis: drilling for oil and gas, pipelines (as a kind of transport), production of special equipment for energy production, transportation, and petroleum chemistry.

The model comprises some peculiarities of energy production and consumption, which distinguishes it from a canonical OMMM:

- oil and gas reserves are monitored: the model fixes the annual output to the volume of reserves ratio; output growth is followed by investment into the reserves;
- diminishing returns to scale in oil and gas extraction sector are included;
- substitution between different kinds of energy is considered: 20 types of technology that produce heat and electricity are incorporated for each region.

The model makes it feasible to evaluate any complex consequences and the efficiency of policy measures in the sphere of energy production, processing and consumption. Earlier, it was applied to evaluate the economic consequence of:

- concentration of energy-intensive production in Southern Siberia;
- gasification in Southern Siberia;
- reduction in energy intensity of production in the national economy;
- introduction of heat pumps technology in different regions.

The latest calculations carried out on the basis of OMMM-Energy were aimed at identifying permissible and economically justified cost limits of installed electricity generation facilities using RES. We made several variants of calculations for each of the region specified in OMMM-Energy to analyze how power generation from renewable sources (RES power generation) could impact on the national economy and regions of such power generation. The technique applied is – the different technologies of RES power generation (RES technologies) were incorporated into the models; on the base of priori guesses, the upper bound of a presumable volume of power generated by untraditional capacities were set; investment intensities of power generation were set with their initial values referred to standard power generation technologies used by traditional thermal stations; and then investment intensities were step-by-step increased to the level when the RES technologies become uncompetitive to traditional ones and, therefore, unavailable in the solution of the problem.

So, two ranges of costs per unit of generation capacity were obtained for each region. The first one is such that power generation from renewable sources is obviously efficient and its application is limited only by technological and natural conditions. Another range is that one when RES technologies can compete with traditional ones and the choice of sources and RES technologies depends on the certain technological, natural, and economic conditions.

Two regions – the European part of Russia and Western Siberia – showed the most interesting results. The results show that both ranges in these regions are nearly equal – the first range, being in the cost of 1 kW, is equal up to US $2.1 thousand and another range – from US $2.1 thousand up to nearly US $3.1 thousand for the European part of Russia and US $3.9 thousand for Western Siberia. Thus, the RES power generation with the cost per 1 kW up to $2.1 thousand could be regarded undoubtedly efficient. The RES technologies incorporated in the model with investment intensities higher than above mentioned are available in the solution with their production lower than their upper limits. At that, if the investment intensity changes from US $ 2.1 to US $ 2.3 thousand the production sharply drops with further retarding deviation from maximum (see Table 10.9). It is just the range where renewable sources can compete with tradition ones as renewables lose their economic attractiveness due to growing cost of the equipment and installation.

For the purpose of our study, we increased the RES investment intensities step-by-step to analyze how they would change the total investment in the economy. Such total investment changes take place mostly due to two factors. The first one is higher investments per RES fresh capacities which make the total investments in the economy higher and the second one – the exclusion of traditional power generation technologies and, therefore, a drop in their fuel supply that results in lower total investments.

To summarize our RES generation efficiency analysis, we have found out that there are two levels of justified cost limits of installed electricity generation for the regions included in the model. The first one equals to US$ 2100 per 1 kW, which equals to US$ 2100 per 1 kW, which means that, given the estimated

Table 10.9 Variants of economic development indices as function of RES generation capacities

European part of Russia					
RES power generation cost, thousands US $*/1 MW	2.1	2.3	2.6	2.8	3.1	
RES power generation, bln. kWh	21.8	8.1	5.8	5.5	1.2	0.0
Incremental GDP growth per 1000 RES kWth, US $ (2007)	19	21	25	38	−3	
Incremental households' consumption growth per 1000 kWth of RES power generation, bln. kWth	7	12	10	4	4	
Incremental investment growth per 1000 kWh of RE power generation, bln kWth	12	9	16	34	−7	
Energy saved per 1000 kWth, toe.	0.160	0.160	0.211	0.254	0.261	

Western Siberia					
RES power generation cost, thousands US $*/1 MW	2.1	2.3	2.6	2.8	3.1	3.9
RES power generation, bln. kWh.	21.8	8.1	7.2	5.6	4.0	1.2
Incremental GDP growth per 1000 RES kWth, US $ (2007)	32	25	27	31	37	3
Incremental households' consumption growth per 1000 kWth of RES power generation, bln kWth	11	16	12	8	3	2
Incremental investment growth per 1000 KWh of RE power generation, bln kWth	22	9	16	22	34	1
Energy saved per 1000 kWth, toe.	0.155	0.219	0.206	0.257	0.303	0.288

* Including cost of installation

Source: Model calculations

long-run *average* conditions, the production technologies of electric energy derived from RES requiring investment per 1 kW that are *lower* the specified level seem to be economically feasible and could dominate traditional generating technologies. Thus, their application is constrained rather by technical and natural conditions. The second level of cost limits equals to US$ 3100 per 1 kW for European Russia and up to US$ 3900 for Western Siberia. That means that given the estimated conditions the production technologies of electric energy derived from RES which require investments that are *higher* the specified levels seem to be neither economically justified nor feasible. The technologies of electric energy derived from RES with the costs of their installation *between* the estimated first and second levels of cost limits of installed electricity generation seem to compete with traditional power generating technologies.

The range between these levels includes the average expected cost on electricity generated by RES, which the State Program of the Russian Federation "Energy efficiency and energy development" establishes at the level of RUB 75 thousand per 1 kW[6]. We believe that this fact shows that probably RES development in Russia requires special attention and support from the government.

Summary

1. Since Russia is an energy abundant country, a number of favorable conditions exist for the development of RES. Russia's extremely large surface area is a specific reason for believing that it will be able to increase both the use of RES and the share of the resources in the energy balance and electricity generation of the country.
2. Although, in general, renewable energy sources are less competitive than traditional energy technologies, there are regions where RES based technologies are effective even at the present time. Probably, in the future, the situation in the country will change to the advantage of RES.
3. It is doubtful, however, that the role of renewable energy sources in Russia will ever be as important as in Europe, Japan, Northern America, or in most other countries, but the importance of RES is highly likely to grow in Russia as well.
4. In order to facilitate RES development, the Russian government should elaborate and carry out drastic measures to support energy produced from RES.
5. The current Russian legislation provides for the possibility to set feed-in tariffs, promises the government's support for the access to grid with budget compensations, and guarantees to oblige network companies to purchase all the RE produced (e.g. through the use of green certificates).
6. The main reason why these institutional regulations in the energy sector do not work is because of the extremely lengthy and expensive certification procedure that they have to undergo. As a rule, local grids are reluctant to connect to RES plants due to what managers believe to be their unstable character and law quality energy.
7. Electricity and capacity supply contracts (which guarantee investment return) on a competitive basis seem to be a key factor in the successful promoting of RES, but the required legislation has not yet been developed.

Notes

1 This concept coincides to energy sector of economy.
2 Russian Statistical Agency.
3 According to another source in 2011 the volume of electricity production from RES increased up to 8.4 billion KWh or about 0.8 percent from the total generation, which equaled 1,058 billion KWh. State Program of the RF "Energy efficiency and energy development" (2013).

4 The solar station of AltEnerg in Belgorod came into operation on October 1, 2010; its peak rated power accounts for 100 kW. It is a pilot plant with two different prototypes of equipment amounting to 1,320 modules, amorphous and polycrystal, with a total active surface of 1,230.2 square meters.
5 Institute of Economics and Industrial Engineering of Siberian Branch of Russian Academy of Sciences.
6 It equaled to about $2.5 thousands as calculated using exchange rate of 2011.

References

Bashmakov, I. Borisov, K., Dzedzichek, M., Gritsevich, I., and Lunin, A. (2008), *Resource of Energy Efficiency in Russia: Scale, Costs and Benefits*, Moscow: Center for Energy Efficiency. Developed for the World Bank.

Granberg, A.G. (1973), *Optimization of Spatial Proportions of National Economy*, Moscow: Ekonomika (*Optimizatsija territorialnykh proportsyj Narodnogo khozjajstva*) (in Russian).

Ickes, B. and Gaddy, C. (2011), "The Russian economy through 2020: the challenge of managing rent addiction," in Lipman, M. and Petrov, N (eds.), *Russia in 2020: Scenarios for the Future*, Washington, DC: Carnegie Endowment for International Peace.

Kozhukhovskij, I.S. (2012), Place of renewable energy sources in the overall energy balance of Russia. International Forum on Renewable Energy and Energy Efficiency, Moscow, June 5–6. www.e-apbe.ru/library/presentations/2012_06_06_REF_ISK.pdf (last accessed on11 December 2013) (Mestovo zobnovljaemykh istotchnikov energii v obschem energetitcheskom balance Rossii. Mezhdunarodnyj forum po vosobnovljaemoj energii i energetitcheskoj effectivnosti, Moskva, Ijun 5–6) (in Russian).

Ministry of the Energy of RF (2013), State Program of the RF "Energy efficiency and energy development," www.minenergo.gov.ru/upload/iblock/d6c/d6c2bd083f7a8 08423b3b21c3069de39.pdf (Gosudarstvennaja Programma RF "Energoeffeknjvnost i razvitija energetiki, "Ministerstvo Energeniki RF, Dokumenty) (in Russian).

Nikolayev V.G. (2013), Status and prospects for the development of general outlay of allocation of wind power stations in Russia up to 2030, www.energy-fresh.ru/windenergy/analitics/?id=3572 (last accessed on 9 December, 2013) (Sostojanie i perspektivy razrabotki generalnoj skhemy razmeschenija vetroelektritcheskikh stantsij v Rossii do 2030 goda) (in Russian).

Nikolayev V.G., Ganago S.V., and Kudryashov, Yu. I. (2008), National Inventory of wind energy resources of Russia and methodological foundations of their determination. "Atmograph," Moscow (Natsionalnyj kadastr vetroenergetitcheskikh resursov RF i metoditcheskie osnovy ikh opredelenija. "Atmograf," M., 2008) (in Russian)

National Human Development Enent Report in the Russian Federation (2009), Energy Sector and Sustainable Development, UNDP, Russia, Moscow.

Pavlov M. (2012), Renewable energy and sustainable economic development. Russian possibilities, http://portal-energo.ru/articles/details/id/521 (last accessed on 11 December, 2013) (Vozobnovljaemaja energija i ustojtchivoe ekonomitcheskoe razvitie. Vozmozhnosti Rossii) (in Russian).

Popel O.S. (2011), "Renewable energy sources in the regions of the Russian Federation: problems and prospects," *Energosovet: Electronic Journal* 5 (18): 22–26, www.energosovet.ru/bul_stat.php?idd=210 (last accessed on 07 August 2014) (Vozobnovljaemye istotchniki energii v regionakh Rossijskoj Federatsii: problemy i perspektivy) (in Russian).

Statistical Compilation/Rosstat-M (2012), *Russian Statistical Yearbook. 2012* (Rossijskij Statistitcheskij Ezhegodnik. 2012: Statistitcheskij sbornik./Rosstat. – M.) (in Russian).

Suslov, N. I. (2005), "What are the conditions influencing efficiency of energy use?" *Northeast Asia Academic Forum* 1(1): 37–45.

Suslov, N. I. (2007), "Energy saving incentives and institutional environment: cross-country analysis," in Babic, S., Cerovic, B., Jaksic, M., and Prascevic, A. (eds.), *Challenges of Globalization and Transition: International Scientific Conference "Contemporary Challenges of Theory and Practice in Economics,"* Belgrade: Economics Department of the University of Belgrade, 341–352.

Suslov, N. (2012), "Rent is all we have" *EKO* 6: 81–93 ("Renta – eto nashe vsjo") (in Russian).

Suslov, N. (2014), "Inter-sector inter-region analysis: estimating consequences of realization of large investment projects in energy sector of Russian economy," in Baranov, A. and Suslov, V. (eds.), *Development of Macro and Interindustrial Methods of Economic Analyses Proceedings of the 21st INFORUM World Conference, Listvyanka, 26–31 August 2013*, Novosibirsk: Institute of Economic and Industrial Engineering of Sib. Branch of RAS (IEIE SB RAS), 188–210.

11 Green growth and low carbon development in East Asia
Achievements and challenges

Akihisa Mori

Introduction

As mentioned in this book's introduction, Northeast Asian countries have been framing green growth and low carbon development as a green industrial policy compatible with conventional export-led industrialization, with a special focus on renewable energy. Through this framing, they have hoped to garner multiple benefits: developing leading manufacturers in prominent industries around the world; increasing green jobs; enhancing the international competitiveness of their industries; reducing carbon emissions; and enhancing their energy security.

This chapter summarizes the findings of the previous chapters and evaluates the Northeast Asian countries' achievements and remaining challenges, with a special focus on energy and trade. Then it explores how green growth, low carbon development strategies can be applied beyond East Asia.

Achievements

Development of renewable energy industries

China and South Korea have dramatically increased their production and export of green products. In Chapter 5, Ogura and Mori showed that the international trade of green products has increased steadily in Northeast Asia, reaching 10 percent of the total trade volume. In particular, exports of renewable-energy technologies and products have risen dramatically.

A remarkable increase can be seen in solar power as well. Chinese manufacturers of solar photovoltaics (PV) modules have capitalized on economies of scale to increase exports. When the Chinese government implemented a feed-in-tariff (FIT) for solar power in 2012, these manufacturers increased domestic supply, accounting for one-fourth of global supply in the same year (Table 11.1). The South Korean company Hanhwa has become a first-tier manufacturer and increased its global market share since it took over the Chinese firm SolarOne and the German firm Q-Cells. Chinese manufacturers have also joined in the more profitable upstream market for polysilicon and silicon ingot (Table 11.2).

Chinese wind turbine manufacturers have also increased production, while have increased export to a lesser extent. Although Chinese state-owned

Table 11.1 Top 10 PV module suppliers in 2012

Ranks in 2012	Company Name	Delivery in 2012 (MW)	Global Market Share (%)		
			2011	2012	2013
1 (3)	Yingli (China)	2300	4.8	6.7	8.2
2 (2)	First Solar (USA)	1800	5.7	5.3	4.2
3 (4)	Trina Solar (China)	1650	4.3	4.7	6.7
4 (1)	Suntech (China)	1650	5.8	4.7	–
5 (5)	Canadian Solar (China)	1600	4.0	4.6	4.9
6 (7)	Sharp (Japan)	1050	2.8	3.0	5.4
7 (11)	JA Solar (China)	994	2.4	2.8	3.2
8 (12)	Jinko Solar (China)	923	2.3	2.6	4.6
9 (6)	SunPower (USA)	912	2.8	2.6	–
10 (10)	Hereon Solar (China)	888	2.5	2.5	–
10 (8)	Hanwha SolarOne (Korea)	750	2.7	2.5	3.3
12 (14)	Kyocera (Japan)	746	1.9	2.1	3.1

Note 1: Figures in parenthesis show performance in 2011.

Note 2: Based on 35.5GW produced in 2012 and 38.7GW in 2013.

Source: Author compilation in reference to RENS21 (2013) and Statista (2014).

Table 11.2 Global top 10 polysilicon producers in 2011

Rank	Company	Capacity (tons)
1	GCL (China)	65,000
2	OCI (Korea)	65,000
3	Hemlock (USA)	43,000
4	Wacker (Germany)	33,000
5	LDK (China)	25,000
6	REC Group (Norway)	19,000
7	MEMC (USA)	15,000
8	Tokuyama (Japan)	9,200
9	LCY (Taiwan)	8,000
10	Woonglin (Korea)	5,000

Source: www.solarpowerworldonline.com/2013/04/top-10-solar-pv-module-suppliers-of-2012/ (accessed July 29 2013).

manufacturers started operation with the aim of rural electrification, they have rapidly acquired and increased production capacity since the Chinese government enacted the Renewable Energy Law, which implemented a renewable portfolio standard (RPS) and mandated that state grid companies purchase from them. Wind power is the second largest category (by number) of Clean Development Mechanism projects in China (Mori, 2011), and this has helped the government recognize that wind power can bring economic and environmental benefits. This provided state-owned manufacturers with opportunities to acquire knowledge and gain economically (see Chapter 4 in this volume). Some of the manufacturers went further, acquiring technology licenses from second-tier foreign manufacturers who had lost in the competition in the European market and had therefore been willing to sell licenses at a cheaper price. These license agreements were used to establish joint ventures in exporting markets to scale up wind turbines and to develop ocean wind power. This has increased the production and export by Chinese manufacturers, and in 2010–2011, they accounted for one quarter of world deliveries (Table 11.3).

As a result, globally, China hires the largest number of people in renewable-energy-related industries. It is estimated that about 2.6 million people work in these industries in China, with 1.6 million people working in solar PV and a further 350 thousand people working in wind power and solar heating/cooling during 2012–2013 (RENS21, 2014).

It was not until 2012, when the Japanese government implemented a FIT for renewable energy and mandated that existing electric power companies

Table 11.3 Top 10 wind turbine manufacturers in 2011–2013

Rank in 2011	Company	Delivery in 2011 (MW)	Delivery in 2013 (MW)	Global Market Share (%)			
				2010	2011	2012	2013
1	Vestas (Demark)	5,211	4,850	14.8	12.7	14.0	13.1
2	Sinovel Wind (China)	3,700	–	11.1	9.0	3.2	–
3	Goldwind (China)	3,584	3,600	9.5	8.7	6.0	11.0
4	Gamesa (Spain)	3,308	1,951	6.6	8.0	6.1	5.5
5	ENERCON (Germany)	3,203	3,657	7.2	7.8	8.2	9.8
6	GE Energy (USA)	3,170	2,342	9.6	7.7	15.5	6.6
7	Suzlon (India)	3,116	2,239	6.9	7.6	7.4	5.3
8	Guodian United Power (China)	3,042	1,419	4.2	7.4	4.7	4.0
9	Siemens (Germany)	2,591	2,587	5.9	6.3	9.5	7.4
10	Minyang Wind Power (China)	1,500	1,242	–	3.6	2.7	3.5

Note: Figures in parenthesis show performance in 2011.

Source: Author compilation in reference to REN21 (2013; 2014) and www.cleantechinvestor. com/portal/wind-energy/10502-wind-turbine-manufacturers-global-market-shares.html (accessed July 29 2013).

purchase all available renewable energy, that Japanese manufacturers recovered their share of solar PV delivery in the world market. Japanese manufacturers used to have the lion's share of solar PV module sales and they have invested in efficiency improvements for solar PV, so some of them have the ability to reverse their decline in global market share, which is caused by slow expansion of the domestic market and fiercer competition in foreign markets. Nevertheless, China's excessive supply of solar PV modules, coupled with uncertainty over policy changes, makes Japanese manufacturers hesitant to make huge investments in capacity expansion. Instead, they are investing in related goods such as power conditioners.

Although no South Korean companies appear in the ranks of global leading wind turbine and solar PV manufacturers, the South Korean government has created industrial parks to attract manufacturers to invest in polysilicon and silicon ingot production for export. This has resulted in creating top manufacturers in this field (Table 11.2). The government has also been pushing a few manufacturers, such as Samsung, to join the ocean wind turbine market as an entry point to a new niche, as well as to increase the availability of appropriate renewable energy sources in South Korea.

Taiwanese companies appear among the world's leading solar PV cell manufacturers, as well as among the leading polysilicon manufacturers (Tables 11.4 and 11.2, respectively). This is due in part to the government's prioritization of solar power through the applicable FIT, which reflects Taiwan's strong foundation in semiconductor production (Lin, 2014). Other environmental industries have grown in Taiwan, but face difficulties in enhancing their international competitiveness due to constraints in the domestic and international markets (Chapter 6 in this volume).

Table 11.4 Global top 10 solar cell manufacturers by capacity in 2011

Rank	Company	Capacity (tons)
1	Suntech (China)	2,400
2	JA Solar (China)	2,100
3	Trina Solar (China)	1,900
4	Yingli (China)	1,700
5	Motech Solar (Taiwan)	1,500
6	Gintech (Taiwan)	1,500
7	Canadian Solar (China)	1,300
8	Neo Solar Power (Taiwan)	1,300
9	Hanwha SolarOne (Korea)	1,100
10	Jinko Solar (China)	1,100

Source: http://energydeals.wordpress.com/2011/12/24/list-of-solar-companies/ and http://pv.energytrend.com/research/20140129-6134.html (last accessed August 22, 2014).

Such increases in production affect the trade balance. Japan has been a net exporter of renewable energy equipment since the early 1990s, and China and South Korea became net exporters in 2007 and 2010, respectively (Chapter 5 in this volume).

Energy system transition for sustainability

China and Japan have shown a significant increase in the installed capacity for wind and solar power. Figures 11.1 and 11.2 illustrate how rapidly the world has increased its supply of wind and solar power during the last decade. Among the listed countries, China has increased its capacity most dramatically. It has rapidly increased the annual installation rate for wind power, surpassing the installed capacity of Germany and the United States in 2010, when it had one third of the world's installed capacity. China has improved its ranking on the installation of solar power since 2011, having the second largest installed capacity in 2013. South Korea, too, has increased its installed capacity, but the scale and speed of improvement has been much more modest than in China. Japan used to have the largest installed capacity for solar power, but the country was left behind recently. This is attributed to the government failing to raise the share of mandatory purchase of renewable energy in the electricity generation market from 1 percent under its RPS. In 2012–2013 however, installed solar capacity in Japan has shown a significant increase after the replacement of the RPS by a FIT, coupled with a purchase price high enough to allow independent power producers to earn a profit. In contrast to solar power, wind power use

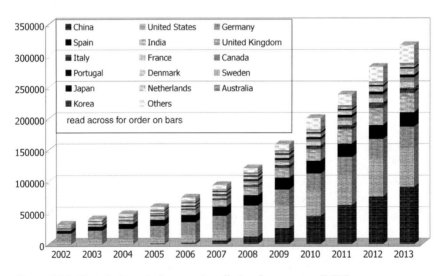

Figure 11.1 Cumulative wind power installation by country (MW)

Source: Author completion in reference to Global Wind Energy Council (2013; 2014).

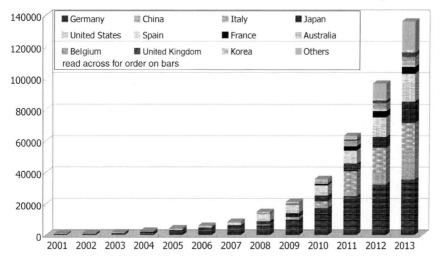

Figure 11.2 Cumulative solar power installation by country (MW)

Source: Author completion in reference to IEA (2013; 2014).

Table 11.5 Share of renewable energy in electricity generation

	2000	2005	2006	2007	2008	2009	2010	2011	2012
South Korea	0.04	0.11	0.13	0.20	0.31	0.40	0.90	1.53	1.69
China	0.05	0.26	0.19	0.34	0.67	1.24	1.88	1.91	2.62
Japan	0.60	0.89	0.92	0.96	0.99	1.10	1.14	1.39	1.64
Taiwan	0.00	0.04	0.15	0.24	0.29	0.45	0.47	0.74	N.A.
Philippines	25.65	17.51	18.52	17.22	18.08	16.79	14.78	N.A.	N.A.
Indonesia	2.66	5.18	5.00	4.94	5.55	5.86	5.86	N.A.	N.A.

Note: Taiwan includes only wind and solar power, while others include geothermal, biomass and waste power.

Source: Author compilation from the information in Agency for Natural Resources and Energy, Japan (2014a; 2014b); Japan Electric Power Information Center (2012); Department of Energy Statistics, National Bureau of Statistics (2013); Taiwan Power Corporation (2007; 2008; 2009; 2010; 2011; 2012); United Nations (2013); and Korean Energy Statistics Information System www.kesis.net/flexapp/KesisFlexApp.jsp?menuId=Q0109&reportId=&ch k=Y (accessed on August 21, 2014).

in Japan has increased only gradually, even after the Fukushima nuclear disaster, which is reflective of its higher transaction costs.

Investments in renewable energy have increased power generation by renewable sources and their share in total power generation. China has raised that share rapidly since 2008, and Japan has done so since 2012, to reach 2 percent. South Korea and Taiwan have much lower shares, but in those countries the renewable energy share has still increased rapidly since 2010 (Table 11.5).

Challenges

Despite the improvements described above, the share of renewable energy in total power generation still lags behind that in other Asian countries, such as Indonesia and the Philippines, which are rich in geothermal power, and far behind the world-leading countries of Germany and Denmark. In addition, the speed of growth is varied. While China raised its renewable energy targets to accelerate installation of wind and solar PV, the South Korean government ended up extending the deadline for renewable energy targets from 2030 to 2035 in the 2014 National Basic Energy Plan. Japan has yet to set a renewable energy target, leaving the growth of installed capacity to preferential prices under the FIT.

In addition to wind and solar power's higher relative costs, there are a number of barriers to widespread adoption of renewable electricity generation. The first barrier is the sporadic nature of renewable energy sources. Renewable energy of most types relies on variable power sources, and an enhanced grid is needed to balance supply and demand at the spot because supply is critically dependent on weather, while demand is not always. The wider the area covered by a distribution grid, the more flexibly its operator can balance supply and demand because it can combine heterogeneous demand and supply. Establishing such systems needs either investment in networking transmission lines or cross-regional coordination of transmission. Under the existing centralized and (regionally) monopolized production systems, incumbent power electricity companies should bear the investment costs and additional transaction costs of adjusting total supply, including volatile supply from renewable sources. However, existing companies have shown themselves unwilling to accept large amounts of renewable sources in their grids, and they refuse grid access by independent renewable power producers because that would deprive them of a source of profit.

The second barrier to the growth of renewable energy is price regulation. In exchanges that allow a centralized regional monopoly on supply, the government keeps strict control on the retail energy and electricity price. Except in Japan, governments offer subsidized pricing for the sake of stabilizing people's daily life, preventing inflation, and supporting industrial development.

Despite its heavy reliance on imported coal, South Korea has offered subsidies to the agricultural sector and industrial energy customers in order to enhance their international competitiveness and protect them from foreign competition (Table 11.6). This policy has increased the presence of energy-intensive industries, such as steel and petrochemicals. The South Korean government kept electricity price stable during the periods of global energy hike (2007–2008) and currency depreciation (2008–2012). This resulted in the wholesale electricity price being lower than the price of imported oil, which generated excess demand that eventually resulted in the blackout of the Seoul metropolitan area in 2011. The policy has also widened the financial deficit of the state-owned Korean Electricity Power Company (KEPCO), which was US$ 2.75 billion in 2011 (Duffield, 2014). This makes KEPCO incapable of investing in a grid and transmission system that could accept massive quantities of renewable electricity.

Table 11.6 Recovery rate of electricity price by sector in South Korea in 2007

Sector	Recovery rate
General	108.4
Residential	99.2
Industrial	90.5
Educational	88.7
Agricultural	39.2
Average	93.8

Source: Author compilation from Jones, R. S. and B. Yoo (2011).

In China, tight price regulation by the government has deterred and curtailed grid connectivity, which has had an adverse impact on the spread of renewable electricity. In the meanwhile, China has refused grid companies' requests to be allowed to pass on the additional costs to consumers. Coupled with an increased coal price, this restriction has deprived grid companies of the financial ability to invest in a unified power grid. Rapid installation of wind power poses additional challenges to grid connectivity in this context because grid companies are required to make huge investments to correct for the geographical imbalance between demand and supply, and the government does not sufficiently compensate this investment. In addition, grid companies must recover losses from paying premium prices to renewable power producers. Even though the Renewable Energy Law requires grid companies to accept increasing volumes of renewable energy, most local grids have refused to establish the necessary connections. The government has not strictly punished the grid companies for this refusal. Coupled with a prohibition against direct provision to end-users, and the numerous small-scale plants that had been installed for the purpose of rural electrification, refusal of grid connection left one-third of wind power plants unconnected to the grid (Fang et al., 2012). Although the rate of idled wind power capacity has dropped to 17 percent in 2012 and to 11 percent in 2013, about 16 TWh were still wasted due to curtailment (REN21, 2014).

Faced with these difficulties, the Chinese government aims to shift the focus from large solar farms to rooftop PV as a way to increase smaller-scale distributed solar PV. These developments provide support for the perhaps optimistic view that idled or unconnected capacity is a temporary challenge that can be solved through future institutional changes and system innovations.

The third barrier to the growth of renewable energy is nuclear dependency. Japan, South Korea, and Taiwan are resource-poor countries that rely largely on foreign imports to meet their increasing energy demand. The two oil crises in the 1970s alerted these three countries to the degree of their vulnerability because of energy dependency, which prompted their governments to diversify energy sources. To enhance energy security and satisfy growing domestic demand, these countries have developed oil reserves, diversified their oil suppliers, which had been mostly Middle Eastern countries, and increased the number and capacity of nuclear power plants. In the process, centralized, monopolized nuclear and fossil fuel-based production systems were established and locked in. Japan implemented an electricity surcharge that was earmarked for local governments that hosted nuclear power plants. Taiwan decided to implement this surcharge several years later to accelerate nuclear development. The electric power companies, politicians at central and local governments, and ministries in charge of promotion and regulatory bodies have grown too close to one another to be truly independent, resulting in a system with insufficient transparency in decision-making and a lack of checks and balances. By 2000, nuclear power accounted for one-third of the total power generation in Japan and South Korea and one-sixth in Taiwan.

Emerging concerns about climate change have spurred the development of nuclear power. South Korean has framed nuclear power as an energy source that can ensure greenhouse gas (GHG) emissions are reduced by the target amount, and as a new export industry. In the 2008 National Basic Energy Plan, the South Korean government set the nuclear share target at 59 percent in 2030, which is up from 33.6 percent in 2007. South Korea rushed to win a competition for the development of nuclear power plants in the United Arab Emirates and is seeking other opportunities. The Japanese government, after committing to a 25 percent reduction in GHG emissions by 2020, has framed nuclear and renewable energy as major vehicles to attain that target. In the 2010 Strategic Energy Plan, the government set the target for the share of renewable at 10 percent of total primary energy by 2020, and that for renewable and nuclear energy at 70 percent of total power supply by 2030. Pushed by South Korea, Japan described the export of infrastructure, including nuclear power plants, as a priority in the 2010 Growth Strategy.

The Fukushima nuclear disaster has had significant effects on nuclear-based production systems in the region. For example, as a result of the tragedy coupled with a series of incidents and local opposition, South Korea lowered its nuclear target from 59 percent by 2030 to 22–29 percent by 2035 in the 2014 National Basic Energy Plan. However, the plan keeps the nuclear capacity target intact. This implies that the government has no intention to compensate for the reduction by increasing renewable energy: rather, it intends to do this by increasing total generation capacity significantly.

The Japanese government decided to suspend all nuclear power plants until they achieve compliance with more stringent safety standards and are certified by an independent Nuclear Regulation Authority. In the meantime, it has attempted to change the decision-making process from one in which climate policy is subordinate to nuclear power development and strategic energy plans to an integrative process in which the government makes a joint decision regarding the above three plans, with a reflection of deliberative opinion polls (Chapter 3 in this volume). In reality, however, the government could not make this decision even at the cabinet level. The decision-making process reverted to its original form when a new administration took power.

The fixed FIT offers an opportunity for renewable energy-rich areas to capitalize on this richness to develop local business, although the success of such attempts is critically dependent on institutional capacity (Chapter 2 in this volume). The ongoing unbundling of regional monopolies on vertically integrated supply in Japan is expected to strengthen institutions that are favorable to the development of a decentralized supply system.

Taiwan, having grappled for a decade with the controversial development of its planned fourth nuclear power plant, has committed to a gradual decrease in nuclear power. It announced the phase-out of plants that have operated for 40 years and the replacement of its first power plant with the planned fourth plant if residents and local governments accept its operation.

Side effects in the globalized world

It is worth nothing that China and South Korea may have realized rapid growth in their renewable energy industries at the expense of other countries.

Development of renewable energy industries in other countries

Export is one of the key drivers of rapid growth in renewable energy industries. These industries enjoy economies of scale that make production more efficient while reducing costs, creating a comparative advantage in international trade. Thus, the bulk of employment in the sector is concentrated in a few countries, such as China, Brazil, the United States, India, Bangladesh, and some countries in the European Union (EU). This is true even in periods when growth in world demand leads to increased prices and profits. Overinvestment by Chinese manufacturers has placed downward pressure on prices since 2010, leading to cutthroat competition. Relative to the 2008 peaks, wind turbine prices fell by as much as 20–25 percent in Western markets and by more than 35 percent in China before stabilizing in 2012 (REN21, 2013: 51). The cost of solar PVs from top Chinese manufacturers approached US$ 0.50 per Watt in 2013 (RENS21, 2014).

This aggressive pricing from China, coupled with policy changes in several European countries, was highly detrimental to wind and solar manufacturers around the world, reducing their revenue margins so much that many have fallen into trouble (Table 11.7). For instance, Suzlon (India), the world's seventh largest wind turbine deliverer in 2011, has lost money for four years running and has struggled with massive debt. Some wind turbine manufactures in the United States have shuttered their factories due to a shortage of new turbine orders. German Q-Cells SE, formerly the world's leading solar PV manufacturer, filed for bankruptcy. This has had an impact on green jobs. Italy was hit the hardest, with 70 percent of those employed in solar power companies losing

Table 11.7 Gross margin of PV modules in the first-tier Chinese supplier in 2012

Company	Net loss (US$ million)	Gross margin
Canadian Solar	−3.9	0.10
Jinko	−20.8	0.13
JA Solar	−33.3	0.06
Hanwha SolarOne	−36.4	0.03
ReneSola	−39.0	−0.02
Trina	−63.7	0.02
Yingli	−103.4	0.04

Source: 'Canadian solar's 1Q13 financial result evaluation: Rise in gross margin lead to decrease in loss,' *Energy Trend*, July 4, 2013. http://pv.energytrend.com/research/20130704-5379. html (accessed July 24 2013).

their jobs. Germany, too, had 22 percent of its green industry workforce, 100,000 people, lose their jobs (IEA, 2013: 62). The larger share that China occupies in the world's renewable energy equipment market, the greater the share that Japan loses in the global market (Chapter 5 in this volume).

Chinese manufacturers have not been immune to the repercussions of price wars. Sinovel (China), which became the leading wind turbine manufacturer, put workers on involuntary leave. Many suppliers in China particularly have been pushed to the edge of collapse, with overcapacity pushing smaller manufacturers out of the market entirely. Suntech Power (China), which was the world's largest solar PV deliverer, declared bankruptcy in 2013, which caused the loss of 200,000 jobs in the solar PV sector in 2012 (IEA, 2013: 62).

Despite these casualties, three Chinese companies remain listed in the global top 10 of wind turbine manufacturers, and six in the global top 10 of solar PV module manufacturers (Tables 11.3 and 11.1, respectively).

By replacing the FIT with an RPS, South Korea is expecting to limit the impact of imported low-price, low-quality renewable energy equipment. An RPS allows Korean electric power companies to procure equipment at their discretion, and so they can implicitly prioritize solar modules that are made of cells, wafers, and polysilicons produced by Korean manufacturers.

Eco-efficiency in resource use

As discussed in the introduction to this book, the United Nations Economic and Social Commission for Asia and the Pacific defines green growth as the eco-efficiency of economic growth (UNESCAP, 2008). South Korea has enhanced its eco-efficiency through international and domestic reuse and recycling of end-of-use goods. South Korea had implemented a waste deposit system to reduce emissions and enhance recycling when faced with the so-called not-in–my-backyard syndrome for developing a waste disposal site. However, Associations of Korean Industrial Companies strongly opposed it, citing its high costs. In response, the government replaced this plan with the Extended Producer's Responsibility (EPR) program. Although imposing on manufacturers the obligation to attain a recycling target for end-of-use electric appliances, it offered export subsidies for international recycling as a complementary measure. This measure may result in the creation of pollution havens impacts at export destinations where environmental governance is too weak to prevent environmental pollution from the recycling and disposal process. In the case of lead-containing used televisions and computer monitors, Korean manufacturers save recycling costs and Korean society gains the benefit of saving on disposal site costs, while Vietnam, the major export destination, gains little from legally permitted reuse (Chapter 8 in this volume).

Product-related environmental regulations (PRERs) can be policy responses to avoid such environmental pollution in countries of weak enforcement. PRERs require significant or complete reduction of hazardous substances that are contained in a product. Nonetheless, PRERs have not always functioned effectively to advance cleaner production and products in such countries, primarily because the use of PRERs has not created globally unified regulations and standards. As a result, several East Asian countries have taken industrial benefits into account when implementing their own PRERs, while others have suffered from a massive influx of 'dirty' products that do not comply with the PRERs of developed countries (Chapter 9 in this volume).

A model worth spreading globally?

Leapfrogging in renewable energy industry

At first glance, it looks easier for developing countries to realize leapfrogging in the wind and solar PV industries. A company can capitalize on production modules to assemble parts, components, and material resources even if it lacks the capacity for a complex production process and has few skilled workers. Because the industry has been previously established in developed countries, some suppliers of machinery and equipment offer a series of production line coupled with operational know-how. This enables manufacturers in any country to enhance production capacity so long as they have a certain amount of capital and educated laborers.

However, companies face difficulties in enhancing efficiency and in upgrading quality by themselves. It was not until they purchased a branch of bankrupted European manufacturers that Chinese wind turbine manufacturers could compete with foreign competitors in the global market.

The Chinese government has played a significant role in fostering domestic manufacturers and protecting them from foreign competition. It capitalized on requirements for local content to the benefit of domestic, state-owned wind power companies. As a precondition to obtain a wind power concession, the government imposed a requirement for 50 percent local contents in 2004, and this requirement was raised to 70 percent in 2005. In contrast, companies were nearly exempt from requirements relating to track record or lifetime turbine performance. State-owned companies capitalized on better relations with the government and state-owned banks to ensure access to substantial amounts of state funding, even while enjoying no or limited responsibility to shareholders. This enabled them to invest in less-profitable projects (Buen and Castro, 2012). In addition, state-owned companies were able to acquire licenses from second-tier foreign manufacturers that had lost in the competition in the European market and were willing to sell licenses at a less expensive price. Under these conditions, private sector and foreign investors won less than 10 percent of the concessions (Li et al., 2010). The winners in the concession are able to obtain financial support for grid connection and access roads as well as preferential loan and tax conditions, which have enabled domestic manufacturers to make massive investment, seeking economies of scale. When the government lifted the local content requirements in 2009, it was confident that domestic manu-facturers had become competitive enough to compete with foreign companies. Although Chinese companies had to accept restrictive terms imposed by foreign companies when acquiring licenses, for example, restricting or prohibiting export of the technology or offering licenses for only turbines below 1.5 MW capacity, they have a first-mover advantage in adapting them to local conditions. In fact, the share of Chinese manufacturers in the Chinese market has increased by 27 percent from 2007 to 2013, when it exceeded 93 percent, and European turbine manufacturers have experienced a decline (REN21, 2014: 58).

It was not just the central government that fostered domestic manufacturers. Local governments have provided land grants and subsidies as measures to boost the local economy. The state Communist party evaluates the leaders of local governments according to economic performance during their tenure when deciding on promotions. This process makes it rational for local govern-ments to take targeted policies toward prominent companies under their juris-diction. This holds true for private companies that have a close relationship with the area.

The Chinese Development Bank (CDB) has provided a massive amount of sub-sidized loans to private solar PV manufacturers that sought the help of foreign investment banks due to a lack of access to preferential treatment or financial support from the central government. CDB subsidized loans of US$ 14.7 bil-lion to clean energy projects and other energy saving projects. In comparison, the European Investment Bank provided 8 billion euros (approx. US$ 10.6 bil-lion) and the US Federal Financing Bank provided US$ 2.12 billion (Sanderson and Forsythe, 2013: 151). Most of the Chinese companies listed in the global top 10 manufacturers of wind turbines and solar PV modules obtained huge credit lines from CDB. The CDB lines of credit had a cowbell effect by provid-ing a guarantee that made commercial banks feel safer lending to these companies, which allowed the companies to obtain cheaper working capital loans from commercial banks. Such loans allowed them to further expand capacity and to drive marginal production costs down.

Local governments and the CDB even rescued these companies when they got into deep distress during 2010–2011. The government of Xinyu city, where the company LDK is based, paid a portion of the company's debt. Yingli sold 1.5 billion yuan (approx. US$ 242 million) of bonds in 2012, with CDB as the lead underwriter (Sanderson and Forsythe, 2013: 154) after it suffered from an annual net loss of more than 50 million yuan (approx. US$ 8.1 million). This government funding has enabled companies to survive in the global market amid plunging prices. CDB went further, providing credit lines that enabled Yingli to purchase a subsidiary of the bankrupted Q-Cells and take a stake in Sunways AG, a German solar panel and cell manufacturer (Sanderson and Forsythe, 2013: 156).

Few countries have local governments and state development banks that can provide such massive financial resources for targeted industries. Besides, massive financial supports have caused trade wars with leading countries. The defaults of US Solyndra and German Q-Cells SE triggered investigation of anti-dumping and anti-subsidy remedies. The United States announced anti-dumping duties of roughly 31 percent on Chinese PV equipment in May 2012, and the EU adopted an average 47.7 percent duty in December 2013. The United States also announced an anti-dumping tariff averaging 25 percent for PV cells and modules produced in Taiwan in August 2014. Australia announced that it was launching an anti-dumping investigation on finished and semi-finished Chinese PV module imports in May 2014.

Energy transition for sustainability

Although centralized, monopolistic nuclear and fossil fuel-based systems for providing electricity have blocked South Korea, Japan, and Taiwan from increasing the use of renewable energy, China has increased its use of renewable energy and reduced its coal dependency, advancing hybridization of its energy infrastructure. Can China be a global model for energy transition for sustainability, and in particular, do its experiences provide useful lessons for developing countries?

At this moment, the answer seems to be no. First, the growth of solar use in China is in part a consequence of the anti-dumping and anti-subsidy duties imposed on solar PV modules by the United States and the EU. The Chinese government intends to exploit the domestic market to compensate Chinese PV module manufacturers for financial losses resulting from the duties as well as the reduction in the size of the European market. China expects that such measures will direct companies to increase the use of Chinese solar cells and polysilicon. Among developing countries, only India and Brazil have markets big enough to take this approach and keep a competitive environment in the domestic market, which eventually offers an internationally competitive price for renewable energy supply.

Second, it is by massively increasing oil and gas imports that China has been able to reduce its coal dependency and emissions of carbon and other air pollutants. To ensure energy access and energy security, China has mobilized massive subsidized loans to oil and gas rich countries that are not locked up by Western countries, ranging from South Sudan and Angola in Africa, to Myanmar, Kazakhstan, and Turkmenistan in Central Asia, and to Russia. It is unlikely that other energy importing countries have a foreign reserve large enough that the government and/or state banks can mobilize the funds needed to enhance energy security in the way that China has. Some energy-rich countries have launched energy-saving measures and renewable energy initiatives to prepare for anticipated energy shortfalls in the future, but many countries still have little incentive to widely adopt renewable energy (Chapter 10 in this volume).

Transition to sustainable development

Although green growth and low carbon development strategy have increased employment in the renewable energy sector in China and, to a lesser extent, in South Korea, they have contributed little, if any, to other dimensions of social sustainability. Instead, local governments in China and the CDB have mobilized massive financial resources at the cost of broadening the income gap and social divide. Companies have used agricultural land and bond issuances to obtain financial resources. This has resulted in capital gains from the development of economic infrastructure near the affected land and the conversion of agricultural land to urban development. In the process, an increasing number of local governments have developed local financial corporations that receive CDB loans and use these to grab lands from farmers, and these funds are spent without audit or oversight. They have forcefully relocated farmers, offering only meager compensation, and this has increased social unrest around China (Sanderson and Forsythe, 2013: 21). In South Korea, a small number of conglomerates have benefited from the renewable energy industry but a large number of small companies have not, and there has been no notable effect on the rising unemployment of the younger generation.

Unlike in Northeast Asia, people in Central and South American countries demand a framework of social institutions that nurture and assist people (Dujon, 2009). Residents of these countries have long suffered from economic, social, and political marginalization under neoliberal market policies. Grassroots movements have raised consciousness about the connections among economic survival, environmental protection, and social justice, and these movements have attempted to democratize the state to redefine the path to social well-being and force the state to increase provisions for broad social well-being (Dujon, 2009).

Because of the very different contexts, it is understandable that Central and South American countries have criticized green growth as not contributing to social well-being, and refused to make it a global goal at the UN Conference on Sustainable Development (Rio+20).[1] To be a globally acceptable agenda, green growth should at least be supplemented by an inclusive growth approach that focuses on a just distribution of resources and on human development.[2]

Concluding remarks

Northeast Asian countries have capitalized on their existing industrial bases to adopt a green industrial policy in the face of the global financial crisis. They have focused on renewable energy equipment industries, such as wind turbine, solar PV cell, and module manufacturing because manufacturers can capitalize on production modules to assemble parts, components, and material resources without needing a complex production process or a mature labor force. The Chinese government and, to a lesser extent, the South Korean government have selectively intervened to foster domestic manufacturers in this industry. Coupled with technological transfer from foreign equipment suppliers, such intervention has created an incentive for many manufacturers to join the market, which has resulted in overinvestment in a limited number of renewable energy equipment types and to price collapses. Although China has avoided inefficient production by the use of protection measures, this has sparked a trade war with the United States and leading countries in Europe. Although lower prices for renewable energy equipment may accelerate a transition to energy sustainability, the incumbent centralized, monopolistic nuclear- and fossil fuel-based energy production systems have blocked such transitions in Northeast Asia.

Northeast Asian countries have legislated recycling acts to increase the eco-efficiency of resource use, but this has had the effect of increasing the international trade in end-of-life goods. These acts have been criticized for transferring environmental pollution to importing countries with weak governance. Import regulations in China and Vietnam, as well as PRERs implemented in many countries, might have mitigated the adverse impacts, but South Korea still promotes the export of end-of-life goods.

Overall, a green growth and low carbon development strategy has succeeded in reframing policies on climate and the environment as industrial policies and in rapidly increasing the production and spread of renewable energy equipment in a limited number of countries. The benefits from approaches have been concentrated on a few industries and manufacturers, while the costs have spread across society and to other countries. To advance the global transition to sustainable development, green growth and low carbon development strategy should be implemented in a way that breaks institutional lock-in, which has blocked such a transition, that minimizes the side effects of change and that incorporates human development and social well-being.

Notes

1 Chung, Rae Kwon. Presentation at the expert meeting on green growth and sustainable development, Sapporo, Japan, 22 August, 2013.
2 The World Bank (2012) adopts the concept of inclusive green growth, paying attention to reduction of poverty and improvement of access to health, education, and infrastructure services.

References

Agency for Natural Resources and Energy, Japan (2014a), *Annual Report on Energy, FY 2013* (in Japanese). www.enecho.meti.go.jp/about/whitepaper/2014pdf (last accessed on July 28, 2014).

Agency for Natural Resources and Energy, Japan (2014b), "State of art and challenges on renewable energy" (in Japanese). www.meti.go.jp/committee/sougouenergy/shoene_shinene/shin_ene/pdf/001_03_00.pdf (last accessed on July 24, 2014).

Buen J. and Castro, P. (2012), "How Brazil and China have financed industry development and energy security initiatives that support mitigation objectives," in Michaelowa, K. and Michaelowa, A. (eds.), *Carbon Markets or Climate Finance? Low Carbon and Adaptation Investment Choices for the Developing World*, Oxon: Routledge, 53–91.

Department of Energy Statistics, National Bureau of Statistics (2013), *China Energy Statistical Yearbook 2013*, Beijing: China Statistical Press.

Duffield, J.S. (2014), "South Korea's national energy plan six years on," *Asian Politics and Policy* 6 (3): 433–454.

Dujon, V. (2009), "In the absence of affluence: the struggle for social sustainability in the Third World," in Dillard, J., Dujon, V., and King, M.C. (eds.), *Understanding the Social Dimension of Sustainability*, Oxon: Routledge, 122–136.

Fang Y., Li, J., and Wang, M. (2012), "Development policy for non-grid-connected wind power in China: An analysis based on institutional change," *Energy Policy* 45: 350–358.

Global Wind Energy Council (2013), *Global Wind Statistics 2012*. www.gwec.net/wp-content/uploads/2013/02/GWEC-PRstats-2012_english.pdf (last accessed on January 20, 2015).

Global Wind Energy Council (2014), *Global Wind Statistics 2013*. www.gwec.net/wp-content/uploads/2014/02/GWEC-PRstats-2013_EN.pdf (last accessed on January 20, 2015).

Institute of Energy Economics, Japan (2013), *EDMC Handbook of Energy & Economic Statistics in Japan 2013*, Energy Conservation Center, Japan.

IEA (2013), *Trends 2013 in Photovoltaic Applications: Survey Report of Selected IEA Countries between 1992 and 2012*. www.iea-pvps.org/index.php?id=3&eID=dam_frontend_push&docID=1733 (last accessed on July 31, 2014).

IEA (2014), *Trends 2014 in Photovoltaic Applications: Survey Report of Selected IEA Countries between 1992 and 2013*. http://helapco.gr/pdf/IEA_PVPS_Trends_2014_in_PV_Applications_-_lr.pdf (last accessed on July 31, 2014).

Japan Electric Power Information Center (2012), *Statistics on Electric Energy Industry in Foreign Countries* (in Japanese), Japan Electric Power Information Center.

Jones, R.S. and Yoo, B. (2011), Korea's Green Growth Strategy: Mitigating Climate Change and Developing New Growth Engines, *OECD Economics Department Working Paper No. 798*. http://dx.doi.org/10.1787/5kmbhk4gh1ns-en (last accessed on May 4, 2013).

Li, J., Shi, P., and Gao, H. (2010), *China Wind Power Outlook*, Renewable Energy Industries Association, Global Wind Energy Council, Green Peace. www.greenpeace.org/eastasia/Global/eastasia/publications/reports/climate-energy/2010/2010-china-wind-outlook.pdf (last accessed on July 31, 2013).

Lin, J.-X. (2014), "Policy target, feed-in tariff, and technological progress of PV in Taiwan," *Renewable and Sustainable Energy Reviews* 39: 628–639.

Mori, A. (2011), "Clean development mechanism policy and sustainable rural development in China," in Sawa, T. et al. (eds.), *Achieving Sustainability: Policy Recommendations*, Tokyo: United Nations Press, 148–161.

RENS21 (2013), *Renewables 2013 Global Status Report*. www.ren21.net/Portals/0/documents/Resources/GSR/2013/GSR2013_lowres.pdf (last accessed on November 3, 2014)

RENS21 (2014), *Renewables 2014 Global Status Report*. www.ren21.net/Portals/0/documents/Resources/GSR/2014/GSR2014_full%20report_low%20res.pdf (last accessed on November 3, 2014).

Sanderson, H. and Forsythe, M. (2013), *Debt, Oil and Influence – How China Development Bank Is Rewriting the Rules of Finance*, Singapore: John Wiley & Sons.

Statista (2014), Global Market Share of Solar Module Manufacturers in 2013. www.statista.com/statistics/269812/global-market-share-of-solar-pv-module-manufacturers/ (last accessed on January 20, 2015).

Taiwan Power Company, *Annual Report 2007, 2008, 2009, 2010, 2011, 2012* (in Chinese). http://info.taipower.com.tw/left_bar/aboutus/Annual_Report.htm (last accessed on August 21, 2014).

UNESCAP (2008), *Greening Growth in Asia and the Pacific*, Bangkok: ESCAP.

United Nations (2013), *Energy Statistics Yearbook 2010*. http://unstats.un.org/unsd/energy/balance/default.htm (last accessed on August 21, 2014).

World Bank (2012), *Inclusive Green Growth: The Pathway to Sustainable Development*, Washington, DC: The World Bank.

Index

Page number in *italics* denote tables, those in **bold** denote figures.